PROFITABLE
RESTAURANT
MANAGEMENT

PROFITABLE
RESTAURANT
MANAGEMENT

Kenneth I. Solomon
and
Norman Katz

PRENTICE-HALL, INC.
Englewood Cliffs, New Jersey

Prentice-Hall International, Inc., *London*
Prentice-Hall of Australia, Pty., Ltd., *Sydney*
Prentice-Hall of Canada, Ltd., *Toronto*
Prentice-Hall of India Private Ltd., *New Delhi*
Prentice-Hall of Japan, Inc., *Tokyo*

Seventh Printing . . . . . June, 1978

"This publication is designed to provide accurate and
authoritative information in regard to the subject matter
covered. It is sold with the understanding that the publisher
is not engaged in rendering legal, accounting, or other
professional service. If legal advice or other expert assistance is required, the services of a competent professional
person should be sought."

*—From the Declaration of Principles jointly
adopted by a Committee of the American Bar
Association and a Committee of Publishers and
Associations.*

Library of Congress Cataloging in Publication Data

Solomon, Kenneth Ira,
    Profitable restaurant management.

    1. Restaurant management. I. Katz, Norman,
            joint author. II. Title.
TX945.S59   658'.91'64795   74-10758
ISBN 0-13-728808-5

This book is dedicated to D.B.S., M.J.S., T.A.S., A.L.K., K.S.K., and R.J.K.

ABOUT THE AUTHORS

Kenneth I. Solomon

Kenneth I. Solomon, a partner in the firm of Laventhol Krekstein Horwath and Horwath, is a graduate with B.S. and M.S. degrees from the University of Illinois, and a graduate of the University of Chicago Law School with a J.D. degree. A former college professor of accountancy and business law, and law school professor, he has written articles in the leading accounting, tax, and hospitality industry publications. He is a CPA in several states and a member of the Illinois Bar. Mr. Solomon is a frequent speaker at professional society meetings and the author of three books on accounting and legal subjects.

Norman Katz

Norman Katz, also a partner in the firm of Laventhol Krekstein Horwath and Horwath, is recognized as one of the leading authorities on restaurant and hotel accounting and as a management advisory services consultant. A graduate of Roosevelt University, he is a CPA in several states. Mr. Katz has co-authored the firm's annual study of restaurant operations, has written articles which have been published in professional and trade publications, and has been a speaker at professional and leisure time industry meetings.

Foreword

Thanks to Messrs. Solomon and Katz, we finally have a comprehensive and practical guide to restaurant management. I am delighted to welcome *Profitable Restaurant Management* because its pages fill a long standing void in our field.

For a business that has grown as rapidly as ours, it is astonishing how few books have been written about it. For those seeking a ready reference, be they practicing restaurateurs or merely curious readers, the written sources have been all too inexact. Most authors have been either too theoretical or too one-sided to paint a valid picture of our business. *Profitable Restaurant Management*, however, avoids both these pitfalls. It guides the readers in all facets of restaurant management—planning, organizing, staffing, directing, and controlling. It demonstrates the interrelationships among them, while also citing the necessary divisions between functions. Each chapter contains need-to-know information for the seasoned veteran or for providing the broader base for the budding restaurateur. The grasp is sure. Most of all, the supporting material is excellent. Its presentation is lucid, its examination is thorough, and the approach is readable.

Theirs is an all too rare response to the problems and situations facing our industry. Messrs. Solomon and Katz present theory, but unlike the average restaurant text I bemoaned above, they don't stop there. They apply theory to arrive at common-sense and practical solutions. And, it's in this vein that they approach the day-to-day operating situations with details in their work.

I was particularly impressed with the case study approach and views of Chapter 5's application of management by objectives. Chapters 8 and 10 dealing respectively with financial analysis and tax matters were equally good and should prove thought-provoking.

This book is a definite must for any library attempting to cover the restaurant field, be it in a unit manager's office or university.

Lawrence Ellman
President
Longchamps Restaurants, Inc.

ACKNOWLEDGMENTS

The authors wish to acknowledge the assistance of many of their partners and colleagues in the international public accounting firm of Laventhol Krekstein Horwath & Horwath, especially Rudy Leone, Jay Brandzel, John Lesure, and Allen Weiss. The authors also acknowledge the important secretarial assistance of Christine Szymkiewicz and her many other efforts on behalf of this book.

How to Benefit from This Book

This book provides the restaurateur with the most modern and topical tools and guidelines available for the improvement of existing operations and the planning of future operations. We have concentrated on the development of a new approach to restaurant management—"optimum customer service." However, as an integral part of this system, we have built in the objective of profit maximization with a minimization of effort on the part of the intelligent restaurateur. How has this sophistication in restaurant management been accomplished? We feel that we have been able to achieve the unique combination of financial analysis, planning, and awareness with sound and practical business judgment in a field where demand most certainly exists but must be properly exploited.

Within the specific context of the individual chapters contained in this book, the following critical aspects of restaurant management are analyzed in detail and presented in a "how-to-do-it" fashion:

1. Food and beverage control, including purchasing, receiving, storing, issuing, specifications, and inventory and reordering techniques. To illustrate, handy tools such as the Daily Flash Sheet appearing on page 35 and the Daily Summary of Food Cost appearing on page 36 are provided. In addition, practical experiences, such as the one demonstrating how to implement a daily purchase journal on page 37, the three cases in point on page 39 demonstrating the real need for storeroom controls and proper purchasing and receiving procedures, and the dramatic "bottom line" example presented on page 41, appear in significant quantity throughout Chapters 2 and 3.

2. Food and beverage cost control, including standard costs, predetermined portion costs, and menu planning. To illustrate, the hard practical look at "things to come" on pages 65 and 66 represent a valuable insight into this phase of profitable restaurant management.

9

3. Restaurant personnel management, employee motivation, and payroll cost control. To illustrate, practical and innovative suggestions are presented through the use of examples such as the following: cash pay for extra work, on page 68; "selling" new ideas to employees, on page 69; reducing restaurant policies to writing, on page 71; imposing fines on restaurant employees to improve service, on page 73; how to correct employee misunderstandings, misinformation and job dissatisfaction, on page 75; what is the best way to train restaurant employees, on page 76; and what does a good restaurant employee want, on page 80.

4. Food service design, encompassing kitchen layouts, proper utilization of space, and control over sales. For example, the unique approach to restaurant layout of the production and food service areas in the form of a "work overlap diagram" is presented on pages 60 and 61.

5. Maximization of operating procedures, with special emphasis upon the vital operational study concept. To illustrate, practical hints on boosting restaurant profits by increasing beverage sales are provided on pages 91 through 94. In addition, the importance (to monitor the results of basic restaurant systems, and hence optimum profitability) of operational surveys is presented in a concise and revolutionary format on pages 94 through 96. Further, the menu cost sheet on page 97 and the comprehensive reference to other interrelated reports and accounting forms on page 96 present the restaurant operator with the required vehicles to determine fastidiously vital operating statistics on a timely and meaningful basis.

6. Restaurant equipment management, related depreciation aspects, modern applicability of leasing devices and the recent impact of the computer and electronic data processing on successful restaurant operations.

7. Management by objectives (MBO), as applied to the restaurant industry. A high point of this book, which goes a long way toward helping to fulfill its promise as "the most modern and topical tools and guidelines available to the restaurateur," is the section on pages 104 through 106 presenting four illustrative case studies demonstrating actual situations for successfully applying MBO to restaurant management with profitable results.

8. Profit planning, projections, forecasts and estimates, as related to improving restaurant profitability. For example, the set of

budgeting and profit planning worksheets presented on pages 143 through 148 are usable for any restaurant operation, large or small. These worksheets provide the most workable format available for the restaurateur to prepare and develop useful budgeting and profit planning information.

9. Financial accounting requirements, profit planning devices, and significant accounting control procedures for successful restaurant operation. We have made an effort to "streamline" restaurant accounting. Specifically the forms and accounting reports, which appear on pages 124, 125, 128 and 131 through 133, constitute key input which must be made available to restaurant management in its constant efforts to make the decisions that will tip the scales in favor of preserving and enhancing profitability.

10. Restaurant financial analyses and ratios and their relationship to sophisticated and profitable managerial decision-making. For example, the break-even analysis for the hypothetical Triple H restaurant which appears on pages 141 and 142, coupled with the graphic illustration on page 143, should be of enormous value in conveying to the typical restaurant operator the mechanics and practicalities of what he may have heard about but yet really be unaware of, the "break-even analysis."

11. The vast scope of tax implications of restaurant operation and management, with significant emphasis on tax-saving and tax-planning devices for the profit-minded restaurateur. To illustrate these practical tax-saving suggestions, several practical examples and tax planning suggestions are contained throughout Chapter 10, such as proper use of the Subchapter S election on pages 175 and 176, how to use multiple corporations to your advantage on pages 178 through 180, some practical hints to avoid the accumulated earnings tax on pages 180 and 181, the tax and financing advantages of leaseback arrangements on pages 183 and 184, properly using the investment tax credit on page 186, tax treatment of restaurant tips and employee meals on pages 187 and 188, and how to save taxes and improve employee morale through bonus programs and profit sharing plans on pages 189 through 191.

12. The industry trends, including highlights of studies of restaurant operations. To illustrate, the Steak and Brew example on page 195 and the "all-you-can-eat" situations cited on pages 194 and 195 present an in-depth and modern analysis of restaurant industry trends.

13. The success associated with the use of convenience foods and the wave of restaurant companies "going public." The central food processing plant concept, as shown by the practical example on pages 203 and 204, illustrates one of these successful approaches. In addition, the up-to-date review of "franchising," on pages 204 through 205, and the "restaurant joint venture" concept, on pages 205 through 206 represent the most unique and "with it" approach to these innovative ideas heretofore presented in any book such as this one.

As can be seen from the above brief summary of some of the topics covered, this book is the most comprehensive publication, to date, dealing with restaurant managment geared to the practicalities of the restaurant business. Quite simply, this is the basic reason for our book and explains why the modern restaurateur cannot afford to be without it.

Each of the chapters contains factual examples and illustrations, as elaborated upon above, of techniques and procedures drawn from both our personal reservoir of experience as well as our firm's many years as the leading expert in the hospitality accounting and consulting fields in the United States and abroad. Actual cases and experiences by restaurant managers and the industry consultants and certified public accountants who advise them on improving management capabilities and increasing profits, while saving time and money, have been implemented throughout our book for the purpose of providing the modern restaurateur with the most comprehensive guide to operating his business more efficiently. While the interrelationship of each chapter in our book to every other chapter is readily apparent, we have made a conscious effort to fortify each chapter with sufficent illustrative and descriptive material and commentary so that it may constitute a self-contained unit to satisfy fully the reader's search for information on any particular subject contained therein.

Kenneth I. Solomon

Norman Katz

Contents

PROFITABLE RESTAURANT MANAGEMENT

CHAPTER 1

Restaurant Formation, Organization, and Management

The success of every restaurant depends substantially upon meticulous advance consideration of every factor which will influence its initial cost, operating expenses, and sales. Planning is the operator's ally in avoiding some problems and in facing others with a sound grasp of alternative courses of action. Superimposed over the entire management and operation of a successful restaurant must be a basic philosophy geared, in our opinion, toward optimum customer service.

Principal considerations are the kind of restaurant to be opened, the kind of market it will serve, and the location from which it can most profitably serve that market. Critically important, also, are the form of business organization to use and the amount of capital that will be required to operate successfully. With a clear understanding of each of these areas, the restaurateur can begin to investigate means of raising the needed capital.

KIND OF RESTAURANT, MARKET, AND LOCATION

The restaurateur has a wide array of opportunities to serve markets ranging from the chic, expensive, four-star *palais de cuisine* to the modest fast-food counter. Between the large plush gourmet place and the small serviceable food counter lies not merely a spectrum of varying size and elegance, but a great variety of specific restaurant types:

Business lunch restaurants.
Homey neighborhood style restaurants.
Fast-food restaurants.
Cafeterias.

Seafood restaurants.

Ethnic restaurants (Italian, French, Spanish, to name just a few of the
   many possibilities).

Health food restaurants.

Cocktail lounges.

Cabarets.

Since eating is one of mankind's most fundamental—and enjoyable—activities, it is
not surprising that the range of options is wide and that the public's taste is subject
to constant change.

To consider the restaurant type most suitable for yourself, you need to
picture yourself in the operation before making your final selection. Does the
restaurant style you have in mind suit you? Does it fit your personality and self-image?
Can it satisfy your ambitions and fulfill your objectives? Having a restaurant that fits
you comfortably is an important part of operating successfully—and enjoying it as well,
which may be equally important.

Whatever type you choose, location will be virtually the most important
single determinant of how successful you can be. The type of restaurant, its location,
and its market are inextricably mixed. For some types of restaurants, it is essential to
be located in the midst of the market. For example, a restaurant devoted to business
lunches needs to be surrounded by business organizations, and a fast-food counter
must be located in a site where vast streams of people constantly pass by.

Thus, the type of restaurant has a distinct influence on how far people are
willing to travel to eat. In the examples given above, businessmen may be willing to
walk a few blocks for a really good lunch at a satisfactory price; for a quick snack, they
will go to the place on the corner—and no farther. The distance people will travel to eat
is very much a function of the restaurant type: people will travel farthest for elegant
dining, not at all for fast-food service, and to moderate distances for restaurants falling
between these two extremes.

Because people's preferences and life styles change, location must be
considered in a broad perspective and in the long term. The choice between a suburban
location and a downtown location is very important today, because the trend has been
distinctly away from the center city. Going downtown is no longer a way of life. This
has occurred simply because department stores, shopping centers—and restaurants—
have followed their markets to suburban locations. Urban unrest and decay have hurt
the center cities, and in the process, people and businesses have moved to the suburbs
in large numbers.

With this as a major and established trend, you must carefully weigh
alternatives between suburban and center city locations. It is important to recognize
that a reversal of the trend has been frequently predicted for the 1970's. High-rise
apartment buildings and condominiums clearly tend to bring people back from the
suburbs. And so long as city housing is available, common life style changes will tend to
encourage people to return, simply because families cease to need all the space available in a house when children grow up and leave home.

Such factors can have a significant influence on the equilibrium between urban and suburban markets. For example, the particularly large surge of postwar babies who reached college age in the late 1960's could precipitate a powerful move to urban high-rise apartments and condominiums in the late 80's and early 90's.

Thus, the flow from downtown to the suburbs could well slow down; the reverse flow could well increase. If so, every restaurateur needs to consider whether a different type of restaurant will be required. Years of suburban experience may well change people's preferences, and they might respond to completely different kinds of food service appeal.

Changes in public tastes may already be showing up in comparisons between small towns and big cities. The differences may be disappearing. The contrast between urban formality and small town informality is declining, and it may legitimately be asked whether things are equalizing at both ends. Formality is less dominant in the cities and more in demand in small towns.

The reasons for this are both changes in promotional methods and changes in people themselves. Differences are becoming less important. Modern promotional methods spread the same messages over broad areas for chains and franchisers with widespread and diverse locations. People will have more common backgrounds as time passes. Education, more extensive travel, and the universality of television smooth out prior differences and raise the general level of sophistication.

Price levels may differ from one kind of area to another, but pricing psychology is similar everywhere. Menu items are priced relative to each other, providing patrons with a range they can match to their pocketbooks. In turn, pricing is frequently constrained by competitors' pricing policies.

Even differences in climate are not as important as they once were. Air conditioning makes dining in New Orleans as comfortable as in Kansas City or Detroit. The great social mobility of recent years has further diminished people's sensitivity to climate and has conditioned them to "eating out" as a common activity. Similarly, population shifts have changed people's life styles to add millions to the food service market.

Location is critically important and requires careful consideration in light of the kind of restaurant you want to operate. Selection of the specific site within the general area you have chosen, however, depends upon developing the utmost information about the market your restaurant will serve. General location, the specific kind of restaurant, and the market are all interrelated factors which need to be examined together before final decisions can be made about any one factor.

Pinpointing Markets

Beginning with the kind of restaurant you want to operate and the general location you have selected, you next need to define the market you want to attract there. What are the characteristics of the potential customers in that area? What are their wants and needs in terms of food, service, and decor, and what quality and price ranges will be acceptable and appropriate?

Since the customer is the final arbiter of the restaurant's success or failure, learning about him, and understanding him is the principal unifying force in the decision-making process. This approach is a fundamental principle in our optimum customer service philosophy of restaurant management.

Architecture, decor, furnishings, pricing, menu-selection, staffing, advertising and promotion all must be geared to customer characteristics, tastes, and known preferences. Each of these factors will determine whether or not he becomes a patron.

In essence, what are we trying to convey? In the final analysis, everything must relate to the customer—this is the thrust of our concern for optimum service to the customer. While his conscious attention is most devoted to the food, the service, and the atmosphere, each of the detailed characteristics mentioned above has an indirect influence on the customer's reaction, and each must be fully compatible with his enjoyment of the food and service alike.

The failure to impose a consistent customer orientation on all phases of the operation and all physical characteristics can imperil a full realization of the market, or even the restaurant's success. For example, advertising that creates erroneous expectations will disappoint customers. If they expect elegance and formality but find hominess and informality, they will be disposed to be dissatisfied with the food and service, and they will not return for a second visit.

Similarly, the surroundings may detract from diners' enjoyment, despite excellent food, The decor and atmosphere must be compatible with the kind of food and service which the restaurant provides. A mismatch detracts from the dining experience—and discourages the diner from returning, even if he likes the food.

Thus, consistency and compatibility of the different elements are important to successful operations. Just as elaborate service for a simple menu and informal atmosphere will not return its high cost, it will also seem inappropriate to the customer, and perhaps even disturb him to the point of not returning.

The nature of the customers in the market to be tapped is the restaurateur's guide to achieving the necessary degree of consistency. This necessitates, in one form or another, a market study, Learning as much as possible about customers in the market is the foundation for establishing clear, integrated objectives and for narrowing down on a specific site which can maximize the sales potential.

The market study must consider potential customers' income level, life styles, types of occupations, ethnic mix, age mix, and a variety of other factors which mold both their preferences in dining out and the relative frequency with which they will dine out. These factors all influence the price range, the atmosphere, the relative elegance and formality, and the kind of cuisine which will most attract customers in that market.

Customers with comparable incomes but different backgrounds may have completely different standards of what they will spend when they dine out. Customers from one background may want a solid, traditional, relatively conservative decor when they dine, while customers from another may want a bright, sleek, modern environment. The former may want discreet, inobtrusive service, while the latter may expect attentive waiters who offer suggestions and show concern about the customer's satisfaction.

Completing a careful market study enables the prospective restaurant operator to forge a single, customer-oriented set of objectives to guide him in making the final decision. These cohesive objectives are the unifying influence that pulls together all the operating considerations and enables the operator to proceed with the odds in his favor.

The principles described here apply to restaurants of all sizes. Small restaurants need this consistent, coordinated approach as much as large ones. Once established, the small restaurant may find numerous areas in which its own operations are simpler than a large restaurant, but in the advance planning, the small operation will require as much detailed consideration of the factors influencing success as the large restaurant. The small restaurant can go astray just as easily as the large one, with the same effect on its customers—and the same drastic financial results.

FORMS OF BUSINESS ORGANIZATION

Careful consideration must be given to the form of business organization that will be most suitable for your purposes. The tax and legal effects differ significantly from one form to another. Most considerations in selecting the form of business organization are common to all businesses, but special factors sometimes enter into the decision for restaurants.

Proprietorship—Sole Owner

The simplest form of organization for restaurants is the sole proprietorship. It is the least formal of all the alternatives and this presents the fewest complications in establishing and operating the business.

Under a sole proprietorship, the owner does business in his own name or a trade name. The trade name must not conflict with another business, but few other formalities apply. The assets are his and the liabilities are his. The profits are unencumbered by the formalities involved in the other forms of business organization.

The sole proprietorship is common for a small restaurant, but this does not mean that it is invariably the most desirable form for the small restaurant, or unsuitable for a larger restaurant. The proprietor must consider the pros and cons of the other forms of organization, and he must particularly allow for the fact that in a sole proprietorship his liability is for all practical purposes unlimited. As a result, all his assets—not merely those involved in the restaurant—are subject to claims against the restaurant's assets. Accordingly, a restaurant operator with relatively limited resources whose prospective restaurant is on the high-risk side needs to give careful consideration to the other forms of business organization before launching a sole proprietorship.

Partnership

A restaurant operator may find a partnership of two or more owners preferable to the sole proprietorship for financial and operating reasons.

The partnership entails some degree of formality, sometimes by legal requirement, sometimes by custom, otherwise as a matter of protecting the rights of the partners themselves.

Using the partnership form of business organization reduces the amount of capital the individual investor must put up and, of course, reduces his dependency upon outside financing. In some situations, the prospective investor in a restaurant may find a partnership a necessity because of the financial requirements of the restaurant operation he plans. In other situations, he might have adequate resources and credit, but he will choose the partnership form over a single proprietorship for other business reasons: to spread the risk, to bring in an experienced restaurant man to help with operations, or simply to share the management with a man motivated by profits, rather than rely on a salaried manager.

The partnership arrangement can be tailored to a wide variety of sharing formulas, depending upon what each partner brings to the operation. The prospective restaurant owner needs to weigh all the considerations carefully and choose the alternative which will most closely suit his objectives. It is often said that a partnership is like a marriage, so in addition to all the legal and business considerations, the personal compatibility of the partners and their character and temperament are important.

The legal liability factor is also important to consider. General partners are *jointly and severally* liable for all debts, which means that each general partner can be held liable for *all* the debts of the business by any creditor. Thus, if one partner's assets are inadequate to meet the restaurant's financial obligations, the other partner's or partners' assets might be subjected to claims by the restaurant's creditors. In such cases, some partners would wind up assuming a liability disproportionate to their share of the business. Accordingly, partners should have relatively comparable resources or the sharing arrangement should take into account the fact that one partner assumes a higher risk.

In contrast to general partners, limited partners can limit their responsibilities for payment of debt, but as in the case described, this factor would be explicitly provided for in framing the sharing arrangement.

The arrangements for distributing profits among the partners are normally covered by a written partnership agreement, which also provides for any remuneration for services to be rendered, terms of dissolving the partnership under various circumstances, conditions for settling differences of opinion, and any other material agreements reached by the partners on the operation of the business.

Consideration must also be given to the continuity of the business in the event of the death of one of the partners. When one of the partners dies, his estate may need cash, which could impose a hardship on the business and the other partners if the survivors lack the liquidity to redeem the deceased partner's share in the business. One common arrangement for dealing with this contingency is a Buy-Sell Agreement funded by life insurance. Insurance proceeds payable to the surviving partner or partners cover all or part of their obligation to the deceased partner's estate for his share of the partnership.

Corporation

The corporation is a legal entity created by the state, functioning as though it were a person. The corporate form has the effect of separating ownership of the business from ownership of the assets. The owners of the business are one step removed from ownership of the assets, and the tax treatment differs significantly from the proprietorship and partnership forms of organization.

The corporation can own assets, assume obligations, sue and be sued. It is a highly formal entity, requiring the filing of articles of incorporation, the issuance of certificates of stock, the appointment of directors, and formal appointment of officers to act as agents of the corporation.

The theory behind the corporation is to allow for multiple absentee ownership and to limit the owners' liability for corporate debt. The limited liability is fully operative with large, well-established companies, but somewhat less so with small corporations. As a practical matter, the limitation is absolute for suits only for bodily injury and property damage. Where a small corporation seeks to borrow money, lenders usually require the major shareholder to sign as co-borrower or guarantor, thus eliminating the shield against his assets outside the business which the corporate form would otherwise provide.

Nonetheless, the corporate form basically limits the owners' liability, and in a going operation not substantially dependent on borrowing, this limitation can be a positive advantage of being incorporated. In case the business fails, the law provides for a so-called Chapter X reorganization in which the courts appoint an administrator to apportion the corporation's assets among its creditors.

For restaurants, the limited liability provisions of corporate law are sometimes diluted by state laws. Where so-called "dram shop" laws exist, operators and owners have larger liabilities than other corporations. If a bar customer leaves in a drunken condition and then injures another party, that party can hold the operator or owner of the bar legally liable for the damages sustained. Thus, the shareholder's protection by the limited liability provisions of corporate law does not insulate him in these circumstances.

The taxation of corporations can be an important factor in considering which form of business organization to use. Since the corporation is legally a distinct person, it pays taxes on its income and the shareholders, in turn, pay taxes on the dividends they receive from the corporation. The net effect is double taxation upon the income generated by the business. For the owners of the business, the after-tax consequences of the corporate form compared with a partnership depend upon the individual owner's tax bracket rate.

Futhermore, the tax law makes special provisions for small businesses to use the corporate form without bearing the brunt of double taxation. By establishing a Subchapter S Corporation, sometimes known as a Small Business Corporation, the owners of a business can control how taxes apply, within reasonable limits. The corporation can elect to pass its earnings along untaxed to its stockholders, who must, of course, report their share as income, just as in a partnership, and pay personal income tax at the appropriate rate.

Although the corporate form of business has complexities and considerable formality, it also has some desirable forms of flexibility. For example, changes in ownership can be effected by issuing or transferring stock to the new interests, whereas a similar change in a partnership requires the preparation of a completely new partnership agreement. Furthermore, corporations are not required to notify creditors of changes in ownership, in contrast to partnerships in which notification could be required in order to relieve a retiring partner of responsibility for debts incurred later.

A prospective restaurant operator must evaluate the alternative forms of business organization carefully in light of his objectives, his financial resources, his credit standing and the variety of other factors which will influence his operations. For two highly similar operations, the form of business organization most suitable for one owner could be quite different from that of another owner because of differences in their financial and personal circumstances.

FINANCING

Even a basically successful restaurant may flounder if the owner does not have adequate capital to meet the operation's cash flow needs with precision. Developing a sound financing plan and making firm arrangements are critically important.

The ratio of debt to capital affects the interest rate, and as debts increase, money is harder to borrow. Furthermore, the last dollar is the most expensive; so by having a clear, accurate advance picture of your needs, you may be able to finance more cheaply than if you have to go back repeatedly to lending sources to seek new infusions of capital.

In considering financing costs, it should be recognized that the interest rate paid on loans is not your total financing cost. Hidden charges are incurred in various forms. For example, the bank account reserves held from borrowed funds have the effect of increasing your actual borrowing costs. To illustrate this, consider a $100,000 loan at 8 percent on which a compensating bank balance of $20,000 is maintained. For all practical purposes, $8,000 of interest is being paid for $80,000 of borrowed money, which means that the effective borrowing rate is 10 percent.

Another hidden financing cost can result when equipment dealers take back notes which include add-on interest. This can become part of your financing plan. But you may find yourself paying higher equipment prices in addition to the nominal interest.

Another indirect form of financing is abnormal credit extended by some purveyors. Here, too, prices may turn out to be higher than they otherwise would be—effectively increasing financing costs.

Reliance upon credit can result in another easy-to-overlook cost: the fee required for audits of your accounts by independent certified public accountants. While such audits bring benefits in other respects, in considering total financing costs, the cost of such audits must realistically be included with other costs of financing.

In planning financing, the prospective restaurant owner needs to consider various alternatives, both in financing sources and in how specific financing transactions are structured.

Although cash financing through loans is important, other forms of financing can play a material role. Restaurants also have available other arrangements—such as turn-key operations and percentage leases—which have the same effect for the operator as receiving cash, since they relieve him of expenditures he would otherwise have to make.

Mortgages

Real estate and chattel mortgages can be valuable financing tools for the restaurant operator by relieving pressures on cash flow during the start-up phase of his business. Real estate mortgages are the conditional transfer of real property issued as collateral for a bond or note. The bond or note represents an indebtedness, effectively deferring costs until some later date or dates. Chattel mortgages on personal property are another way of deferring costs: equipment or furnishings may be the subject of a conditional transfer accompanying a loan.

In some situations, the operator may be barred from chattel mortgages by the terms of the lease he negotiates with his landlord. Some leases provide landlords with the protection of holding restaurant property and giving the landlord rights to lease it to others in the event of non-payment of rent. In such cases, of course, equipment and furnishings could not be encumbered with a chattel mortgage because the lease requires that they must remain free and clear. In lieu of such a lease restriction, a security deposit is often required by the landlord which serves as an alternate measure of security.

Special Restaurant Arrangements

For restaurants, special non-cash financing arrangements have been developed over the years. Turn-key operations, percentage leases and excess rental arrangements will be described in detail in Chapter 7, but we would like to give some brief idea of the role the typical turn-key arrangement can play in restaurant financing at this point. The turn-key operation requires no financing at all by the operator. He simply takes possession and manages the restaurant under a lease agreement. A turn-key operation is not ordinarily available to small operators. Only a large operator can expect a landlord to offer such a lease, for obvious reasons.

In cash borrowings, various alternative transaction forms apply. Some may be optional and some may be conditions imposed by the lender. Common to all loans are:

1. The loan principal: the amount borrowed.
2. The interest: payment for use of money, over and above return of the principal amount.
3. Interest add-on: the difference between the amount received by the borrower and the face amount of his note.

Some of the important variations in borrowing conditions lie in the repayment timing, the use of collateral, and the involvement of third parties as guarantors.

Repayment Timing

Aside from variations in the repayment schedule when the installment method is used, loans can sometimes be repaid in a single lump sum at an agreed-upon date. Clearly the financing cost will vary significantly from one payment method and period to another. Although cost will be a significant factor in establishing repayment terms, cash flow in the years ahead will be a material factor—and frequently, the single determining factor.

To the extent that the borrower has flexibility in negotiating repayment terms having accurate cash flow projections can be very helpful in keeping borrowing costs at a minimum. (Conversely, of course, they can prevent difficulties if the business is not going to generate enough cash surpluses to maintain the repayment schedule.)

The repayment schedule should be set at a rate that will leave adequate cash reserves for operating contingencies and yet not leave substantial amounts of cash idle, since those idle funds are really incurring a cost (by not earning a return).

Collateral

Cash financing is sometimes faciliated by the use of collateral. This may be a necessity where the borrower's credit standing is weak. Or it may be a device used by the borrower to reduce his financing costs. Collateral is property owned by the borrower but held by a lender as a protection against loss through default in repaying the loan.

The use of collateral is one of several forms of creative financing the businessman can use to minimize financing costs, or to raise capital needed for a prospective investment in circumstances where lenders are not beating down the door. Accordingly, as you determine your capital needs for a new restaurant, you need also to review your assets for property which can be used as leverage in raising funds through its being pledged as collateral.

Guarantor Loans

In some cases, lenders may be willing to grant a loan without additional collateral by requesting third party cosignatures to indemnify the lender in case of default by prime borrower. Where the borrower is a corporation, a stockholder owning a major interest in the corporation may be asked by the lender to guarantee the corporation's borrowings, thus eliminating the limited liability protection usually afforded to the owner by operating in the corporate form. The use of guarantors is not necessarily confined to mandatory requirements by the lender, but can sometimes be used by the restaurant operator as a device for increasing loan size or decreasing loan costs.

These various financing alternatives enter into the restaurant operator's considerations not merely in the initial stage, but also in subsequent operations. For expansion, replacement of facilities, and other needs that enter into the operation over a period of time, you may need interim financing. In turn, with seasonality, fluctuations in sales volume, and other situations which may put a strain on your cash flow, you may need short-term loans to tide you over periods in which liquidity is insufficient. Accordingly, you need to be on good terms with lending sources and to anticipate needs carefully in order to avoid default on existing loans which would discourage lenders from advancing additional financing.

SOURCES OF FUNDS

Banks are the major standard source of funds, and it is important to document your needs meticulously. Recent earnings statements, balance sheets, and projections of your income and cash flow for the future are the bank's basis for the loan decision. They reflect your ability to repay the loan and demonstrate your command of the situation.

Both the detail of your documentation and timing are important in dealing with banks. You should allow the bank sufficient time to consider your application, avoiding emergency situations in which your various reports show an urgent short-term need. Your foresight in planning puts you in a better light and generates confidence in your ability to produce performance according to your projections.

In connection with initial borrowing for a proposed restaurant, the restaurateur must have an economic feasibility study ready for banks and other lenders. The feasibility study, normally performed by an independent outside firm, is an investigation which carefully considers all the factors entering into the relative economic prospects for a restaurant of the type envisioned at the planned site. The study analyzes the market, evaluating the location in general, the competition and start-up costs and estimating the sales volume that may be expected.

The feasibility study offers the prospective lender independent evaluation and analysis in support of your loan application, and it expresses findings in terms of capital requirements, projected earnings, and cash flow as measure of ability to repay.

The feasibility study is the basis for initial financing, but once you have a going operation, you will need clear financial records to enable you to anticipate any additional need to borrow. Miscalculation of existing liquidity can be fatal. Running in at the last minute as though you were caught short or didn't expect to need money can impair your bank's confidence in your managerial capabilities.

Preserving this confidence is an important asset to your business, and thus you need to be sure that you have adequate information available at all times to manage your funds well.

Another important source of funds is the Small Business Administration, a federal agency established to help small businesses which cannot obtain full financing from banks. To qualify for an SBA loan, a restaurant's sales must be $1 million or less. SBA loans are made on three different bases:

1. By SBA guarantee of a loan made by a bank.
2. By a combination of both a bank loan and SBA participation loan.
3. By a direct SBA loan.

Under the first, the SBA may guarantee up to 90 percent or $350,000, whichever is less. The limits on participation and direct loans are $150,000 and $100,000, respectively.

SBA loans may run for as long as six years and, in special circumstances, for ten years. Collateral is required, usually in the form of real estate or chattel mortgages or third-party guarantees.

The interest rate on SBA loans is low. For example, when bank rates were running at 9 percent and higher, the ceiling on SBA loans was 5½ percent.

SBA loans for a new venture require that the borrower provide approximately half the total funds required, and he must provide it from his own resources. In all cases, the SBA is a secondary resource, since the SBA will provide financing only if financing is not available to the borrower from private lenders.

Expanding to a Second Restaurant

At some time, the successful restaurateur, and even some not so successful operators, decide to expand by opening an additional restaurant. At this critical point, an important evaluation must be made. Do you have the capability to run two operations which are separate geographically and in concept? The answer to this question requires a completely objective approach, without being swayed by the opinions of others. Take a personal skills inventory at this time. You will in the long run, save a great deal of trouble, distress, and possible failure.

How good a manager are you? Self-analysis is one of the means through which sound and accurate decisions are made. It is critical that this be done at the outset of the venture. Even more critical, this self-analysis must be undertaken with objectivity, which is extremely difficult to achieve.

Once these decisions and analyses have been made, the remaining problems are no different from those facing the restaurateur who is forced to confront the many decisions centering around his initial operations. These include finding the proper location, defining the market to be served, determining whether to rent or buy, arranging financing, designing the kitchen, surveying the labor market, developing the proper accounting and reporting mechanisms, and all of the other ingredients which have been discussed elsewhere in this chapter.

AVOIDING PROBLEMS

You have carefully investigated your market, selected a site, obtained financing and signed a lease, and you're now in the restaurant business. You must at all times, and particularly during the first year, realistically recognize the fact that some restaurants do not make it! Restaurants are prominent among businesses which have a high failure rate. This is not intended to discourage you—only to educate you to the cold, hard facts of life.

Accordingly, you need to be aware of some of the most common problems and causes for failure. For example, a Dun & Bradstreet study of 10,748 business failures showed that 43.3 percent of all failures were retail stores among which restaurants were very much included. Inadequate sales were the principal reason for the failure in 45.2 percent of the cases, and competitive weakness the reason in another 24.1 percent. The only other causes with any significant percentage were: poor location, 6.4 percent; inventory difficulties, 6.2 percent, and heavy operating expenses, 6.5 percent.

It is important to note that misjudgments of the market were clearly a major factor in more than 50 percent of the cases (inadequate sales and poor location). These cruel facts should dramatize the need for intensive advance study of the market and its potential, as carefully reviewed in depth earlier in this chapter.

In working with restaurants, we have found certain management and financial problems, that vary depending on the size of the restaurants. These problems sometimes reach such a severity that the restaurants simply cannot survive.

Among small restaurants, staffing is one of the major problem areas. Hiring, turnover, and absenteeism can be seriously disruptive of the owner's routine, whether he is normally present at the restaurant or not. Frequently, finding himself forced to handle many routine duties himself, the owner-operator may be unable to give sufficient time to more critical matters.

In turn, small restaurants frequently suffer from a shortage of cash. The failure to anticipate working capital needs can impair the ability to replenish inventories properly and even to meet payrolls—with disastrous results!

For medium-sized restaurants, undercapitalization and weak management are the two major causes for failure. Cash requirements prove to be larger than expected, thus swamping the restaurant during the start-up period when operating losses eat up the available cash. At the same time, the owner or owners frequently have not organized operations with sufficient depth to keep the business running smoothly. With limited personal experience, the owners may underestimate the importance of a system that ties together all the employees and all the different aspects of operations into a cohesive package.

Large restaurants which fail have usually incurred problems of a more sophisticated nature. Frequently, the basic problem has been traced to a fundamental error in defining the market or designing the facility and preparing a menu that will attract customers in that market. Another major weakness we have observed over the years is a lack of coordination of the diverse activities involved in running a large restaurant. Large restaurants are necessarily much more complex than smaller ones because functions which are relatively simple and quickly handled in small restaurants are more formal, complex functions in large ones. Thus, they require full-time staffs to handle, and a carefully designed system to integrate, all direct and support functions into a smoothly operating whole.

By having a familiarity with these sensitive areas from the very day you first consider starting a restaurant and throughout your initial operations, you can be on guard against the mistakes which have made others go under—and thus assure yourself of a greater chance of making a success of your restaurant, perhaps even where others have failed! It is precisely with this theme that we intend to provide such familiarity with every facet of restaurant operations and management in the following chapters.

CHAPTER **2**

Food and Beverage
Cost Control

CHAPTER CAPSULE PREVIEW

Prime cost, consisting of food, beverages, and payrolls, is the largest expenditure of a restaurant. This prime cost usually constitutes 65¢ out of every dollar of restaurant sales. Fortunately, these items, the ones most in need of control, are susceptible of control by techniques that lie within the reach of restaurateurs. This chapter will be devoted to the control of food and beverage costs.

Food and beverage control extends through a series of activies from purchasing to serving meals and drinks to customers. Each stage has its own peculiarities and its own needs, but there is a common need for documentation and records through all the stages.

A quality control function is also geared to timeliness. Inspecting, testing, and measuring while things are happening, quality control offers assurance that management's standards are being observed and its objectives carried out. Quality control provides "feedback"—which is essential to the overall control over the day-to-day operations of the restaurant enterprise.

All of the food and beverage control devices and techniques set forth, explained and examined in this chapter are keyed to the development and maintenance by restaurant management of a watchful eye directed toward maximization of restaurant profits.

CONTROL MEANS LIFE OR DEATH FOR THE RESTAURANT

Typically, food costs run from 30 percent to 40 percent of food sales; and in many restaurants the percentage is higher. The magnitude of the outlay for food is in itself a sufficient reason to focus attention on it. In addition, a steak or a roast is subject to pilferage and is readily usable. Similar observations apply to beverages, with the added characteristic that familiar brand names make them more easily salable to third parties.

When a single item accounts for a large part of the outlays of business, a small percentage loss incorporated in that outlay can make a substantial difference in earnings. If food and beverage costs amount to 40 percent of sales, and 5 percent of the cost of food and beverages is lost, then 2 percent of sales is lost through faulty control procedures; and a loss of this size could cut a restaurant's potential profit in half.

Such a situation can develop quite easily. Let management neglect part of the operations of the business, and that part is likely to suffer. If food and beverage costs are not kept under surveillance with a watchful eye, the very survival of the restaurant can be jeopardized.

Delays in detecting and correcting problems in food and beverage control can be expensive. For, not only do the losses mount up, but there is also a likelihood that further slippage will occur; that poor practices will grow worse, causing losses of serious dimensions.

Avoidance of unnecessary loss demands prompt action to remove difficulties, to correct abuses, to tighten up wherever practices show signs of loosening. In other words, control, itself, requires *prompt action* to be fully effective.

But in order for corrective measures to be prompt, they must be activated by a system that ensures *early detection* of developing problems. Early detection, then, is a crucial prerequisite to prompt action to minimize losses. Accordingly, a system for reporting is essential to effective control. The reporting system must make available to management all the information it needs to alert it to problems; and the information must be made available quickly so as to prevent or minimize costs at each stage in the flow of food.

The nature of the reports to be issued will vary from one kind of operation to another, and from one kind of organization to another. For instance, if foods are stored under lock and issued on requisition, then information pertaining to issues will be available for control reports; but if physical controls are lacking, and people help themselves to meet their needs, then a different report must be devised, one that attempts to fill a more urgent information gap in light of less available information.

The size of a restaurant and the equipment it uses in its data processing will also influence its reporting. Data that are available to some restaurants in one day may require a week of preparation time in other restaurants. A restaurant may have three kinds of reports on food costs, reflecting data gathered in three different ways, each with its own time requirements. For example:

  A daily flash food cost report shows the aggregate of requisitions plus purchases (as for bread, rolls, and milk) and compares the total cost with food sales.
  A daily summary of food cost (sometimes a semi-monthly, weekly, or ten-day report) shows actual food consumption and cost by category for comparison with sales in both current and previous periods.

A monthly consumption report, based on physical inventories, discloses inventory shortages and also prevents revised cost figures for analysis and comparison.

The following Daily Flash Report presents a useful illustrative tool for use by the restaurant operator:

ANY RESTAURANT
DAILY FLASH SHEET

TODAY'S DATE_____

FOOD AND BEVERAGE COST SYNOPSIS

	TODAY	*TO DATE*
FOOD COST	_____%	_____%
BEVERAGE COST	_____%	_____%
COST OF SALES	_____%	_____%

LABOR COST SYNOPSIS

	TODAY	*TO DATE*
FOOD LABOR COST	_____%	_____%
BEVERAGE LABOR COST	_____%	_____%
ADMINISTRATION LABOR COST	_____%	_____%
COMBINED COST OF LABOR	_____%	_____%

	TODAY	*TO DATE*
SPOILAGE REPORTS	_____%	_____%
LOSS & DAMAGE REPORTS	_____%	_____%

	TODAY	*TO DATE*
EMPLOYEE CAFETERIA	$_____+	$_____+
STEAK CONTROL REPORT	_____-	_____-

Submitted by: _____

Distributions:

Figure 2-1. Daily Flash Sheet.

The next form (Figure 2-2) is the Daily Summary of Food Cost, as discussed above:

There are economic considerations governing information systems themselves. Roughly stated, the system must not cost more to maintain than the output is worth. Adequate information should be sought, not a superabundance; and the cost must be held within reasonable bounds. In general, simple presentations help to achieve these goals. Elaboration should be questioned whenever it occurs.

In judging the reasonableness of the cost of a proposed or actual report, its preparation cost must be weighed against its value. Its value, in turn, is measured by

	THIS MONTH		TO DATE		RATIOS TO TOTAL SALES			
	TODAY	TO DATE	LAST MONTH	LAST YEAR	TODAY	TO DATE	LAST MONTH	LAST YEAR
KITCHEN & PANTRY								
BEEF								
VEAL								
LAMB & MUTTON								
PORK								
POULTRY								
SEAFOOD								
SUB-TOTAL								
VEGETABLES								
SALADS & RELISHES								
FRUITS								
MILK & CREAM								
EGGS								
CHEESE								
BUTTER								
SHORTENING & OIL								
COFFEE, TEA, COCOA								
STAPLES								
BAKE SHOP								
PASTRY SHOP								
ICE CREAM								
D. R. BUTTER								
D. R. GROCERIES								
TOTAL COST								
LESS EMPLOYEES' COST								
NET COST								
TOTAL SALES								

STATISTICS

	TODAY		TO DATE					
			THIS MONTH		LAST MONTH		LAST YEAR	
	COVERS	SALES	COVERS	SALES	COVERS	SALES	COVERS	SALES
TOTAL								

DAY_____ DATE_____   _____

Figure 2-2. Daily Summary of Food Cost.

the uses to which the data are put. In making decisions that are influenced by the report, the entrepreneur must inquire how much is at stake? In controlling costs with the help of the contemplated report, he must ascertain what risks are avoided?

Too much reporting can be uneconomical. It is unsound to gather and present data at a cost that cannot be recovered in the ultimate practical use of the data. The data should be capable of either leading to changes that will promote efficiency or controlling outlays and avoiding losses. In other words, the restaurateur should not get carried away and must constantly avoid the trap of "over-reporting" under the false label of control.

It should also be remembered that decisions are made and control is exercised by people. Reports must be understandable to the managers before they can be used properly in the accomplishment of management's objectives. It is futile to offer managers more data than they can digest. or to present them with data they do not know how to analyze. If a report is potentially valuable but susceptible to misunderstanding, its issuance may have to be accompanied by discussion, explanation, and perhaps reorientation.

In the initial stages, an information system should report on operations fully, presenting all the useful data that can be economically justified. This kind of reporting has educational value: it familiarizes managers with aspects of their operations that they may not have perceived quite so clearly before. It may also lead them to question practices that had been accepted previously, and to notice relationships that had gone unobserved. In short, it can enhance management's understanding of that nebulous all-encompassing element—"operations."

Case in Point:

We would like to share with you our experience involving the operator of a 200-seat restaurant who waited until the end of the month to obtain his cost percentage(for all food items lumped together) by dividing his sales for the month into the total purchases of food. This restaurant operator computed his cost incorrectly because he did not take into consideration the variance between the opening and closing inventories, did not maintain his cost by commodity breakdown and determined his cost only at the end of the month. Since this resulted in his finding out that costs were too high after it was too late to react, and since the individual food items—such as meats, fish, and vegetables, poultry, etc.—were lumped together making it impossible to identify the specific items that were out of line, we advised the operator to implement a daily purchase journal. This journal separated the cost of food items going directly to the kitchen from the purveyor and the cost of food items issued to the kitchen from the storeroom. These costs were recorded on a daily basis by commodity groupings.

Full reporting, however becomes wasteful, even self-defeating, when it is overdone. It should be supplanted in time by the method that has come to be called "reporting by exception." In essence, reporting by exception is a matter of reporting only those variances that are noteworthy. Everything else goes unreported, so that management relies on a "no-news-is-good-news" concept. Because reports are short, and they concentrate on problem areas, managers are promptly and effectively alerted to situations requiring their attention as decision-makers.

While reporting by exception is simple as a theory, its practical day-to-day implementation demands that certain preconditions be met. First, characteristics must be capable of measurement, and actual measurements must be made. This requirement presents no problem in reporting food and beverage costs: they can certainly be measured. Second, standards must exist for comparisons to be made; and variances between actuals and standards must be calculated. Third, tolerable limits must be set for variances, in actual amounts or percentages. Exception reports show only those variances that exceed the established limits, or parameters.

Standards are often thought of in connection with details: for example, the standard cost of a portion for each menu item. And such standards are certainly most useful in analyzing costs and investigating variances. But rough guides may serve a purpose too. And they may facilitate more timely reporting, especially in the smaller restaurant.

We noted earlier that a daily flash report of total food cost, a sample of which appears earlier in this chapter, can be useful to management. Daily control procedures can be improved still further by adhering to a standard for purchasing the main ingredients of the most popular dishes on the menu. While this method of food control is admittedly basic and crude, it has the great advantage of operating to control purchasing while it is in progress. There can be no more timely method: in effect, a control device built-in to the purchasing function.

HOW COST CONTROL HAS SAVED MONEY
FOR RESTAURATEURS

In many instances that we have witnessed, restaurant operators have first been alerted to leaks and deficiencies in their purchasing, storing, and consumption of food and beverages by reports that indicated excessive costs or erratic cost behavior. Having had their suspicions aroused, they then either found the cause of the problem or tightened up their security precautions until the problem disappeared. In these cases, analysis of data came first, followed by investigation.

How could losses have occured despite reasonable physical protection? There are many ways. Collusion between people can defeat many well-designed systems. To protect against all possibility of collusion is frequently too expensive a project to be worth undertaking. Any time two people are involved in a transaction in such a way that each provides a check on the other, there is a possibility that they will collude and share the proceeds of their illegal venture. And three people can beat almost any system. The concern of prudent management should, thus, be with probabilities and not possibilities.

Collusion is not always confined to employees of the restaurant. Outside deliverymen and salesmen have on several occasions been known to conspire with receivers and bookkeepers on the inside. Thus, receivers have signed for thousands of rolls their restaurants never actually received. With equal frequency, suppliers of food have been paid for greater quantities than they delivered or for which they could show receipts.

It is worth repeating that collusion is very difficult to guard against and that the first indication of a problem has often come through careful analysis of reported data. But even in the absence of collusion, there are still many ways for losses to occur.

A system that is designed to protect against pilferage may fail on account of negligence. If the person with the key to a storeroom walks away leaving it unlocked, or if he is careless in checking quantities removed against quantities requisitioned or signed for, there may be pilferage. Take it from us, these things have happened—and more than once!

Case in Point:

We have witnessed the failure of a popular family-style restaurant due to an inadequate storeroom system, because the storeroom clerk (and ultimately restaurant management, which must bear this responsibility) did not control issuances of food items from the storeroom and did not keep the storeroom locked at all times, allowing food items to leave without requisition.

Another Case in Point:

We should like to share with you an experience involving a 320-seat surburban steak house which suffered significant financial setbacks due to abnormally high prices. This resulted from kickbacks to the food buyer from the restaurant's meat purveyor, based on a percentage of the purchase price.

A Final Case in Point:

We encountered a similar problem in the case of a medium-sized neighborhood pancake house which had a system under which the storeroom clerk accepted food items that were not counted or weighed and did not check spoilage, conformity to specifications, damage in transit, or improper grades of merchandise. Since the pancake house restaurant's profitability was dependent on the cost per edible portion, over and above the mere purchase price of its food items, this lack of proper receiving controls and procedures was observed by us to represent the cause of financial distress to the restaurant. Fortunately, in this case, our analysis of the situation and the ultimate installation of proper receiving procedures saved this operation before it was too late.

Errors have been made by accounts payable bookkeepers quite honestly and unintentionally. Mistakes in bills do go undetected, especially where bad handwriting makes figures ambiguous. Bills are sometimes paid twice. This kind of error can get by more easily when the same amount recurs frequently in a vendor's bills, a circumstamce that must be expected in the average restaurant, where similar quantity, kind, and grade of food and beverage purchases recur on a fairly regular basis.

Carelessness in dishing out portions can also cut into profits. Many times this sort of difficulty has gone unnoticed until the existence of a problem was indicated by a reporting system, and subsequent investigation disclosed the nature of the problem. Although standard portions had been established in many cases, the portions that went out to customers were larger and more costly than they should have been. We are aware of countless instances where this was discovered only after management was alerted to the fact that actual food costs were running high.

Cost control has saved money for restaurateurs by protecting them from the danger of severe and unanticipated loss. Whether higher costs are incurred through careless, inefficient practices, or dishonesty, leakages are detected by the methods of cost control. Prompt disclosure, followed by prompt action, has often avoided additional loss.

BOOSTING PROFITS WITH PREDETERMINED PORTION SIZES

We have noted that carelessness can dissipate profits in spite of properly predetermined portion sizes. It should be obvious that, in such cases, the existence of standards makes it easier to pinpoint the specific cause of excessive food costs.

Moreover, there are other good reasons for establishing standard portions. Profit-planning will be discussed at length in a later chapter. Suffice it to say here that standard portions are the keystone of profit planning. Effective restaurant management contemplates that portion size, food cost, and menu price are fixed simultaneously for each menu item. Then, forecasts of sales and direct labor costs lead to estimates of the contribution margin available to meet all other so-called "indirect" expenses and, hopefully provide a net profit. Portions must be standardized and costed in advance, in order to predict whether margins will be adequate to cover expenses and allow a profit to be earned. Food cost and portion size are a pivotal factor in management thinking and planning for profitable operations.

Looking at the matter another way, both prices and portions have to be competitive with other restaurants in the neighborhood. That being the case, both prices and portions must be established with the market in mind—and with the intention of providing consistent portions at fixed prices.

Whichever way you look at it—from the standpoint of either marketing policy or cost control—portion sizes must be established and adhered to if a restaurant is to attract customers to (and through) its doors and serve them profitably. Furthermore, changes in raw food prices and changes in meal prices require careful and immediate recalculation of margins and reconsideration of portion sizes. Once portions are predetermined, they can be converted into standard costs per meal of each type. Standard costs are then available for control reports, as discussed earlier.

Example:

We encountered a medium-sized downtown restaurant which specialized in chicken dishes and established specifications for purchasing chickens between 2 and 2½ lbs. Under the normal specifications, 100 lbs. would yield approximately 45 chickens. However, because the purveyor included ten three-pound chickens, this yielded only 42 chickens which resulted in a loss of three chickens to the restaurant. This situation showed up dramatically on the bottom line!

HOW TO USE COST ACCOUNTING TO CUT COSTS

There are various ways to keep track of the transactions that occur in the course of business operations. Accounting systems classify and gather data for assets, liabilities, income, expense, and net worth so that the details can be summarized in regular periodic reports. Cost accounting systems carry the classification of income and expense items to departmental activities as well as objectives (or "natural expenses"), for internal management purposes.

In a restaurant, the goal of a cost accounting system is to accumulate data pertaining to revenues and expenditures for individual activities: bar sales, food sales—regular and banquet, take-out sales, counter sales; food preparation costs, serving, bookkeeping, selling promotion, and so on. Labor, a natural expense, is normally charged to many different departments by way of a labor distribution sheet.

Since food and beverage control is our primary control in this chapter, let us focus on cost accounting for food and beverages. First, how many categories of food should be recognized? That depends on the nature of the operation, the menu, storage facilities and procedures, and the relative need for control. If there is a separate counter for delicatessen meats, then the category delicatessen meats becomes a candidate for a category of its own. If the menu stresses seafood, with only a limited number of meat items, then beef, veal, lamb, and pork may comprise a single category, even though the usual practice is to give each a separate cost category. Frozen foods may have their own categories because of special storage facilities, and also because an analysis of combined labor costs and raw food costs may be desirable for these items. Bread and rolls may be delivered to serving areas, bypassing the restaurant's regular receiving, storing, and issuing procedures, In that case, management may find the need to control bread and rolls carefully, and to count them as a separate cost category.

To illustrate, examine the following sample form (Figure 2-3) which we developed for use by a state university dining system for cafeteria and fountain food cost reporting:

Second, how many activities should be recognized for purposes of control? Here again, restaurant accounting must be adapted to restaurant operations. If food is served from a number of counters, each with its own cash register, and food control overlaps with cash control, then each counter must be charged for food issued to it and credited for cash collected at its register. To illustrate further, the earnings of a catering

REPORT ON FOOD COST

WEEK ENDED _____ 19____

COMMODITIES	CAFETERIA COST THIS WEEK	TO-DATE	CAFETERIA RATIOS TO TOTAL SALES THIS WK.	TO-DATE	LAST MO.	LAST YR.	FOUNTAIN COST THIS WK.	TO-DATE	FOUNTAIN RATIOS TO TOTAL SALES TO-DATE	LAST MO.	LAST YR.
MEATS											
POULTRY											
SEAFOOD											
SUBTOTAL											
FRUITS AND VEGETABLES											
BUTTER											
EGGS											
MILK AND CREAM											
ICE CREAM											
BREAD AND ROLLS											
PASTRY	x x x x	x x x x									
COFFEE, TEA & COCOA											
STAPLES AND GROCERIES											
PIZZA	x x x x	x x x x									
SOUP AND SAUCES	x x x x	x x x x									
PICKLES AND RELISH	x x x x	x x x x									
BEVERAGE SYRUPS	x x x x	x x x x									
TOPPINGS	x x x x	x x x x									
GROSS COST											
LESS: EMP'L. MEALS											
NET COST											

STATISTICS

	SALES THIS WK.	TO-DATE	LAST MO.	LAST YR.	MEAL PERIOD	COVERS THIS WK.	TO-DATE	CHECK AVERAGE TODAY	TO-DATE
CAFETERIA					CAFETERIA				
CLUB					LUNCHEON				
PARTIES					DINNER				
SUBTOTAL					PARTIES				
FOUNTAIN					CLUB				
CIGARETTES					SUBTOTAL				
CANDY AND OTHER					FOUNTAIN				
GRAND TOTAL					GRAND TOTAL				

Figure 2-3. Report on Food Cost.

service can be measured only if the catering department is charged for all foods issued to it. Similar considerations apply to a banquet department. Likewise, profits by meal period can be ascertained only if the records segregate food costs by meal period.

Consider, for example, the following form (Figure 2-4) which was developed to assist in the segregation of food costs applicable to the banquet department of a hotel

These considerations all lead to a basic principle of cost accounting: expenses are charged to those activities that are responsible for incurring them. In a restaurant, food is charged to responsible activities, and these activities are relieved of their accountability when they move food on to other activities. Thus, the storeroom is charged for stocks of food received and credited for food issued to kitchens, bars, or counters. A kitchen is charged for food that it receives, and it is relieved of responsibility for meals checked out to customers or employees. A waiter is responsible for meals checked out to his customers, and he is relieved of accountability for checks turned in to the cashier for payment. At this point, the cashier is accountable for the cash value of checks turned in to her. (This is one link between food control and cash control.) In effect, accountability for the cost of food and beverage items should follow the physical flow of those items through the restaurant.

In the foregoing illustrations, another principle of control is exemplified: wherever possible, individuals should be held accountable rather than whole departments or groups. For instance, each waiter is properly charged for meals checked out to him. Carrying this principle a step further, each shift should be responsible for its own activities: in the kitchen, each chef, for example, should bear this responsibility during the time he is on duty.

Responsibility accounting leads ultimately to reports that reflect the operating results of individual areas of responsibility—normally termed departments in the restaurant industry. From such reports, a restaurateur can obtain specific information on which to make decisions that will affect his earnings. He can tell, for example, the contribution that the breakfast period makes toward overhead and profits, the relative contributions of the bar, of banquets, catering, and take-out products. He can plan for each activity on the basis of its own track record.

Futhermore, accumulated records for each activity over several periods permit comparisons to be made. If something unusual occurs, something that may require attention, it will be brought out more certainly by departmental figures than by totals that lump together the operating results of all departments. Likewise, developing trends manifest themselves more readily in departmental figures than in aggregate data which may well serve to hide rather than highlight offsetting trends.

Notwithstanding the fact that historical cost data by responsibility has many uses, the best way to control costs is by planning first and then matching performance against the plans. In other words, comparison of a department's results in one period with its own record is not as effective a method of control as comparison of the same actual data with standards that are designed in advance to achieve management's objectives.

ORGANIZATION_____
LOCATION_____
BARTENDER_____
CASHIER_____
DATE_____

Units	ITEM	Original Issue	Additional Issues	Total	Total Returned	Consumed	Item Cost	COST

Figure 2-4. Banquet Requisition.

This observation leads us to the most important use of cost accounting: to accumulate data for use in profit planning. Not only are cost data useful in constructing a profit plan, but newly accumulated cost data are also used in analyzing variances from the profit plan while it is in operation, and they are used again as feedback in adjusting the new profit plan the next time around. The most effective use of cost accounting is in establishing and testing standard costs and reporting variances between actual and standard for various operating periods.

Insofar as profit planning for food operating is concerned, standard costs relate to predetermined portions, volume forecasts, and estimated prices for raw foods. Whenever these variables diverge from their predetermined values, profits are affected sometimes drastically.

Brief mention must be made at this point of the importance of butchering and cooking tests for the purpose of determining ingredient cost and establishing properly marketable *and profitable* portion sizes. We have too often observed in practice that these easily applied butchering and cooking tests are ignored or overlooked by the typical restaurant operator, despite the obvious control benefits to be derived from their sensible and cautious utilization.

Hence, control becomes a matter of noting specific deficiencies quickly, developing supplementary information, if necessary, and acting to correct problem situations. Variance analysis, which critically depends on cost accounting, is the principle step in this sequence of events.

If variance analysis seems to be a long-drawn-out affair, consuming much time (which is often found to be the case) then let us remember the importance of timeliness in controlling activities. Daily flash reports may lack many things: detailed analysis, supporting evidence, complete accuracy may all be missing. But there is a net gain in trading these things for immediacy. A flash report should present whatever information is available quickly, including variances that have not yet been analyzed— *hopefully early enough to be controlled.*

BOOSTING PROFITS BY AVOIDING SPOILAGE AND WASTE

It hardly needs to be said that food is perishable, or that the degree of perishability varies. Fruits, bread, and milk deteriorate rapidly, while refrigerated meats and shortening have a longer life, and frozen foods last longer still. Although these groups have some spoilage problems (and solutions) in common, there are other problems they don't share.

To begin with, there is overbuying, which may result from poor purchasing practices, inadequate information, or forecasting failures. Quantity purchases at favorable prices, with lower shipping costs per unit, may lose their attractivemess when the costs of prolonged storage are considered; and they may prove to be unsound investments if they result in spoilage. Excessive purchase may bring about spoilage among other items by overtaxing the storage facilities, so that equipment works below normal efficiency (if, indeed it doesn't break down) or standard procedures are suspended due to difficulties in reaching items that should be used first.

Poor records may result in overbuying, especially if they co-exist with haphazard storage procedures. Food buyers must know what is on hand before they place new orders. This simple fact is essential and cannot be overemphasized, yet it is surprising how often it is overlooked.

Since purchases are made in anticipation of need, accurate forecasts are essential to effective inventory management: The harm done by a bad forecast is most severe, of course, when highly perishable items are bought, because there is no time limit to correct such mistakes. Consequently, it is the daily forecast that is most critical. Unfortunately, it is the daily forecast that is also the most subject to the vagaries of weather and the impact of fleeting factors, implying a strong need for refined methods and exceptional care in forecasting.

Spoilage can occur for reasons other than overbuying. Lax inspection on the part of receivers may permit inferior merchandise to come in without challenge and be stored. Frozen foods that have begun to thaw may deteriorate rapidly. Some of the effects of careless receiving practices may not be felt until much later, and in such cases the receivers may not be held suspect even then.

Storage space of one kind or another may be inadequate for the handling of normal purchases and normal inventories. A situation of this kind can develop rather rapidly if volume surges upward or practices change in the kitchen. For example, there may be a shift toward frozen foods that cannot be accommodated properly in this freezer space that is available. The temptation under such circumstances is to overstack a freezer. It would be far better to respect the limitations of existing equipment and to arrange for more freezer space.

Care of equipment involves more than just proper use. There must be a regular program of preventive maintenance to detect incipient troubles before they create serious problems. As part of the maintenance routines, controls should be checked periodically to ascertain that they are functioning properly. An erratic thermostat can endanger large quantities of food stored in a refrigerator or freezer. In particular, when meat becomes unfit for use because of alternate freezing and thawing, the condition is not observable until the damage is done.

Despite all precautions, despite careful use and preventive maintenance programs, we have witnessed failures that may occur. Sometimes external conditions, such as power shortages or floods, cause damage. There should be a plan to go into effect in each situation that can reasonably be anticipated; and the procedures for carrying out the plans should be readily available in writing. They should be known to, and understood by, all parties concerned with implementing them.

Finally, food can be kept from spoiling in storage by ensuring that storing and issuing procedures move the oldest items out first. When a new shipment arrives, it should not be stored in such a way as to block or hamper accessibility to the remaining stock from previous shipments. In addition, everything should be dated; either at the receiving location or on being moved into storage. Each shipment of a single item should be kept together; and when its turn comes, it should all be used up in its entirety before turning to another shipment. Dates of foods in storage should be examined periodically to confirm that stocks are being rotated in accordance with established procedures.

When foods and beverages are moved into or out of storage, as well as during the various stages of preparation, there are chances for breakage and spillage to occur. Many containers, particularly beverage containers, are susceptible to these types of losses. Proper equipment helps to reduce breakage and spillage. Hand trucks, racks, and vessels should be of appropriate sizes, and they should be used correctly. A safety program, while intended primarily for other purposes, will act as a prophylactic measure against breakage losses. Careful employees, working with suitable equipment properly maintained, and finding fixtures and materials readily accessible, should be able to bring spillage and breakage down to minimum levels. The real problem in this regard is for management to take the little bit of extra time and expend the marginal effort toward such a high standard of care.

There is considerable potential for spoilage and waste in the preparation of foods. When too much food is prepared in advance, and large quantities are left over at the end of the day, the fault may lie in a forecasting error or in a failure to relay information properly to the chef. Once again, we find that it is a critical matter to forecast as accurately as possible, not only total volumes, but the demand for specific menu items. Having made a detailed forecast for the day, the next step is to convert it into work orders to prepare so many roasts, so many turkeys, so many legs of lamb, and above all, to transmit these work orders to the kitchen as authorization to requisition items needed from storage.

Waste can also result from preparing the wrong item. Cooks prefer to hear and see each other: they want the servers to call out orders and also present a customer check for each one. The use of numbers for menu items provides added protection against misunderstanding. And, of course, legible writing helps, too.

Overcooking can ruin the best foods. It may be caused by unfamiliarity with the equipment, faulty temperature controls, poor timing, or just plain neglect. A customer may complain of overcooking if his concept of rareness differs from the chef's concept of the term, or if a server mixes up orders. A helpful and inexpensive operating hint is in order: with an adequate supply of coded plastic markers to indicate whether steaks are rare, medium, or well done, such mistakes should not occur.

Nevertheless, records should be kept of customer complaints leading to spoilage or waste. Such records provide symptoms of underlying problems: poor quality foods, poor storage conditions, overcooking, errors, or inferior service.

Service is at fault when items are permitted to stand too long. The cause may ultimately be traced to bad layout, inadequate facilities, shortage of help, or lack of supervision. Perhaps procedures can be changed or duties adjusted to prevent recurrence.

ESTABLISHING DEPARTMENTAL RESPONSIBILITIES
AND PROCEDURES

In any restaurant, regardless of size, certain functions must be carried out. Food must be purchased, received, stored, prepared, and served. In a large restaurant, each of these functions will be handled by a separate department, with its own staff and departmental supervision responsibilities. In a small restaurant, one person may wear several hats, supervising and/or participating in several activities, so that lines of demarcation become blurred. But in all cases, the functions do exist, and they can be observed separately, allowing for an effective delegation of specific duties.

In describing the activities of a small restaurant, it is helpful to focus on functions instead of individuals. Where several functions are handled by one person, it is easier to follow the logic of the organization structure by relating functions to each other than by relating individuals or their titles. In these situations, titles can be most misleading.

In what follows, therefore, operations will be analyzed by function rather than title. The principles and recommendations are applicable to small restaurants as well as large ones.

Avoiding Pitfalls in Purchasing

The buyers of food must be experienced people with a thorough knowledge of quality and grades of food, and also of industry practices. There being many temptations in the path of buyers, they must be people of unquestioned integrity, with no conflicts of interest.

Records and systems serve two purposes: to facilitate buying by making readily available information concerning food requirements and sources of supply; and to encourage honesty among buyers.

There should be a card file or loose-leaf book of specifications for all raw foods purchased. Each specification card or sheet should describe the item fully, including grade, size, style of pre-preparation, and container. And each specification should bear evidence of formal approval by the chef and the general manager.

To illustrate what we mean by "specifications," the reader should refer to the following sample specifications for breast of chicken cacciatore (in this case the specifications relate to an advance-prepared frozen convenience food):

SAMPLE SPECIFICATIONS FOR PRE-PREPARED
FROZEN CONVENIENCE FOOD

Breast Of Chicken Cacciatore

NET WEIGHT: 5 lbs.
PACKED: 4 Trays per case
GROSS SHIPPING WT.:   22 lbs.
PORTIONS PER TRAY: 10
RECOMMENDED portion size: 8 ozs.   (Breast average weight 4 ozs. cooked)

PRODUCT DESCRIPTION: Tender half chicken breast prepared in a delicate Italian tomato sauce with just the right touch of seasoning.

INGREDIENTS:	Chicken breast with ribs, tomatoes, chicken stock, onions, tomato paste, sweet peppers, flour, carrots, starch, rice flour, salt, red wine, celery, monosodium glutamate, flavorings, hydrolyzed plant protein.
INSPECTIONS:	U.S.D.A. inspected for wholesomeness #P-89.
COOKING DIRECTIONS:	Remove label, loosen aluminum lid. Preheat to 450°F. CONVENTIONAL OVEN: Heat for 60-70 minutes depending on oven load and recovery time. CONVECTION OVEN: Approx. 10 minutes less than above. Recommended minimum serving temperature—161°F. Lid should be removed 10-15 minutes to enhance flavor and appearance by browning.
CAUTION:	1. DO NOT refreeze product that has been completely defrosted.
	2. Once product is removed from the freezer, it should be held at a temperature no higher than 40°F. and should be used within 24 hours. Reduce oven temperature by one-third (1/3).

A file should also be maintained for suppliers, both actual and potential. Each supplier card should record name, address, telephone number, categories of foods purveyed, terms, salesmen's names, and pertinent information regarding deliveries, reliability, and special characteristics. Such a file can be helpful to a buyer who has to make new arrangements, or to a substitute during the buyer's absence.

A system of purchase orders should be fully operative. Daily deliveries should be covered by long-term purchase orders; and new ones should be issued whenever changes are made. Some items are ordered by telephone for immediate delivery, and it may be convenient to confirm all of these transactions with purchase orders. Nevertheless, purchase orders should be issued whenever it is practicable to do so. The number of purchases without written documentation should be held to a minimum.

Examples of Purchasing Problems:

Consider the following practical examples of purchasing problems which we have encountered during our experience as consultants to the restaurant industry:

1. A restaurant manager in a large downtown restaurant, relying primarily on luncheon business, believed that if specifications were drawn up properly, he did not have to spend a lot of time learning to identify the various grades of meat. He couldn't have been more incorrect. We have personally toured packing houses and have witnessed unbelievable variations within the same "U.S. Choice" grade of hanging beef. Had the manager selected his own meat, rather than blindly ordering a "U.S. Choice" grade, he would have without doubt obtained a much higher quality of meat.

2. Consider the case of the small neighborhood 80-seat restaurant whose operator purchased meat in wholesale cuts. This turned out to be a serious economic error since he would have to purchase pre-fabricated meats in light of his high labor costs and limited menu. A much larger operation is better equipped to purchase wholesale cuts of meat since that can utilize the leftover pieces for preparing other menu items and employee meals.

3. We must relate our experience with an otherwise competent restaurant manager who failed to give proper attention to reordering points and purchasing. He found himself in serious financial straits as a result of his failure to consider present quantities on hand in making purchase decisions, with a consequent duplication of ordering and excessive quantities of certain items on hand, resulting in unnecessary spoilage and being forced to carry an inventory far beyond the restaurant's financial capability. This type of disregard for proper purchasing controls and procedures can be a large step down the road to disaster.

Over and above this need for written documentation in purchasing, several bids should be sought on each item at regular intervals, and the dates and bids should be recorded. A minimum of three bids is appropriate. The frequency will depend on price stability, volume, and changes in order quantities. The rules on competitive bidding must be enforced, or else the effort is merely a sham.

Written procedures should cover every aspect of purchasing. The procedures should be kept current by regular updating, and they should be accessible to the buyers. Likewise, there should be written procedures for all other functions as well; and these must also be updated, with copies available to the people who are to follow them.

RECEIVING

Written procedures for receiving should cover weighing, counting, measuring, physical handling of goods, and routines regarding receiving tickets. Inspection for quality must also follow established routines. The performance of each task requires a person who is qualified by training and experience. It is management's responsibility to see that people with such qualifications regularly carry out their instructions in compliance with the existent written procedures.

Receivers should have quality standards in writing readily available. For frozen and refrigerated foods, these standards must include criteria for temperatures and packing materials. Inspection methods should also be specified in detail.

Where large quantities are received, sampling methods are available for ascertaining at minimal cost that shipments are up to established standards. While sampling methods are applicable in some situations, their detailed application and other related intricacies are beyond the scope of this book.

A pre-numbered, three-part receiving ticket should be issued for each delivery. One part of the three-part form should go to the accounts payable bookkeeper, a second part to the purchasing department, and the third part should stay in the receiving area, where it should be filled for subsequent reference as needed.

To illustrate the daily recap of goods received, the reader should refer to the Receiving Sheet form (Figure 2-5):

STORING AND ISSUING

Storage requirements should be estimated far enough in advance to take steps to provide adequate space of all kinds to meet anticipated demand. When estimates show a developing need for additional space of a particular kind, top management should be informed immediately, in order to allow as much time as possible for planning, getting estimates, awarding a contract, and having the new storage space built with the least interruption of normal operations.

All storage areas should be kept locked, with keys in the possession of authorized storekeepers only. Issues should follow a regular schedule, so far as possible; and they should be made only on written requisitions approved by department heads.

Physical inventories are taken at regular intervals; and shortages or overages are calculated and investigated before adjusting the records. Issues are priced out and summarized daily as part of the procedure for controlling food costs.

PREPARATION

In the food preparation function, documentation calls for a file of standard recipes and another file of portion sizes, including specifications for vegetables and garnishes for each plate. Seasonal factors and erratic price swings may dictate temporary adjustments or long-lasting changes. These modifications, too, should be recorded in the files, and adherence to the new standards should be enforced.

Production should be guided by, and based on, detailed forecasts and production orders. Whether requirements can be anticipated within narrow limits, as in the case of a banquet for a given number of reservations, or estimates are subject to wide margins of error, as at a seashore resort subject to changeable weather conditions, there is far less risk in making the best possible forecast than in allowing production to be governed by guesswork on the part of people who are neither adequately informed nor especially well qualified in the techniques of forecasting. A forecast of total demand should be analyzed into forecasts for all menu items. These detailed forecasts, in turn, must be converted into production requirements.

QUALITY CONTROL

When a restaurant has established standards, recorded them, and made them available to its operating personnel, it has taken a long step toward systematic management. But even the best systems need to be continuously watched and controlled. No system can be entrusted to work automatically; nor can management afford to abdicate its vital control function.

Standards must be enforced through quality control at every stage: through purchasing, receiving storage, production, and serving, At each stage there are specific standards to observe.

DATE _____ 19____

Form 441-1, A, Medlar Co., Omaha, Neb.

Quantity	Unit	NAME AND DETAILS	Unit Price	AMOUNT		DISTRIBUTION				
				Extension	Total	Food Direct to Kitchen	Food to Store Room	Cigars	Sundries

Figure 2-5. Receiving Sheet.

The grades and sizes that are specified in purchase orders must conform to the purchasing specifications on file. Quality control begins here.

Receivers are responsible for inspecting and measuring incoming goods to see that the restaurant is getting what it is paying for. A quality control activity devotes part of its energies to making sufficient tests to assure management that the receivers are actually carrying out their responsibilities.

Foods in storage must be kept at proper temperatures, free of contaminating odors, and accessible for issuance on a first-in first-out basis. Also, certain foods must be separated from others while in storage.

Quality control involves inspection of storage areas and of stored foods to detect indications of unsanitary conditions, infestation, incipient spoilage problems, excessive length of storage, or the absence of receiving dates on specific items.

Adherence to recipes and portion sizes in the preparation of foods is also a concern of quality control. In addition, meals being served should be subject to scrutiny for taste, visual appeal, temperature, and cooking time in conformity with customer requests.

The techniques of quality control vary with operations and conditions. More time has to be allocated to critical matters than to ordinary things. A new refrigerator, or one that has recently been repaired, may demand more frequent temperature checks than one that has been functioning well. A newly hired receiver may have to be watched a little more closely than an experienced man who is thoroughly familiar with the restaurant's routines.

Certain precautions are necessary in making observations. The times for checking temperatures should be varied. Heavy movements of food into a refrigerator may cause its temperature to rise. If this should occur daily at approximately the same time, then consistent observations at an earlier time would miss an important fact about temperature fluctuations.

Tests of received merchandise are made after approval by the receivers. The timing of these tests should follow no predictable pattern, lest the receivers get into the habit of exercising care at certain times only.

Destructive tests should be avoided. If inspection requires that a package be broken open, then the food in it should either be used immediately or repacked carefully. Waste is costly!

It is unnecessary for a quality control individual or group to inspect every item at every stage. Rather, they should rely on samples. To derive the greatest benefit from sampling involves the use of techniques that are beyond the scope of our discussion, belonging in the realm of statistical quality control. In a large restaurant or chain, it would be a sound investment to provide training in statistical methods.

The quality control function needs documentation as much as any other activity—more, in fact. All the precedures for selecting and testing various kinds of samples, for scheduling observations and readings, and for taking measurements, should be spelled out precisely. In addition, records should be kept, at least for one month, of all readings and the results of all tests. Before quality control can be expected to function effectively, it must keep its own house in order.

PROFESSIONAL IN-DEPTH STUDIES

Food and beverage control is a broad subject, covering so many of a restaurant's activities and involving so much of its costs, that efforts to improve performance in this area may take many directions and still be rewarding. A professional in-depth study will be methodical, and it will identify and concentrate on those functions that are most in need of corrective action.

Characteristically, such a study by outside consultants, experts in the industry, defines existing problems. Symptoms are often deceptive, and the underlying causes may have to be uncovered by intensive study of operations. But as in medicine, treatment of a symptom may allow the disease to go unchecked. If a patient has the measles, it is futile to treat him for a rash.

Once the real causes have been precisely defined, solutions must be sought. This process involves a methodical search for alternatives, followed by a careful selection of options to achieve the desired results. While the decision-making function must always remain as a prerogative of management—not to be abdicated—consultants can assist in the process by presenting alternatives, along with their advantages and disadvantages.

When a particular solution has been selected, procedures must next be established for implementing it. This task also falls to professionals in the field. During the period of implementation, they can offer advice and help to overcome problems that arise.

Finally, consultants should follow up to assure themselves and management that troublesome conditions have indeed been corrected. During this follow up, divergence from the planned solution can itself be detected and rectified.

CHAPTER 3

How to Streamline Material Handling and Food and Beverage Procedures

CHAPTER CAPSULE PREVIEW

Material handling procedures influence a substantial portion of a restaurant's costs, and thus its profits. Accordingly, management needs assurance in its operations that it is using equipment and facilities which will most efficiently realize its marketing concept to the fullest utilitarian fruition. Even the most advanced labor-saving setup, however, will not do the job alone. Staffing policies, scheduling, and meticulous supervision are also critical. Finally, a well-designed layout and effective procedures are needed to blend the whole into a smooth operating unit which minimizes cost and maximizes customer satisfaction.

Restaurant profitability depends substantially upon the efficiency of handling food, beverages, and other materials and supplies. Accordingly, planning for such handling must begin early.

The basic planning ingredients are the market concept and the menu. The market concept determines the menu, and the menu in turn determines both the various categories of food and materials needed and how they must be stored and handled.

Thus, this chapter will consider:

Interrelations of food handling with markets and menus.
Layout considerations for storage, preparation, service and sanitation.
Utilization of staff and facilities.
Future trends.

INTERRELATIONS OF FOOD HANDLING
WITH MARKETS AND MENUS

The planning of kitchen equipment and layout needed is substantially dependent upon the advance planning of market segments to be sought after, general menu content and the type of overall service planned for the market. The restaurateur, regardless of the type of restaurant operations involved, must continuously consider *"a minimum of effort with a maximum of efficiency"* as his guiding philosophical principle.

Therefore, the restaurant must be assured of having equipment which will maximally facilitate rapid economic delivery to the public. This means having the right equipment in the right amount and the right place, because each factor substantially influences labor costs. Inadequate equipment means extra labor, and even if equipment needs are fully met but the individual pieces of equipment are not related to each other satisfactorily, employees will use extra time in using the equipment, in moving from one piece of equipment to another, and in performing other functions related thereto.

For example, convenience foods require special equipment. Without the proper facilities, the advantages of convenience foods cannot be fully realized. Their advantage to the public is based upon quick and economic service. If service is not quick, sales will be lost. If service is not economic, profits will be lost. Inadequacy in any single piece of equipment can hamper the entire operation. Everything else may be satisfactory, but if food warmers cannot keep pace with the demand, the whole operation inevitably suffers.

Throughout the whole spectrum, ranging from convenience foods to a gourmet cuisine, the configuration of basic equipment and storage facilities varies significantly, and the design significantly influences profit margins. The restaurateur must use a meticulous systems approach to ensure that all the pieces fit to form a unified, consistent whole. The system must translate the menu into its constituent elements, purchasing units, storage requirements, and processing steps. A given level of sales of a given menu will determine both the amount of individual food items needed and the nature and volume of individual work steps.

Thus, by using a systems approach, the restaurant can establish equipment needs and layout. A limited menu can hold equipment needs down; an elaborate menu calls for complex processing and storage equipment. Flexibility in the kitchen will permit later adjustments of the menu, should they prove necessary or desirable. The basic processing system is an outgrowth of the basic menu, however, and the greater the departures from the menu for which the system was designed, the greater the chance that the kitchen will be less than optimally efficient.

In order to apply a systems approach to a new restaurant, the restaurateur needs to translate the menu into work steps, storage requirements, and equipment. Each menu item has its own logistical implications, from the receipt of food supplies, their storage, and their issuance into production, through the delivery of the meal to the table. Analyzing the menu in terms of the work steps involved is the basis for determining equipment needs and its placement for minimizing labor costs.

This applies both to processing equipment and storage equipment, which also can significantly influence labor cost. Storage equipment must be designed with a careful consideration of nearness and accessibility for two functions:

1. Movement into storage from the receiver; and
2. Issuing out of storage to production.

The flow from receiving to storage to production must be designed in terms of work steps, with distance and the frequency of performance determining relative efficiency of a prospective layout. Clearly, issues from storage, and thus access for production is more important than access for receipts.

Storage is linked to the menu, because the kinds of food to be served determine storage requirements. For example, the ratio of space for frozen foods and space for general refrigeration—or simple shelf storing—can vary widely from one kind of menu to another. In turn, the nature of storage space can be influenced by trends in the industry. The growing trend towards pre-portioned food and frozen meats can influence both the nature of shelving and storing and the ratio of freezer space to general refrigeration.

PREPARATION AND LAYOUT

Just as the menu determines the kind of equipment needed for the most economic preparation of meals, it also determines how that equipment is used. In turn, efficient use depends upon how the various pieces of equipment are located in relation to each other.

Since the food preparation process is composed of a great number of individual work steps using a great variety of utensils, as well as the major pieces of equipment, facilities layout is critically important. The labor cost includes a substantial amount of time used just for moving supplies from one location to another. Unless all facilities and supplies are favorably located, a large amount of unnecessary time can be used. Because of the large number of variables involved, the cumulative effect of poor layout could be substantial.

Work Centers

The basic principle of a well designed kitchen is the establishment of individual work centers for specific food preparation functions. Work centers common to most restaurants are:

A pantry area to prepare salads, desserts, and sandwiches.
A broiler station.
A fry/cook station.

Whatever the menu style, these stations operate with separate equipment and supplies and, therefore, have no direct interdependence.

Each work center is a self-contained unit, but not separated from others by walls or visual obstructions. Work in one situation is unencumbered by work in the other stations, but workers have no sense of isolation, and they are accessible to the necessary supervision and coordination.

Each work center has its own crew of workers, each of whom is trained to perform all the functions of that particular work center. This is important in order to avoid fragmentation of duties and its effects on performance, and in order to minimize waiting time. Since the individual work steps vary in length, assigning individual employees to individual work steps would result in each step taking as long as the longest. Having each employee perform all functions also prevents excessive movement and handling of food, and it prevents monotony and boredom among workers.

Worker Movement

Within each work center, the kind and placement of utensils are also important to efficiency. Workers should have to move minimally for access to the utensils needed in each work step, and the utensils should be arranged to correspond to the sequence of work steps, from the receipt of food supplies to the issuance of the completed menu item.

Equipment in each work center needs to be installed with a view to worker convenience. All work surfaces, valves, controls, and appurtenances must be easily accessible and at the right levels. They should be easy to reach without strain, and they should be far enough from any related activity to insure that each of the work steps will not interfere with the others.

Installing equipment is always a process of achieving a judicious balance between providing *enough* space and *not too much*. The greater the available space, the more workers have to move from one activity to another and, thus, the more time consumed. Yet, condensing the work space within a work station (and between stations) reaches a point of diminishing economic returns when workers' freedom of movement is impaired. If workers get in each other's way, smaller walking space provides no advantage.

Accordingly, the space allocated to individual work stations needs to balance the two considerations and to allow for peak operational levels: the greatest number of workers most fully occupied. During a restaurant's development period, capacity operations may be rarely or only briefly reached; but unless facilities are adequate for capacity, marketing success can result in reduced efficiency.

Equipment installation must also consider worker comfort. Efficiency also depends on good working conditions: temperature control and the other amenities contributing to a pleasant working environment.

Relating Work Centers

Just as work centers must be laid out for an efficient flow of the individual work steps, their relationship to each other must be carefully designed to facilitate the flow from station to station and to the dining room. The same principles apply but with some additional factors influencing the placement of facilities: the relationship to the storage area and the dining room and the sequence within the total meal. The kitchen should be able to operate as a production line. The meal preparation should be a smooth flow of work with successive stages of production accomplished as materials move along, without "backtracking" or duplication.

While the finished meal may seem relatively simple, the work steps which go into it are anything but simple, and thus meticulous systems analysis is needed in kitchen layout design. An effective tool for this purpose is the "work overlap diagram". By superimposing flowcharts of the preparation steps of each menu item on a drawing of a planned layout, it is possible to identify and eliminate flow problems before the equipment is installed. This is important because a layout may be satisfactory for individual menu items and yet conceal problems. Work overlap diagrams test the way work steps of different menu items interact with each other and hence expose bottlenecks which will arise in that layout.

Illustration:

Examine the diagram (Figures 3-1A and 3-1B) which was prepared to lay out the production and service areas for the employees' food service facility of a large insurance company

The anaylsis of the food preparation process used in designing the kitchen must be hard-headed and practical. Since it has served as the basic assumption underlying the final layout, it should be adequately documented so that employees may be trained in the procedures which have been established as most efficient for the operations they are putting into practice.

Service And Layout

Kitchen layout relates directly to customer service because it determines the relative speed and efficiency with which customer orders are received, processed and delivered. Thus, the kitchen layout flows directly into the layout of other facilities:

1. The service area, where servers deliver orders, pick up foods, and assemble everything needed for delivering the complete meal to the customer.
2. Supplies of linen, flatware, condiments, and other service-related items.
3. The dishwashing and storing facilities.

These facilities are the bridge between the kitchen and the dining room, and must be laid out with the appropriate mixture of convenience and access by both the kitchen staff and serving staff. The menu and the kind of service offered the public determine what this mixture should be.

For example, with counter service, the dishwashing and supplies are outside the kitchen, whereas their placement in table service restaurants varies with the nature and complexity of service. With gourmet cuisines, appearance and arrangement of the

L E G E N D

1. RECEIVING
2. TRASH
3. OFFICE
4. MALE EMPLOYEES' TOILETS & LOCKERS
5. FEMALE EMPLOYEES' TOILETS & LOCKERS
6. WAREWASHING
7. CART & DISPENSER WASHING
8. CART PARKING & BULK COFFEE PREPARATION
9. DRY STORAGE
10. FREEZER
11. REFRIGERATOR (MEAT)
12. REFRIGERATOR (VEG.)
13. REFRIGERATOR (COOL)
14. BAKE SHOP PRODUCTION
15. BAKE SHOP DRY STORAGE
16. BAKE SHOP REFRIGERATOR
17. BAKE SHOP FREEZER
18. DAIRY & BEVERAGE REFRIGERATOR
19. VEGETABLE REFRIGERATOR
20. COLD FOOD ASSEMBLY
21. SCULLERY
22. PREPARTION
23. HOT FOOD PRODUCTION

Figure 3-1 (A).

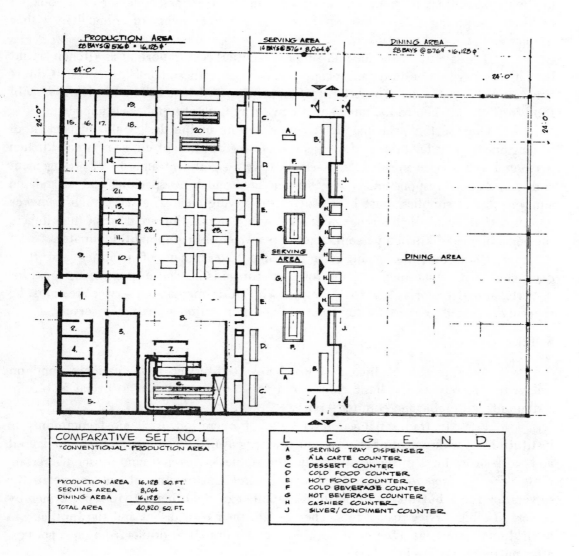

Figure 3-1 (B).

food are so important that the assembly of the various items on a plate is done in the kitchen (in contrast to some exotic dishes which servers assemble—or even cook—at tableside) requiring greater kitchen access to principle items of china than with a simpler menu.

The layout of service and support facilities is as important as kitchen layout both because waste-motion factors apply and because these facilities represent direct contacts with customers. The benefit of an efficient kitchen will be lost if the flow of food from the kitchen to the table—or the two-way flow of supplies—is impeded.

One of the principal determining factors in the design and placement of serving and supply facilities is the separation or distribution of duties between kitchen personnel and service personnel. If servers have a significant amount of arrangement and preparation responsibility, the serving area must be spacious and all related equipment and supplies must be close to the serving area. *The servers' convenience dominates!* If, instead, all arrangement and serving preparation are done in the kitchen, the convenience of kitchen personnel in the placement of equipment dominates.

Here, too, the menu is a principal determinant of facilities and their placement. With some menus, some form of storage is needed in the serving area, for desserts, appetizers or salads, for example. With other menus, the service area must be specially designed to allow for final assembly or preparation activities by servers.

Self-Service

As a means of increased efficiency, self-service is increasingly common today, not merely as the basic cafeteria style set-up but also as a special feature in restaurants with table and counter service.

For the traditional cafeteria style of operation, used most commonly in institutions, a wide range of special equipment is available; and, of course, the layout and work procedures differ significantly from table-service and counter-service restaurants. *The fundamental principle is labor-saving!* Customers not only come to the servers for food, but they also perform a number of the other activities performed by servers in table service restaurants. They obtain their own dishes and flatware, and in institutional cafeterias, they even pour coffee and draw soft drinks from taps, perhaps after putting ice cubes in a glass.

The traditional line between full service and self-service is becoming increasingly blurred. In addition to the introduction of such familiar practices as soft drink vending machines, restaurants have begun to introduce such innovations as salad centers in table service restaurants and the use of table servers for desserts and beverages in cafeterias. In the former arrangement, customers are offered the convenience and economy of cafeteria service coupled with some of the amenities of table service.

Sanitation

Keeping a restaurant immaculately clean and safe is an increasingly important consideration today. Always as important to a restaurant's appeal as the food and decor, sanitation is achieving a new significance in public attitudes as a result of growing awareness of ecology. Even the practical and legal significance of poor sanitation has changed. For example, in New York city, the names and addresses of restaurants with violations of the sanitation code are sometimes broadcast on television Being a good neighbor has now become good business!

Sanitation considerations range from prompt removal of soiled dishes and flatware from the dining area to garbage disposal, and sanitation measures must be considered throughout the planning and layout phase of profitable restaurant management. Since restaurant operations constantly desanitize and constantly generate garbage, adequate equipment and procedures must be used from the beginning.

The layout must allow for the most economic way of moving dishes and flatware from the dining area to washing equipment and for storing garbage before removal. If the washing equipment is a significant distance from the dining area, a conveyor system may be preferable to manual busing, In some operations, disposables may be preferable to permanent wares because savings in capital equipment, labor, and space may offset the added cost of disposables.

The layout and facilities must also allow for multiple garbage collection and transfer to the storage point: garbage from the dining room and from the individual work stations. The collection point must be, at the same time, accessible and adequately insulated from food storage and preparation. Procedures must provide for periodic removal of garbage to the storage area where it is retained until disposal. Facilities must be adequate to control odors both on and off the premises.

Similarly, the restaurant needs effective control procedures and supervision for the handling and storing of food and for cleaning throughout the premises. Kitchen work surfaces should be immediately cleaned when not in use, and extra perishables should be returned promptly to refrigeration. Rules on freshness should be established, clearly communicated to all employees, and stringently enforced.

Slackness in sanitation can pose significant problems, from consumer resistance to the need for costly remedial measures. The effort and expense of eliminating a sanitation problem are frequently grossly disproportionate to the effort of avoiding it. For example, eliminating insects or rodents, which can result from poorly enforced food and garbage handling procedures, can take a long time and greatly complicate sanitation controls thereafter. In turn, such lapses not only imperil customer relations directly, but also indirectly through legal sanctions and fines.

UTILIZATION OF STAFF AND FACILITIES

Profitability depends substantially upon effective utilization of staff and facilities. Convenience foods and special equipment are available to keep costs low, but they call for different staffing and special training and supervision measures.

Because of the wide swings in customer flow, restaurants need to use a variety of work leveling methods. A basic principle is to shift as much work as possible away from peak meal periods. Thus, kitchen workers are assigned to advance preparation and partial preparation for the next meal period.

Advance Preparation

Advance preparation entails a risk of over-production and waste, which varies significantly from menu to menu. On the one hand, little advance preparation is possible with some foods, such as grilled steaks and chops; on the other hand, a very wide selection of menu items reduces the likelihood that any individual item will be ordered, also limiting advance preparation possibilities.

Nonetheless, a certain amount of advance preparation is either necessary or desirable, and every effort should be made to identify items which may optionally be prepared in advance and to determine sales patterns as a means of scheduling reasonable amounts which may be safely prepared. An irony here is that convenience foods, which save money through lower labor costs, decrease the potential for assigning workers to advance preparation.

Partial Preparation

Partial preparation is an important measure of minimizing staff idleness, and the menu should be carefully analyzed for preparation steps which can be performed in advance. Whether it be cutting vegetables, setting up salads, or transferring desserts to service area storage, every conceivable step which does not depend on an immediate meal order or immediate serving after preparation should be performed before the meal period.

Planning and supervision are important in this area because a slack period tends to be self-reinforcing. Unless procedures clearly call for specific preparation work and supervisors are alert to short-term opportunities for such work, it can easily be overlooked.

Similarly, as much as possible of "housekeeping" activities such as cleaning, garbage transfer, and "work station maintenance" should be systematically scheduled for slack periods.

Staggered Shifts

Because of the peaks and valleys in manpower needs, restaurants can benefit from staggering work shifts. Building up staff to correspond to volume results in a lower payroll during slack periods, both preceding and following peaks. Staggering of shifts results in a tapering off of the staff level following the peak and, hence, is a valuable cost-saving device. Such staff scheduling minimizes idle time and excessive payrolls.

Labor-Saving Operating Procedures

Operating procedures must be carefully designed to build in every possible method of saving time and thus holding labor costs down.

For example, chef orders of food from storage for delivery to the kitchen should cover all requirements for the meal period. Piecemeal ordering uses extra labor and this incurs unnecessary costs for the restaurant.

Similarly, phasing out service areas by closing down counters or groups of tables as customers dwindle after the meal period peak can reduce the distances servers have to travel.

Pursuant to the broad management principle that "time is money,"operating procedures should be designed to speed service during peak periods. The higher the turnover per seat, the higher the profits. Accordingly, except for luxury dining, restaurants should carefully control all the factors which contribute to prompt service, in both the dining room and the kitchen. Servers should take orders promptly, deliver them quickly to the kitchen, and deliver completed orders to customers as quickly as possible. Every operational factor that could contribute to slippage should be controlled.

The avoidance of slippage is the critical factor, because speed of service must be largely invisible in all but "quicky"-type lunch operations or very special situations. Thus, the objective is to avoid *unnecessary* waiting of time between the different steps of meal service. From the restaurant's point of view, slippage in this waiting time can also be nearly invisible, because it is compounded by such a great number of variables. And sometimes, even though it may be visible, its origin may not be immediately identifiable.

Identifying its genesis is important, however, because it is the extra meals served during peak periods which make up, as a practical matter, for idle seats between meals. Increasing sales during slow periods may take many months of promotional efforts, but opportunities to increase sales during peak periods are immediate and conclusively realizable.

Accordingly, astute restaurant management must be constantly alert to service slippage and reasons for it. Because sales patterns vary, some slippage will be unavoidable, such as when the distribution of sales among menu items is skewed significantly from the usual pattern, for example. Nonetheless, delays in any restaurant operation should be investigated and remedial measures taken. For example, a kitchen delay in delivering orders may be found to originate in inadequate advance preparation or an unanticipated shortage of materials or rising sales of a particular menu item—any one of which might call for specific changes in kitchen procedures.

By making necessary marginal adjustments in operating procedures, restaurant management can sustain or increase turnover per seat. This, in turn, directly boosts gross revenue.

THINGS TO COME

Restaurant operations are never constant, and the shrewd restaurant owner or operator must be alert to trends which could influence future operations. Equipment and food preparation methods are subject to change. Being prepared to respond properly to those changes can be an important, even critical part of remaining competitive and profitable.

Recent years have witnessed an increasing reliance on foods prepared in factories equipped for mass production. The result has been economies in preparing food for serving; but ultimate dollar realization of that result will more and more depend upon special equipment and methods and upon different work procedures. As noted before, the very advantages of convenience foods can be fraught with the danger of increasing the spread between manpower needs in slow periods and manpower needs in peak periods.

Accordingly, staffing methods may change significantly, and one approach which may achieve increasing frequency is to operate restaurants exclusively with part-time workers. Restaurants already operate with more part-time workers than most other industries. As manpower needs during slow periods decline, the pressure to rely even more so on part-time help will increase.

Some of the dissatisfactions inherent in restaurant work may be unavoidable, and part-time workers may well be able to bear them better than full-time workers. In turn, restaurants may seek out new sources of part-time help; these sources could well grow in great measure in the "seventies."

Housewives with free time for part of the day are increasingly particularly attracted to part-time work. They may want to work; yet with children in school, they cannot take full-time jobs.

"Moonlighters" are another future source of part-time restaurant workers. The practice of taking a second job has been growing in recent years, and various factors seem to reinforce the trend. The basic motivation for taking a second job is either to raise family living standards or to save money for a specific purpose. Inflationary pressures and growing human wants and needs may sustain workers' interest in second jobs; the shortened work week of the seventies on the first job may make a second job even more feasible.

Students may also become more interested in part-time restaurant work. They are interested in earning extra spending money and sometimes need extra income solely to meet rising costs of education.

Another trend which could begin to have a significant effect on restaurant operations is an increased staggering of meal periods in industry. The result may well be staggering of demand and a consequential reduction of the time between restaurant peaks. Restaurant employees would then be less able to go home between shifts. It might, then, become preferable to hire separate crews for each shift and to lengthen each shift.

CHAPTER 4

Improving Restaurant Personnel Relations and Motivation

CHAPTER CAPSULE PREVIEW

Personnel management is one of the most important factors in a restaurant's success. Profitability, in most instances, depends critically on employee productivity.

Sales per employee per year in restaurants have been regularly among the lowest of any industry in the U.S. economy, according to the Bureau of the Census. The restaurant industry has continually experienced long-term persistent labor shortages, high turnover, high absenteeism and tardiness. Major contributing factors for these results over the years have been poor working conditions and low pay. Restaurants enjoy the advantages of a special exemption from federal minimum wage requirements, but it may well have worked against the industry in the long run, and at least some of the personnel problems common in restaurants may be directly attributable to the pay structure which has evolved as a result of minimum wage exemption.

Accordingly, restaurant owners are challenged to establish effective wage-administration programs from the beginning and to develop measures of satisfying and motivating employees in order to maintain the utmost productivity.

FAIR WAGE DILEMMA

Every industry seeks capable motivated employees, and paying a fair wage is an essential prerequisite, but restaurants face a competitive dilemma in laying this foundation for employee satisfaction. They are competing directly with other restaurants for customers, but they are also competing with other industries for employees.

In order to be competitive with other industries in attracting workers, restaurants (or any other industry) should ideally meet prevailing pay scales. In order to be competitive with other restaurants, however, a restaurant must pay for labor on a comparable basis—which of course is partially determined by the minimum wage exemption.

As a result of this dilemma, restaurants tend to have a persistent disadvantage in their competition with other industries, and they therefore need to compensate through their wage administration and personnel management policies.

These policies should be aimed at satisfying employees' needs so that they in turn will satisfy the needs of their employers. Industrial psychologist Maslow has defined workers' needs as a hierarchy, somewhat like a pyramid:

Need for self-actualization
Need for esteem
Need for belongingness and love
Safety needs
Physiological needs

Employers should recognize these needs and design policies to fulfill them as fully as possible, allowing for the fact that satisfaction at each level depends on satisfaction at the next lower level. Thus, the foundation on which the rest of the pyramid is based is a fair wage.

Unless employees feel wages are fair, efforts to satisfy the needs higher in the hierarchy will not be effective. By matching adequate wages with equivalent productivity, the restaurant operator can at the time demonstrate the fairness of wage rates and exercise effective control over payroll costs.

Example:

Consider this very practical example demonstrating that money isn't everything, but it helps an awful lot! The manager of a large downtown restaurant which services many private parties told us frankly: "Make extra hour work more attractive by paying for it on the spot in cash instead of including it in the weekly paycheck. Many of the male employees turn their paychecks directly over to their wives who handle the family's fiscal affairs, and they appreciate the chance to get extra cash for their own pockets instead of having it included in their paychecks. The extra bookkeeping is more than offset by the psychological appeal that 'cold cash' has for many workers."

IMPROVING PRODUCTIVITY

Every activity in a restaurant influences productivity and thus profits; therefore restaurant operators should consider the effect on productivity of all policies.

Each activity should be evaluated in terms of revenue or covers served per man hour, thus providing a measure of how well each employee is performing. This also shows the employee what is expected of him and an indication of how well he is fulfilling that expectation.

By providing for feedback and periodic reports on revenue or covers served per man-hour, management can maintain a constant watchfulness over productivity. Knowing revenues or covers served per man hour can serve several purposes:

1. A measure of the restaurant's overall effectiveness.
2. A measure of the effectiveness of individual activities performed by several employees performing the same basic job.
3. A measure of the effectiveness of individual employees.

With this knowledge, management can keep its finger on the pulse of the business, identify problems as they rise, rather than after difficulties have been experienced and plan remedial measures promptly. Significant changes in revenue per man hour overall or for particular activities can be a signal to increase or decrease staff, investigate why a particular employee's productivity has fallen, reward an employee whose productivity has increased notably, or other suitable managerial response.

BOOSTING RESTAURANT EMPLOYEE PERFORMANCE THROUGH BETTER COMMUNICATIONS

A fair wage and productivity controls are only the foundation on which measures to fulfill other employee needs are built. The principal means of implementing such measures are good communications and employee relations.

A Practical Illustration:

The president of a nationwide family restaurant chain has on many occasions related his conviction that employee performance, and hence his restaurants' profits, have been effectively enhanced because he "sells his ideas to his employees the same way as he does to his customers!" He explains that he accomplishes this by telling his employees what is being done now, how management thinks it should be done, what can be expected by doing it differently, and what it can mean in savings in time, labor, and eventually, more money for the employees.

A restaurant is never too small or too large to show concern over proper handling of employees. Good two-way communications may be relatively easy in small restaurants, but in the larger restaurant, top management can easily lose touch with employees. This is a danger to be avoided, because knowing employees and how they feel about their jobs is important to minimizing problems.

Unless management knows employees well, problems may arise unexpectedly, or only surface problems may be recognized in time for action. Many employee dissatisfactions lie below the surface for a while before erupting into a significant problem for management to cope with. Catching incipient problems before they grow serious can prevent them altogether or minimize their consequences.

Accordingly, it is important to know how employees feel about their jobs, both generally and specifically. How they feel depends on their relations with other employees, and with you, their bosses, but it also depends upon their overall expectations about their jobs and how well their expectations are met. If most of these expectations are reasonably well fulfilled, the normal frictions with other employees which occur in every job will rarely cause serious difficulties. If, however, an employee is basically dissatisfied, even a minor friction can lead to a substantial problem.

Industrial psychologist Frederick Herzberg analyzed employee attitudes through questionnaire responses and determined that employee satisfaction and dissatisfaction arise from highly complex factors. Applying his findings, however, can be both simple and highly useful.

Herzberg discovered that although we think of satisfaction and dissatisfaction as opposite conditions, the absence of one in a job situation does not lead to the other but rather it just leads to neutrality. Thus, the opposite of dissatisfaction is *no* dissatisfaction, rather than satisfaction. And the opposite of satisfaction is *no* satisfaction.

While this seems paradoxical at first, considering satisfaction and dissatisfaction in a practical context shows the validity of Dr. Herzberg's conclusions. Just because something doesn't cause us dissatisfaction doesn't mean that it will cause us satisfaction. And just because something doesn't yield us satisfaction doesn't mean that we will be actively dissatisfied.

Dr. Herzberg concluded that satisfaction and dissatisfaction operate independently of each other and are influenced by completely different factors, one set dependent upon job *content* and the other dependent upon job *context.*

Job content, or substantive factors, which Herzberg lists as determining satisfaction are as follows:

Achievement
Recognition
Work itself
Responsibility
Advancement
Growth

Job context or environmental factors which Herzberg classified as the principal sources of dissatisfaction are as follows:

Company policy and administration
Supervision
Working conditions
Interpersonal relations (with superiors, subordinates and peers)

Salary
Status
Job security
Personal life

Designing personnel administration methods to allow for these factors can go a long way toward avoiding problems which are likely to arise, because when the basic job *content* satisfies the employee, he is much less likely to react strongly to the provocations which will always occur occasionally in even the best regulated of job environments.

Thus, jobs should provide employees the opportunity to *achieve* through completing a task, solving problems, seeing the results of their own efforts, etc.

Accomplishments should be specifically *recognized*. The *work itself* should be varied and interesting, offering sufficient challenge to allow for achievement but not so much challenge that the employee will frequently face the disappointment and dissatisfaction of failing. The *responsibility* should take the form of giving the employee adequate control over his own job and thus the opportunity to fulfill all the other satisfiers, and to achieve the *advancement* and *growth* which such fulfillment can produce.

By organizing jobs in this way, the employer gives workers the chance to realize true satisfaction from their jobs, but he must also do everything he can to control the job context factors which can produce dissatisfaction. Working conditions must be pleasant, company policy and supervision must be neither too strict nor too lax, and overall personnel administration must take individual personalities into account so that interpersonal relations can be kept as smooth as possible. Sometimes a highly capable individual can be aggressive or r oversensitive, or moody, or simply hard to get along with. It's worth a special effort in supervision or job assignments to allow for these individual idiosyncrasies in order to minimize dissatisfaction in such an employee (or the dissatisfaction he may induce in others!).

As an extra dimension, it can also be useful to relate Herzberg's *satisfiers* and *dissatisfiers* to Maslow's hierarchy of needs, particularly for restaurants. Except in very large restaurants, most jobs do not lead to a high level of self-actualization, therefore, fulfillment of the needs at the second and third levels can be particularly important: the need for esteem and the need for belongingness and love.

The question has frequently been raised by restaurateurs concerning the desirability of reducing to writing restaurant policies relating to employee performance. We believe that in today's climate the preferable approach is best illustrated by the following example.

Example:

The Vice-President-Personnel of a large regional restaurant chain phrased it like this, based on his vast reservoir of on-line practical encounters: "Don't rely on verbal instructions and information in the case of new—or older—employees. Put company or individual restaurant policies in writing in a manual or booklet. When you rely on verbal instructions, you can never be sure that you covered everything you should have or wanted to. With instructions in writing, the employee can never say 'Nobody ever told me.' Discuss written instructions point by point with every new employee to make sure each point is completely understood."

These can be particularly important in the context of the high turnover rate which applies in the industry. A management which imbues its employees with a keen sense of the importance of their jobs and a warm feeling of being liked and accepted can expect to keep the turnover rate at a minimum. A dramatic example of this—and the rewards it can pay—occured in 1972 when the Schrafft's chain in New York had to close a restaurant which had been operating since before 1920, because the land was sold for a skyscraper. On the final day of business, waitress and customers of decades' standing unexpectedly held a sentimental ceremony commemorating years of mutual loyalty to the restaurant.

Obviously, some of the aforementioned theories of personnel management must be tempered with practicality when applied to certain job responsibilities with the typical restaurant. For example, the applicability of context enriched may be limited in the case of a dishwasher as compared with an effort to make the job of a chef more meaningful from a context standpoint. In other words, the application of these principles to typical restaurants must be influenced with a practical sense of awareness of the relative importance of the various jobs.

Personalizing Employee Relations

Because restaurants depend upon their employees' direct relationships with customers, personalizing employee relations is particularly important. Relations should be based on two-way communication, with effective listening always being an important factor. Management and supervisors always need to keep a careful balance between disclosing too much or too little, and for purposes of evaluation and feedback, formal procedures for reporting at regular intervals are needed.

Under these procedures, goals which employees are expected to fulfill should be clearly understood on both sides, and both employees and supervisors should participate in setting those goals. Proper standards and measures accepted on both sides can be valuable means of avoiding disputes, hurt feelings, and even abrupt resignations, because deficiencies or superior achievement can be clearly and objectively recognized. Fairness in all particulars is an important part of avoiding dissatisfaction (including employer dissatisfaction!) and formalized standards and measures are a valuable way of building fairness right into operations.

Closely related to formal standards are organizational lines of communications, which need to be clearly drawn so that each employee knows what information must regularly be distributed to whom. Organizational lines knit the group together in an effective network that keeps responsibilities clearly divided and at the same time makes sure everything gets done.

People will surely communicate across organizational lines of course, and every group of people will develop an informal network— the grapevine—which will transmit a lot of information of its own, sometimes at an astonishing speed! But don't try to fight the grapevine; live with it and remember to use it yourself when it suits your purpose to get something across fast but informally or in advance of a final announcement. Sometimes when you're in doubt about how a prospective policy might go over, put it on the grapevine discreetly, and you won't have to wait long to find out how employees feel about it.

Letting the Employee Know He Belongs

There are many ways of fulfilling the third level of Maslow's hierarchy of needs: letting the employee know he belongs. Encourage suggestions from workers. It's an effective motivational device, but it can also be a fruitful source of ideas. Things can be done in so many different ways that management and supervisors are not necessarily going to see them all. Futhermore, employees are involved in vastly more details and thus can see things which their bosses might not notice.

When an employee makes a good suggestion, adopt it and be sure to give him plenty of credit. It will make him feel good—which can help build loyalty, and it will motivate others to make constructive suggestions.

When you're unable to use a suggested idea, explain why. Show an interest in the employee and his ideas, and appreciation of his thoughtfulness and an openness to further suggestions.

Remember that changes in operations can be unsettling and, therefore, people need to be prepared to accept it. What might be a temporary disadvantage can be turned into an advantage by having employees participate in the decision and implementation plans. Explain the purpose of the change, show how it will (or will not) affect employees and invite suggestions on how the change should be put into effect. This can help remove causes of apprehension and at the same time give employees a sense of being part of operations.

Giving employees a sense of belonging is important in more than the sense of individual employees. If they feel they belong, they develop a certain loyalty to the restaurant, but they develop at least as strong a sense of being part of a group which accepts them and which they accept. Most of their hour-to-hour, day-to-day and week-to-week relations are with co-workers, who become important to them. When there is good *esprit de corps* and the group is well knit, the individual wants to belong and will hesitate to take a stand which differs from the majority.

Example:

While there seems to be a side divergence of opinion, we have been very impressed with the success experienced by a 560-seat, first class suburban restaurant in the Philadelphia area which imposes fines ranging from $1 to $10 on its employees to improve service. The fines, which are designed to penalize for failure to provide required services for guests, are assessed by the head waiter or the chef, and the waiters and cooks police themselves. The fines are paid into an employee welfare fund.

Thus, the group plays a key role in setting and enforcing standards, and the employer's motivational efforts should be devoted to winning over the group and holding its loyalty. The desire to belong will keep all but the most obstreperous worker in line most of the time.

Building the Employee's Self-Esteem

While the group is important, the nature of the group relationship is particularly intensive in restaurant work where there is a constant flow of relationships, frequently under pressure, from workers in one kind of job to another. Accordingly, restaurant employees have a particular need to be differentiated and to have their own identity as individuals recognized.

Management, therefore, should take particular pains to treat each employee as an individual. Under the stress of peak-hour traffic, relations between employees and between employer and employee easily become impersonal. By learning an employee's responses to stimuli, management and supervisors can recognize their specific needs and quietly and effectively personalize relations when the pace has slowed.

Treating each employee as an individual satisfies his general needs and helps you to recognize when an employee is beginning to get restless or losing interest in his work. Job enlargement and job rotation can give the employee new stimulus and thus revive his interest and satisfaction.

By using job enlargements, you enable an employee to change his duties and thus benefit from a change of pace. Any extra training needs are repaid by flexibility in your operations: you get built-in substitutes for absent and vacationing employees. However, this rotation may be limited by union restrictions. The restaurant operator needs to be continuously alert for opportunities for job enrichment: incorporating a recognizable unit of work into an employee's responsibilities. The unit of work must be meaningful, of course, amd when it is, it can help compensate for the defects of work fragmentation. When a job consists of only a small part of some overall activity, employee morale often falls. Additionally, fragmentation frequently leads to a real loss of time because of the necessity for repeated setup time.

Building the employee's self esteem gives him pride in his work and motivates him to perform better. The restaurateur should seek to instill pride in work wherever possible, for example by associating an employee's name with a dish he made: such as Elsie's salad, Dora's cole slaw or Frank's pâté.

Employees in Their Relations with Others

Your employees *are* your restaurant. They can make or break you. If they're unhappy, their dissatisfaction and indifference will show up, sooner or later, as a minus on the bottom line. Employee attitudes will inevitably produce a response of one kind or another in customers. That response can be either favorable or unfavorable, and its variance on either side of the ledger can have a direct influence on overall sales.

A superb cuisine cannot, for long, override persistently negative customer-employee relations.

Example:

Some now defunct jet-set restaurants have learned this after a policy of intentional condescension to non-celebrities drove customers away in droves!

Conversely, strongly positive employee-customer relations can create long waiting lines for a restaurant which will never win a four-star award.

Accordingly, the restaurant operator's interest in having satisfied and well-motivated employees is highly practical and the foundation on which the restaurant builds its relations with the public. Training employees in customer relations can be very valuable, but it is rarely enough by itself. Employee selection, supervision, and overall management policy must first be successful before training can improve relations with the public by adding specific skills in handling people.

A Practical Guide!

Consider the following suggestions, set forth in the February 1973 issue of *Restaurant World* (Vol. 2, No. 5), for correcting employee misunderstandings, misinformation, and job dissatisfaction:

1. *Employee meetings.* Meetings on employee time can be one of the greatest causes of dissatisfaction with a job. But to avoid more unhappiness, they must be held on your time, not employees' time.
2. *Regular or irregular letters from management* on operation matters that will give the employee a better insight into your business and why things are done in a certain way.
3. *Employee publications.*
4. *Annual, semi-annual or quarterly reports on financial facts* of your business, such as the chains produce for their stockholders. A good employee invests his future in your operation. Consider him a valuable working "stockholder" as deserving of knowledge as the stockholder who just invests money.
5. *Films* on restaurant operation or salesmanship that emphasize the importance of the industry and the people who make it up.
6. *Bulletin boards.* If you don't have one, set one up at once. And maintain high interest in it by using it for news matters, jokes and personal items as well as to inform employees of your operation's aims and goal.

   And remember, a program to eliminate misunderstandings and misinformation can never be a one-shot thing. A program that takes 2 weeks or 4 months and then ends is only a temporary cure. The program must be continuous to produce continuous results.

Human relations is like advertising. You can never relax and feel you have accomplished the job for all time.

Supervision is so critical that training at the supervisor level can often be more important than training at the level of employees who will be in most frequent sustained contact with customers. Management policies must be followed down the line, and thus supervisors are management's key link to how the public will react.

A Case In Point!

A highly successful restaurant operator, who now has "graduated" into an equally successful executive position in a restaurant construction firm, related his experience in this regard to us which we wish to share with you. He has proved the validity of his theory that training a restaurant employee for management responsibilities is completely wasted if the person shows no signs of managerial talent. In looking for management talent, he insists on checking the employee's record from school days to the current time because of his belief that if the person has talent, he will have shown traces at times, in school and off or on his job. Further, our experience in the restaurant industry has proved you must recognize different mental capacities in training restaurant employees. Some can learn twice as fast as others. Slow learners, many times, have proved to be better workers than ones who learn fast. For best results, therefore, we have found that training periods should be spaced and not crammed—many of those who have successfully developed restaurant talent have often told us, in concurrence with our belief, "30 or 60 minutes of training a day can be more effective than longer periods in most cases."

By training first-line supervisors in management and supervision, restaurant operators can build in the skills needed to keep employee-customer relations predominantly positive. If supervisors are trained in the techniques of on-the-job training, they can both conduct formal training programs for employees and modulate the flow of operations to minimize friction with customers and show employees how to handle different situations.

Because of the critical role which supervisors play, their selection is a major determinant of success and, thus, restaurants need to exercise particular care in the people they select for supervisory and management jobs.

Interest in people is a major criterion for selecting supervisors. Such an interest indicates that they will recognize what is important both in their own relations with employees and in turn in the employees' relations with customers. Having supervisors with such an interest can create a favorable atmosphere and effectively implement a policy of satisfying employees' personal needs such as belonging and developing a strong self-esteem.

Example:

Consider what a leading metropolitan area restaurateur has said about the ideal restaurant manager: "He must treat the employees fairly and must be frank about their problems. He may be considerate and understanding but his fuse should be short over shortcomings in service and he can't hide it. When it comes to talking with the customer, apologizing if necessary, he earns his title. If we're wrong, it's his fault. He says so, even though the employees may know differently. When there are compliments on food or service, he thanks the customer and says that he'll tell the chef or waiter, *and he does!*

Satisfying Employee Needs for Self-Realization

In both the Maslow and Herzberg concepts of employee motivation, the need for advancement, growth and self-actualization ranks high, yet compared to large highly structured organizations, restaurants are at a disadvantage in fulfilling an important need. Accordingly, restaurant operators need to be all the more alert to realizing their limited opportunities to enable employees to move upward. The National Restaurant Association has identified the lack of employee advancement as one of the industry's principal problems.

In efforts to satisfy employees' needs to belong and to develop strong self-esteem, management will tend to identify employees with high motivation and high capability, and to the extent possible, such employees should be rewarded with additional responsibilities appropriate to their growth. They should be considered as prime candidates for more responsible jobs which open up, and they should be groomed for such jobs as early as possible in their careers. The rewards can be substantial, if intangible. Compared to an outside individual of similar ability and experience, they have the advantage of already knowing your operation, your own special needs, your customers, and your other employees. Their gratification for being moved upwards in the ranks results in a special kind of loyalty which simply cannot be expected from a new employee.

Improving Union Relations

Employee relations are not merely a matter of direct relations with employees, but also, frequently, of establishing and maintaining a good rapport with union representatives. Maintaining friendly relations is an asset, not merely in wage negotiations, but also in day-to-day operations.

Grievance procedures should be followed closely. Good employee relations are not intended to replace normal union procedures when grievances develop, but they are a good foundation for negotiating disputes which arise.

When a situation arises which cannot be settled through informal employer-employee relations, the employer should be prepared to negotiate in good faith and abide by decisions.

The restaurant owner must recognize that every job decision may be subject to union review and possible wage renegotiation. For example, in enlarging a job to include an additional activity as discussed above, it may be necessary to negotiate a new wage rate that takes into account the higher pay that some tasks earn over others. In such cases, the advantages of combining tasks may justify paying the top rate for the enriched job: paying the higher rate may be preferable to having employees remain idle for part of the time.

OBLIGATIONS OF AN EMPLOYER IN
THE RESTAURANT BUSINESS

The special concessions allowed the food-service industry create particularly complex problems in wage administration for restaurants. They are regulated by minimum wage laws, child labor laws, standards for working conditions, and prohibitions against discrimination in employment.

Further complicating matters is the need to comply with requirements of several different regulating agencies within both the federal government and the state in which they operate. For example, they must meet the requirements of both the Internal Revenue Service and the Social Security Administration in the federal government, and they are at the same time subject to the Fair Labor Standards Act and to unemployment tax requirements of the Department of Labor.

While meeting minimum wage requirements is perhaps the most important basic concern, restaurant operators must also make sure that they comply with state and local requirements on working conditions, child labor, and discrimination. Many state laws make special provisions for minors, such as limiting the hours they may work and establishing special overtime rules.

Minimum Wage

The federal minimum wage is applicable to restaurant employees. Tipped employees may be paid less, however, except where employer and employees agree that all tips are to be turned over to the employer and treated as part of his gross receipts.

Where the employee is permitted to keep the tips himself, the employer may pay as little as 50 percent of the applicable minimum wage. In addition, the employer is allowed a credit for meals and lodging he provides, at the "reasonable cost" to the employer, *NOT* to include a profit. State laws vary, from making no provision, to setting specific maximum hourly limits.

The application of tips against the minimum wage is discretionary with the employer for all employees who regularly receive more than $20 per month in tips and may be determined on an individualized basis for each employee.

The treatment of tips is a major administrative consideration also, because of various reporting requirements. Each employee must furnish his employer with written reports of tips for each month in which he receives at least $20 a month. The tax treatment and reports required for such restaurant tip income are discussed in detail in Chapter 10. If the employee can show that he is receiving less in actual tips than the amount credited, the employer is required to pay the difference so that the employee receives at least the minimum wage in the combination of both wages and tips.

The employee's tip reports are important because taxes to be withheld must come from the employee's cash wages in order to avoid the employer's having to lay out tax payments from his own funds. Thus, taxes due on tips must be withheld from the cash wage in the employer's possession.

Child Labor

Whenever a restaurant hires employees under 16 years of age, it must comply with federal and state child labor regulations. The Fair Labor Standards Act provides that 14- and 15-year-old employees may not work:

After 7 P.M. or before 7 A.M.

More than three hours per school day and 18 hours per school week.

More than eight hours per non-school day and 40 hours per non-school week.

In some states, stricter requirements apply, both as to hours and as to age, with limitations on hours applicable to any employee under age 18.

Discrimination

Under federal discrimination provisions of the Fair Labor Standards Act, equal pay for equal work by waiters and waitresses is required unless it can be conclusively demonstrated that physical strength is inherently required.

Posted Notices.

Under the Fair Labor Standards Act, each restaurant is required to post an official "Notice to Employees" where employees can readily see it. This Notice is supplied by the Wage and Public Contracts Division of the U.S. Department of Labor. Similar requirements apply in various state and local jurisdictions.

As a result of these various complex requirements, restaurants must keep meticulous records in order to comply with the various laws, and of course to be able to substantiate compliance. Specific requirements for such records are provided by the U.S. Department of Labor in the Regulations for Part 516 of the Fair Labor Standards Act. Where local jurisdictions have similar requirements, the design of adequate records can be an important consideration both in the avoidance of problems and in effective overall payroll administration.

Compliance with the laws is a basic necessity and involves several areas: payroll taxes, minimum wages, working conditions, records, reporting, remitting, posting of notices. And from this necessity, a natural outgrowth is a corollary necessity to establish and maintain an effective system to tie everything together.

Motivation of employees is a management function. Building upon a foundation of a fair wage, management needs to treat individuals with fairness and respect, to recognize differences in individual requirements, and to implement that recognition with advancement wherever appropriate. The rewards are productivity and good customer relations, which are keystones of success in the restaurant business as in any other.

A FINAL CORNERSTONE IN IMPROVING RESTAURANT PERSONNEL RELATIONS

Remember the following guiding principles, excerpted from the February 1973 issue of *Restaurant World* (Vol. 2, No. 5), in continually trying to answer the question, "What Does A Good Restaurant Employee Want?"

1. *Opportunity*. Not necessarily the rags to riches type, but the opportunity to lead a full, productive life.
2. *Recognition*. From day to day, every time it is deserved; not at the end of 10 or 20 years with a pin or a watch. Acknowledgement and appreciation of a job whenever it is well done.
3. *Participation*. Knowledge that he is part of a team and that what he does is important to all.
4. *Security*. Knowledge that his income is regular and that he will not be laid off or have his hours cut after he has bought a new car, washing machine, TV or refrigerator.

CHAPTER 5

Maximizing Operating Profits

CHAPTER CAPSULE PREVIEW

The key to profit maximization is profit planning. In the final analysis, profits are compounded of dozens of marginal differences throughout operations which combine into a total positive result at the end of the year. While the profit and loss statement shows two simple figures: R amount of revenues less C amount of costs—both R and C are built up a little at a time. Meticulous planning can help add to R and subtract from C throughout the year, and thus maximize profits.

Accordingly, profit planning is divided into two principal categories:

1. *Marketing*—the development, adoption, and implementation of policies and techniques which will yield the greatest amount of sales from the market, and
2. *Cost control*—the development, adoption and implementation of policies and techniques which will minimize costs at every level of operations.

In establishing a new operation, these two categories are relatively distinct and have a relatively equal weight. Once the operation is firmly established, however, they are more intermingled, and cost control predominates more. Revenues reach a fairly stable level which may not be very susceptible to influence upward, whereas costs may reach a fairly stable level but can all too easily slip upward if operational systems do not keep them in check.

Thus, some of the principal techniques of profit planning by restaurants are as follows.

Market Analysis—determination of the market potential and a detailed strategy for realizing that potential.

Cost Accounting and Control Systems—the translation of the market into expected costs and systems for recording and controlling those costs.

Budgeting Control—the translation of expected revenues and costs into a future time frame (months, quarters, years, or even multi-years), and control standards;

Management by objectives—the identification of long-term and short-term objectives and cost goals and the related activities involved in meeting those goals;

Department Control—the translation of objectives and budget into terms of the individual operational departments, and

Periodical Operational Surveys—the review and analysis of how well all aspects of operations are performing in terms of goals, personnel, systems, layout, cost control, efficiency, etc.

These techniques apply one way to the advance consideration of a prospective restaurant operation and in another way to on-going operations, but ideally, a clear continuity from one phase to the next ensures consistent control of the factors which will determine profitability.

This can be graphically illustrated by means of the "Financial Management Flowchart": (Figure 5-1).

MARKET ANALYSIS

A critical factor in capitalizing on a food market is knowing its approximate potential size and nature, in order to have facilities which are adequate but not excessive and which suit the market taste. A knowledge of the various market segments and their potentials provides the basis both for investment decisions and for operating policies and decisions needed to reach selected market segments effectively.

Market analysis is the only basis for setting realizable goals and effective policies, because those goals must be based on the public's expectations from a restaurant. Thus, restaurant operators need to determine various characteristics of the area's population and local industry. Income levels, education levels, spending patterns, age distribution, and other characteristics are all factors which influence the incidence of eating out. The character of local industry, institutions and sites which attract daytime visitors influence the potential for luncheon trade.

Geography and nearby traffic patterns influence the extent to which outside patronage may be expected—or perhaps attracted by effective promotion. Local restaurants which will compare are a guide to various market characteristics and careful review of their operations may indicate needs and wants which are not yet being met in the area.

Market information has to be translated into expected sales volume, the kind of menu and service that will maximize that volume, and the kind and size of facilities needed for that menu and service. Because initial decisions are critical, they should be based on the most precise determinations available, including such techniques as statistically based forecasting, regression analysis, macroeconomic analysis, and input/-output analysis. Decisions will determine operations for several years ahead, not merely as they exist initially, therefore those decisions should be as soundly based as possible.

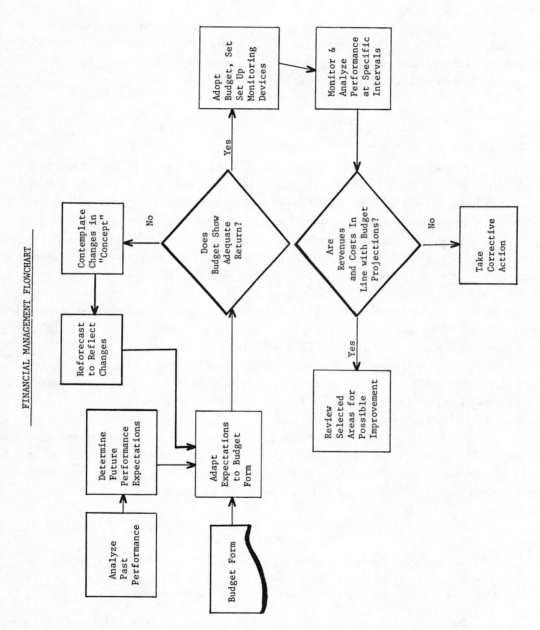

Figure 5-1. Financial Management Flowchart.

Once the basic broad decisions are made they must be further refined into explicit details of how the market will be served, prices, decor, equipment, staff, layout, business hours, promotional programs, etc. These details are the basis for determining costs and thus the relative profitability of the planned restaurant at the expected revenue levels.

Market analysis is most intensive, of course, in the planning phase for a new restaurant, but should be a continuing management tool, thereafter, to keep operations attuned to demand and thus to be prepared for changes that may be needed in response to trends which will influence the market, its tastes, etc.

COST ACCOUNTING AND CONTROL

The market, menu, and operation methods incur costs which need to be standardized as operating controls. Standard portion sizes need to be established for each menu item, as well as standard kitchen preparation and serving procedures, so that costs will be known with sufficient precision to determine profits at various sales levels.

Initially, cost standards when combined with all other operational costs serve as a measure of feasibility. As a practical matter, such cost determinations in the feasibility stage become part of the final determinations of how the prospective restaurant will operate. Individual menu items will be traded off against each other, operating procedures will be refined to achieve economies, prices will be adjusted, equipment and layout will be modified to improve efficiency, etc. The net result will be a sounder operation than if costs were not precisely analyzed.

Once the restaurant is operating, cost standards and adequate accounting to apply those standards are an important profit control tool. Since significant variations of cost from the standards have a direct influence on profits, periodic comparisons of actual costs with standards are necessary.

Accordingly, restaurants need a feedback system to report variances. This system need not be elaborate. Timeliness and consistent attentive review are more important than precision. To delay reporting for the sake of greater accuracy defeats the whole purpose. Such reports may be of little more value than yesterday's newspaper.

Illustration:

Take, for example, the following Daily Departmental Personnel Report (Kitchen) and Daily Departmental Payroll Report (Beverage), both of which forms are designed to provide such "feedback" quickly to restaurant management.

In turn, the *trend* of variances is usually more important than an individual variance for a particular period. Special circumstances may result in large individual variances with no long-term significance. Smaller variances consistently above or below standards may need serious attention. For example, overages without increased materials cost or overtime or other visible explanation may be evidence of leaks and losses, requiring action. Since profits are composed of dozens of marginal differences,

ANY RESTAURANT

DAILY DEPARTMENTAL PERSONNEL REPORT

Date _____

Dept.: KITCHEN

	Regular Hours	Overtime	Total Hours	Rate	Amount
CHEF'S OFFICE					
GENERAL COOKING					
DINING ROOM LINE					
CAFETERIA LINE					
BANQUET COOKING					
BUTCHER					

Actual Hours   _____

Scheduled   _____

Dollar Amount Today _____

Figure 5-2. Daily Departmental Personnel Report.

being overly attentive to cost variances is distinctly preferable to being overly-inattentive.

The standards themselves should be revised at reasonable intervals to reflect changes in the underlying assumptions—or errors that may have been made in estimating costs. Keeping standards current is a basis for prompt price changes when appropriate and necessary. Delay in price increases directly reduces profits. Delay in reducing prices may lose sales which otherwise would have been made.

Portion-size standards must be adequately known and enforced in the kitchen, and particular care should be taken when employees change.

BUDGETARY CONTROLS

A year's revenues and a year's costs determine profitability, and just as standards are needed for short-term operations, overall standards are needed for each

ANY RESTAURANT

DAILY DEPARTMENTAL PAYROLL REPORT

Date _____

Dept.: BEVERAGE

	Regular Hours	Overtime	Total Hours	Rate	Amount
Beverage Office					
Other Side - Bartenders					
Bar Boys					
Cocktail					
Service - Bartenders					
Bar Boys					
Banquet - Bartenders					
Bar Boys					

Actual Hours   _____

Scheduled Hours   _____

Amount   _____

Figure 5-3. Daily Departmental Payroll Report.

year. By estimating the coming year in terms of expected sales and the resultant costs expected for each operating department, management has a method of measuring progress each month and quarter and taking any action that may be needed.

A budget system coordinates all activities and ensures consistency in planning all operations. It is also a basis for achieving consistency between short-range and long-range planning. For example, a restaurant opens with certain assumptions about long-range market potential and realization. Each year's experience tests those assumptions and provides a basis for estimating the future more accurately and revising expectations about individual market segments.

The budget is based on an expected level of sales and the department by department costs that will be incurred at that level. Individual department budgets based on the overall budget provide the means of meaningful monitoring of operations during the year, comparable to the process of reviewing variances of actual experience from cost standards. By comparing actual departmental costs with budgeted costs and adjusting for the variance of actual revenues from projected revenues, management has a means both of anticipating the year's profits and of determining how well individual departments are performing. Thus, if sales are on target but kitchen costs are substantially over budget, kitchen operations need careful review. Food costs may be up substantially but since this would have been likely to show up in a review of variances from cost standards, labor excesses are more likely, and management will need to review whether procedures are being followed, whether supervision may have slacked off or some other operational breakdown may have occurred.

Budgets should preferably be flexible in recognition of the fact that sales projections are only estimates and that costs do not vary totally with sales, but rather move in steps. Thus, a given level of staffing various departments will be able to accommodate a range of sales without being increased or decreased. Thus, it is more useful to establish budgets on a range of sales expectations. One approach is to budget at two, or possibly three levels:

1. Most optimistic sales expectations.
2. Most pessimistic sales expectations.
3. Most likely sales expectations.

The third category is, of course, the budget level that would be established for a single fixed budget, and perhaps it should be the basic standard for comparing actual period performance with budget. Estimating most optimistic and most pessimistic sales levels, however, has the advantage of requiring explicit conclusions about market factors which generate sales. These explicit, quantitative conclusions provide a valuable frame of reference for judgments and decisions whenever actual sales vary widely from the basic budget figure ("most likely" in this case). Outside sales estimates (and the market assumptions on which they are based) can facilitate rapid management decisions in response to wide variations from the budget, because they provide instant standards which would otherwise have to be developed each time a budget variance occurs.

The mechanics of, and related forms used to implement, budgeting and profit-planning for restaurants are set forth in great detail in Chapter 8.

MANAGEMENT BY OBJECTIVES (MBO)

In the final analysis, profits depend upon people and performance. Decisions made at each level and in each department influence profits, and the operating decisions depend on clear goals to give each decision-maker both an incentive and a frame of reference for his decisions. Thus, expressing operations in terms of individual departmental objectives can build in a valuable operational discipline.

Management by objectives begins with a translation of long-range objectives into departmental terms. This is then broken down into individual short-range plans which must be fulfilled in order for long-range objectives to be fulfilled. The basic principle is that each activity has its own objective as part of the whole. By giving the manager in charge of each activity specific results he is expected to achieve in a given period, management both compels detailed consideration of the operational steps needed to achieve those results and establishes explicit goals which the individual manager will be expected to meet.

Such an approach provides benefits already at the planning stages, because the individual department manager can determine all the implications of meeting a particular objective better than an outsider. Thus, by inducing each department to consider the results of particular objectives, management can refine plans and assess their operational results in advance.

By having explicit objectives to meet, department managers coordinate all expenditures of time, money, and efforts to keep costs within the limits. Thus, throughout the restaurant's day-to-day operations, each responsible executive is constantly motivated to act promptly on conditions which will change the realization of objectives. Therefore, any significant revenue changes which affect operations and costs will be observed and acted upon throughout the organization, and management will have an additional means of recognizing any condition which will significantly affect profitability.

To illustrate further how MBO is being used with profitable results, four case studies of MBO applied to restaurant management appear as the final section in this chapter.

DEPARTMENT CONTROL

The most valuable effect of management by objectives is that it builds sound management principles into each operating department. Making that management work effectively depends upon establishing effective departmental controls.

With the framework of the budget system and the objectives established, each department head participates in determining his own objectives and the explicit departmental controls and plans needed to implement them. Translating these into financial terms provides a basis for responsibility accounting to serve both management and department heads.

Under responsibility accounting, information is accumulated by centers of responsibility, enabling each department head to evaluate his own department's performance in relation to budgets, standards, and objectives and to take any necessary action.

While responsibility accounting is basically financial, supervisors can also use the established budget standards and accounting reports to plan, schedule, and assign work; to evaluate employee performance; to evaluate overall departmental performance in terms of observed variances from standards, and to control activities. Out-of-control situations can be quickly recognized and remedial action promptly undertaken.

Responsibility accounting is also a valuable tool for management to judge the quality of performance by various employees, since it provides objective standards which management can relate to the traditional qualitative judgments used for assessing performance.

Maximum Profit from Menu Pricing

The menu is one of several major marketing tools available to the restaurant operator. The price range and appeal of menu items will be important determinants of the size and type of clientele attracted. Once patrons have been attracted, prices of individual items surely play a part in determining what items a patron will order.

Ideally, a menu should be priced so that the items ordered frequently offer the maximum contribution toward profit. However, even in restaurants where the average menu price and selection of items are well suited to the clientele, many menus are not priced in a fashion consistent with this profit maximization objective. The most frequently encountered reason for this failure is excessive price spread among menu items, particularly entrees. While excessive price spread may not result in losses, it inhibits making maximum profit from the menu.

Assuming all items offered are appealing, excessive price spread among entrees encourages patrons to order lower priced items. The spread in prices makes the lower priced items seem like a relative bargain considering that the same service and atmosphere go along with them as with the higher priced items. The concentration of orders among low priced entrees is generally undesirable because the low priced entrees offer a smaller contribution toward fixed costs and profits, even though the contribution as a percentage of sales may equal that from higher priced items.

Example:

With the exception of food cost, the costs of selling an order of chicken for $2.50 are likely to be nearly identical to the costs of selling a steak for $6.00. Assuming a 40 percent food cost for both items, the steak would offer a $3.60 contribution toward costs and profits, while the chicken would offer only $1.50 contribution. Pursuing the example further, if costs, other than food costs, of serving an entree were $1.00, profit of $2.60 would be made on the steak, but only $.50 would be made on the chicken.

There are two major causes of excessive price spread. The first is pricing according to competition. If there is not any one establishment in the area with a similar menu, prices may be drawn from several types of establishments with differing levels of service, atmosphere and price. The second is arriving at prices solely by marking up food cost. In the previous example, steak and chicken prices were arrived at by marking up food costs 2½ times, thus resulting in 40 percent food cost.

The optimal pricing structure will, of course, differ from establishment to establishment, but the presence of two circumstances should provide an indication of excessive price spread to most operators. If the most expensive entree item is more than 200 percent (or 2 times) of the price of the least expensive item, and there is a definite concentration of entree selections among the less expensive items, excessive price spread probably prevails.

The solution to the problem is to make the high priced items less expensive and the lower priced items more expensive, while keeping previous quality and portions the same.

Another Example:

Suppose, to continue with our example, chicken was raised in price $.75 to $3.25 and steak was lowered $.75 to $5.25. Food cost percentages would then be 31 percent for the chicken (assuming $1.00 food cost) and 46 percent for the steak (assuming the $2.40 food cost). Contribution toward other costs would then be $2.25 from the chicken and $2.85 from the steak. One advantage gained would be that steak would not be more attractively priced relative to chicken, and more people would probably order it. Additionally, those guests who ordered chicken at the revised price level would be contributing more toward costs and profit than was the case previously.

To demonstrate the effect of such a price change on profits, let us assume that, at the original menu prices, 25 percent of the orders were for the $2.50 chicken entree, while only 5 percent of orders were for the $6.00 steak. Assuming 100 customers per evening, sales would be as follows:

Chicken
  $2.50/order X
    100 customers X 25% = $62.50
Steak
  $6.00/order X
    100 customers X 5% =   30.00
              Total Sales $92.50

With a 40 percent food cost, a dollar food cost of $37.00 would result. Thus $55.50 would be left to cover other costs and profit. These amounts were computed as follows:

Sales $92.50
Less Food Cost
  (40% X $92.50)   37.00

Remaining contribution
  toward other costs and
  prices $55.50

Now assume prices are changed, raising chicken in price to $3.25 and lowering steak to $5.25. A few chicken customers might conceivably be lost to other establishments, but some additional steak customers should be gained. Thus, let us assume that the restaurant could still expect 100 customers per evening.

Suppose at the new prices chicken and steak become equally desirable, each attracting 15 percent of the orders. With a 31 percent food cost for chicken and 46 percent food cost for steak, the contribution toward other costs and profit would increase to $76.50, computed as follows:

Steak
Sales
  (15 orders X $5.25) = $78.75
Less food cost
    15 X $2.40) =   36.00

Contribution toward other
    costs and profit $42.75
Chicken
Sales
    (15 orders X $48.75 = $731.25
Less food cost
        15 X $1.00) = 15.00
Contribution toward other
costs and profit   <u>$33.75</u>
                              <u>$76.50</u>

The result would be an increased contribution to fixed costs and profits of $21.00, a percentage increase of 38 percent. If we assume costs, other than food costs, relating to the preparation and service of the 30 meals had amounted to $1.75 per meal, a profit of only $3.00 would result at the original menu prices, while a $24.00 profit would result at the revised prices.

This illustrative increase in profit is based on the assumption that steak and chicken become equally popular at the revised prices. If more than 15 percent continued to order chicken and fewer than 15 percent ordered steak, the increase in profit would be somewhat less. If more than 15 percent ordered steak, the increase in profit would be somewhat less. If less than 15 percent ordered steak, the profit increase would be greater.

The example we have dealt with was limited to two items for simplicity of explanation. Parallels could be drawn between other menu items.

INTEGRATED PROFIT PLANNING SYSTEMS

Market analysis, cost standards and control, budgeting, management by objectives and responsibility accounting combine to provide management with an integrated profit planning system which ensures a clear continuity of policy and action from broad long-range planning down to relatively detailed day-to-day operations. Each facet of the system flows through to the next, and the system overall is internally consistent.

Basing management on well-designed systems rather than on unstructured subjective judgments provides management with a substantial degree of control and a clear frame of reference both for adjusting existing plans for changing circumstances and for developing new plans which are promptly responsive to developing trends. In effect, planning systems and operational systems are integrated into each other.

Boosting Restaurant Profits by Increasing Beverage Sales

Liquor sales are high profit margin, and servers must be continuously made aware of the importance of serving drinks with dispatch. Immediately after a party has been seated, the server must proceed to try to take a drink order by asking, "May I serve you a cocktail" or a similar question. After the first round has been consumed, the server must approach the table again and ask, "May I serve the same?" When the party is thus approached, usually a second round of drinks will be ordered; it is all too frequent a complaint that the patrons did not order a second round of drinks, because it took too long for the first to be served, or they were not approached to place an order for a second round. Employees can also be motivated when it is emphasized that the importance of these potential additional drink sales also means an additional 10 ¢ or 15¢ in gratuities per drink. However, the server must be warned not to "push" drinks to a point where a patron feels uncomfortable.

THE CONTRIBUTION OF WINE SALES TO RESTAURANT PROFITS

Wine can be sold only when such sales are properly promoted, through wine display at the entrance, through a wine list, and through special incentives for servers. The importance of wine sales lies in the fact that these sales are usually above and in addition to, *and not instead of*, hard liquor sales.

HANDY REMINDERS ON SETTING OF WINE GLASSES

All wine glasses are placed on the table in the same order as the wine is served. All wine glasses appear to the right of the water goblet—the only glass to the left of the water is the cordial glass and port wine glass. In a formal setting, the glasses would appear as follows, starting at the right:

Sherry glass
White wine glass
Champagne saucer or goblet
Water goblet
Port wine glass
Cordial glass

To promote wine sales, personnel must be adequately trained so they can make recommendations and answer questions intelligently. It is advisable to have a limited wine list rather than one that is so comprehensive that it would take an expert to know the difference in varieties.

A PRACTICAL GUIDE TO PROFITABLE WINE SERVICE

What type of wine to serve, when and with what food?

Sherry Wine, a fortified wine served before a meal instead of a cocktail, also with certain appetizers and soups. Served in A SHERRY GLASS.
Dry White Wine, may also be served with certain appetizers and soups, particularly sea food, caviar, and other non-sweet appetizers. Served in an ALL PURPOSE WINE GLASS.
Dry or Semi-Sweet White Wine, may be served with all fish dishes and shell fish. Served in an ALL PURPOSE WINE GLASS.

Dry, White Wine, Light Red Wine, or Rose Wine, may be served with all white meat poultry and light meat such as veal. Served in an ALL PURPOSE WINE GLASS.

Full-Bodied Red Wine, may be served with all red meat, game, and dark meat poultry. Served in a RED WINE GLASS.

Rose Wine, Sparkling Burgundy, and Champagne, may be served with all meals and with all courses. Rosé wine is served in an ALL PURPOSE WINE GLASS, sparkling burgundy and champagne are served in a CHAMPAGNE GOBLET or CHAMPAGNE SAUCER.

Dry Red Wine, may be served with cheese. Serve in an ALL PURPOSE WINE GLASS.

Wines can be served only after they have been sold. It must become a standard procedure to ask the patron *after the food order has been taken,* if he desires some wine. And with this question, present the wine list, or draw his attention to the wine selection on the menu.

Once an order for wine has been taken, the server must proceed immediately to prepare for such service so that the wine may be served when it is appropriate. The proper glassware must be placed on the table immediately and the ordered wine obtained from the bar. Wine glasses, except for the port wine glasses, are always placed to the right of the water goblet.

White Wine, Rose Wine, Sparkling Burgundy, and Champagnes
Take the selected wine to the table and present it to the person who has made the choice so that he may "approve" the bottle. After approval, place the bottle into the wine bucket on stand next to the table. The wine bucket should be filled three-quarters with ice and some water, to facilitate the bottle sliding into the ice. Place napkin, folded lengthwise, over the bucket and let it stand until needed. White and rosé wines may be opened just prior to serving the meal or course. Champagne and sparkling burgundy may only be opened immediately after the given course or meal with which the wine is to be served has been served.

First, serve a sip to the host to try the quality of the wine. When approved, proceed around the table serving the ladies first, then the gentlemen, and last the host. Wine glasses are filled only three-quarters full and never to the brim. After serving, return bottle to the wine bucket.

Red Wine
Take the selected wine to the table and present it to the person who has made the choice so that he may approve the bottle. (When red wine is served, it must be placed into a wine basket immediately and should be moved as little as possible in order not to stir up any possible sediments.) After approval, proceed to open the bottle immediately and leave standing on the table in the wine basket. Red wine is opened immedately and left standing so that the wine may "breathe." Actually, the wine absorbs oxygen from the air, and this oxidation process activates the development of the bouquet and the aroma.

Red wine is served at room temperature or at approximately 65 degrees. Immediately after the meal or course has been served with which the wine is to be served, proceed with the wine service in the same way as for white wine.

Opening the Wine Bottle
First of all, provide yourself with a good corkscrew. A good corkscrew has sharp thin screw edges that bite into the cork and pull it out. A cheap corkscrew has rounded edges, and since it cannot bite into the cork, it will pull out of the hole without pulling the cork. When cork is removed, it should be placed above the set plate of the person ordering the wine or the host.

All still wines are opened exactly the same way. Place bottle on firm level support and immediately cut, not tear the tin foil around the neck of the bottle with a sharp knife, just below the protruding edge. Wipe the top of the bottle, particularly the now-exposed cork, keeping the bottle at all times in an upright position. Insert the corkscrew all the way straight into the cork as far as it will go and pull out in one smooth movement. After removal of the cork, wipe the inside of the bottle neck for any possible particles inside it. When opening champagne and sparkling burgundy, first remove all foil or tin foil around the cork and upper part of the neck of the bottle. Remove the wire holding the cork in place. Hold bottle at a 45-degree angle and proceed to push the cork out with the thumb, turning the bottle slightly. At all times, keep the bottle at the same angled position after the cork is forced out, to allow inside pressure to adjust to outside pressure. Holding the bottle at an angle, to avoid spillage of the wine, proceed to serve the same way as for a still wine.

Always serve wine from right and food from the left. The wine stand should always be placed to the right of the host or person ordering the wine.

If the above guidelines are scrupulously followed, we guarantee that the restaurant's bottom line will benefit from the increased *profitable* sales of wines.

Operational Surveys

In applying, interpreting, and monitoring the results of the basic systems, management should remember that a substantial part of operational effectiveness still depends upon qualitative factors which must be reviewed and controlled separately from the basic systems. Furthermore, since circumstances and operating conditions are not constant, the systems themselves may need to be changed from time to time to ensure optimum effectiveness.

Accordingly, management should conduct periodic operational surveys to determine how well systems and personnel are performing. At their most comprehensive, such surveys are all-embracing reviews of policies and procedures for their cost-effectiveness, leading to recommendations for improvement wherever needed.

At their most ambitious, such surveys should be conducted by outside consultants who can bring both detachment and various forms of expertise to the survey. In the absence of major symptoms trouble, such surveys can be effectively performed internally. In large operations, the internal systems staff or audit staff may assume the responsibility for the review. In smaller operations, management may undertake the investigation themselves.

For restaurants, the principal areas of investigation for an operational survey are:

    Personnel evaluation.
    Accounting procedures evaluation.
    Internal control evaluation.
    Management policy.
    Financial analysis and industry review.
    Layout review.

The basic methodology is a series of interviews, observations of operations and analysis of systems, policies and procedures. This approach permits the identification of symptoms which might not otherwise be recognized and the identification of causes and potential solutions.

Effective operational surveys are a valuable management resource for keeping systems finely attuned to changing needs. Clearly, elaborate formal surveys relying on outside consultants will not be needed frequently, but a careful internal review of each area, at least, annually, can be valuable insurance that various small problems will not mushroom into larger problems.

Personnel Evaluation

Of all the qualitive areas of operations, few depend more on intangible factors than personnel, and restaurants have unique challenges. Working hours differ from most industries, the work load has usually wide variations from peak to valley, and restaurants rely on an unusual mixture of skilled and unskilled labor. As a result, turnover is high, productivity hard to control and effective systems and supervision are unusually important.

Since turnover is costly and productivity hard to control, restaurants need to emphasize motivation and employee satisfaction. The suitability of incumbents for the jobs they hold should be reviewed both in terms of efficiency and the possibility of the employee's potential for assuming greater responsibility. Where employees are performing satisfactorily but not likely to advance to another job, management must assure itself that the employee is reasonably content and not likely either to work below desired productivity or to leave the job.

Where a survey shows significant morale problems or low productivity, management needs to review the adequacy of the job structures. The job structure should provide for doing the right things in the right ways, and if circumstances have changed, the job structure itself should perhaps be changed. Employee satisfaction is closely allied to organization and motivation.

Restaurants, more than most businesses, may benefit from individualizing operations. They are uniquely dependent on key people (head-waiter, chef, managers, etc.) and they neither need the relatively rigid job structure which may work well in other industries nor will they suffer from a job structure which allows for the personal characteristics of key individuals. The higher the cuisine, the fewer the job candidates who will adequately run the kitchen. Thus restaurants need to motivate key employees and inculcate a management viewpoint and loyalty in such employees.

Accounting Procedures Evaluation

At the root of both planning and all financial decisions are the accounting procedures and systems. The efficiency of record-keeping operations plays a key role in profitability. Thus, these procedures and systems must remain responsive to management needs in the light of changing circumstances.

As management reviews the results of operations through various accounting reports, as will be set forth in the samples presented throughout Chapter 7, it must also consider how well they are operating and whether they can be improved.

The principal criteria are:

Does the system provide useful data and analysis as quickly as needed?
Is the information accurate and quickly intelligible?
Is the information functional?
Can it be produced more efficiently?

Accounting information is the basis for cost standards, budgets, departmental controls, and a key factor in judging whether all these are working well is whether responsible department heads are using accounting reports as a basis for controlling operations. If reports are being largely ignored, they may be providing too little or too much information, or they may be poorly organized. More often, they may simply have become obsolete for one reason or another, so that department heads no longer rely on them. If the individual manager must make several mental adjustments in order to use reports, he may simply cease to rely on them.

Example:

Take, for example, the menu cost sheet, Figure 5-4, If used properly, this report can be of invaluable aid to the restaurant operator in determining his per portion cost of various menu items, then computing his actual cost per dollar of sales, and finally in matching the actual number of portions which predetermined estimates thereby obtaining relative indices of menu item popularity, However, as in the case of the daily flash report presented in Chapter 2, the daily beverage personnel and kitchen payroll departmental reports presented earlier in this chapter, and the several accounting reports and forms illustrated throughout Chapter 7, these forms are of little value unless they are critically used and relied upon by the restaurant operator and department heads.

The calculation of the cost of each portion sold for the various menu items is directly related to our discussion of standard costs earlier in this chapter. Such a calculation, of necessity, presumes standard methods of preparation, adherence to standard portion sizes, and standard recipes. As noted in earlier chapters, these standards are buttressed and maintained by cooking yield tests and butchering tests and samples.

Thus, an important part of a review of accounting systems and procedures is ensuring that they are up to date. As circumstances change, information needs change and keeping accounting procedures responsive can easily be ignored. The accounting department and operating departments must keep clear channels of communication open so that anything which affects the utility of accounting reports is promptly reflected in the procedures and systems.

Accounting efficiency is always an important concern. On the one hand, costs can escalate unnecessarily if reports are not kept to the level of information that

MENU COST SHEET

RESTAURANT _____ 13570

DINING ROOM _____ MEAL _____ DAY _____ DATE _____

ITEM	PRINCIPAL INGREDIENTS					SECONDARY ITEMS							TOTAL DIRECT COST	UNPRODUCTIVE ITEMS	PER PORTION				TOTAL			COST PER $ SALE	NUMBER OF PORTIONS		POPULARITY INDEX
	COST	PER	PER PORTION		COST	SOUP AND/OR APPETIZERS	GARNITURE AND SAUCE	VEGETABLE	POTATO	SALAD AND/OR RELISH	BREAD AND BUTTER	DESSERT	BEVERAGE			COST	SELLING PRICE	COST	SELLING PRICE				ESTIMATED	ACTUAL	
			QUANTITY	UNITS																					

Figure 5-4. Menu Cost Sheet.

is truly needed. On the other hand, systems are constantly susceptible to improved efficiency through advances made in the use of computers. Where systems are operated manually, management must remain constantly alert to the possibilities of computerizing the system. Mini-computers already can afford substantial benefits in small operations, and with the further development of software programs for use with mini-computers and the further refinement of services offered by computer service bureaus, the use of EDP becomes all the more appealing.

THE FLOW OF PAPERWORK

Even the most efficient accounting system will lag if the flow of paperwork delays input into the system. Thus a periodic review of how expeditiously information moves to where it is needed is an important management consideration.

The basic tool for evaluating the paperwork flow is Flow Charting, which traces each document visually and thus quickly identifies bottlenecks, duplications, omissions, etc. The system must always walk a tightrope between having too much and too little paperwork and, accordingly, a comparison between practices from one period to the next can be a clue to how well the flow is working. If new reports have developed or if existing reports are now going to additional users, the changes are likely to have developed informally and thus without regard for the overall system. With changed needs, the distribution system may need to be changed, to include more or less information and to include broader or narrower distribution.

In reviewing paperwork, the objective should be the utmost integration of forms. Frequently, several different reports can be integrated into single, more useful and quickly comprehensible reports. The result is both greater economy of preparation and stronger assurance that the affected departments will use reports effectively. Integrated forms eliminate backtracking and fragmentation and thus enable the department head to absorb quickly the information he needs for action.

DOCUMENTATION

Many aspects of operations depend upon documenting procedures and policies which must be followed for efficient operations. As needs change, this documentation can become obsolete; thus a periodic review is needed. For example, cost standards will be more easily infringed if changes in portion-sizes, ingredients, or kitchen procedures are not accurately reflected in the guidelines kitchen personnel use.

Similarly, procedures for training new employees must be up-to-date in order to ensure that new employees will be endoctrinated in methods and procedures on which the restaurant currently relies.

INTERNAL CONTROL

The accounting system and the paperwork which serves it operate as an internal control and as a constraint upon irregularities. Such internal control also depends substantially upon other factors, however, and the internal control system should be periodically reviewed to determine whether:

Appropriate procedures are being followed, and
Those procedures are themselves adequate.

Despite the rising incidence of credit card sales, restaurants remain predominantly cash operations and, therefore, stringent controls on cash receipts and disbursements are essential.

Such controls depend upon both careful supervision and meticulous sales check control at each stage from writing up the order at the customer's table to receiving and recording the cash receipts at the cash register.

Similarly, controls over inventories must be stringent, because restaurant operations are particularly vulnerable to pilferage, loss, and spoilage. Broad period accounting reports may be a rough indication of how effectively controls are working, but for day-to-day operations, some kind of inventory reporting system and procedures for controlling disbursements and kitchen procedures are essential.

Both purchasing and production control have built-in bias toward high inventory where a restaurant is large enough to have separation of production and purchasing responsibilities and where food and beverage control department heads have direct responsibility for inventory control, yet every decision to buy, which the purchasing department head makes, is also an inventory decision.

We have found that one of the better ways to attain greater efficiency and restaurant profits from proper inventory management is by use of the ABC system of restaurant inventory management.

Example: The ABC Analysis

Analysis of a restaurant's dollar usage of inventory will usually show, on the one hand, a large percentage of annual dollar usage applicable to a small percentage of the number of items, while, on the other hand, there will be a large percentage of the number of items contributing relatively little to dollar usage. Although the degree of concentration will vary greatly between different types of restaurants, a typical relationship is shown in the bar chart (Figure 5-5) where 10 percent of the number of items accounts for 65 percent of the annual dollar usage, and 65 percent of the number items accounts for only 10 percent of the annual dollar usage.

In most instances, the restaurant's *investment* in its inventory closely follows its inventory *usage* value.

Although the percentage of inventory investment for low- and medium-value items can normally be expected to increase, the result is an overall decrease in inventory investment brought about through a closer control of high-value items, offset only partially by the increase in Class C inventory items. By reducing receipt quantities and safety stock levels of high-value items while, at the same time, increasing receipt

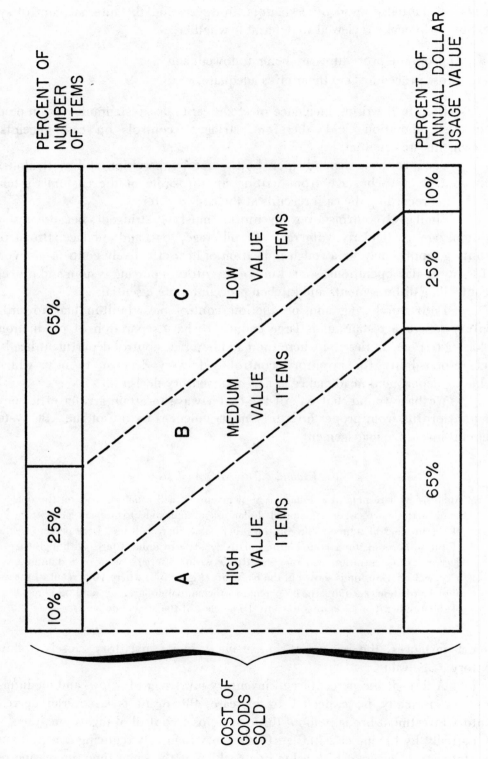

Figure 5-5. The ABC Analysis

frequencies, the turnover can often be almost doubled and the inventory almost halved.

Once a restaurant can identify its A (high usage volume), B (medium usage value), and C (low usage value) inventory items, its inventory control policies can then be formulated differently for each class of items, probably characterized by the following comparative inventory control policies:

For "A" items
—Frequent deliveries
—Maintain minimum safety stocks
—Maintain strong purchasing control
—Review records frequently.

For "B" items
—Maintain strong purchasing control
—Record pre-determined reorder points based on average usage
—Review records on an "exception" basis and arbitrarily determine safety stock.

For "C" items
—Receive 3 to 12 months' supply (assuming staples if food stuffs) at a time
—Use physical reorder points
—Exercise less control over purchasing

As should be perceived from the above analysis, one of the important advantages of the ABC method of inventory classification for restaurants is the reduction in record-keeping costs for the large number of Class C items which can be removed from purchasing control records and put under physical control. Clerks, once they are freed from the task of keeping records of the many immaterial items in an inventory, can devote more time and greater attention to purchasing and reorder control systems for the A and B items of inventory in which dollar usage is greater.

USE OF A SERVICE PAR STOCK INVENTORY TO MAXIMIZE EFFICIENCY AND PROFITS

The size of a restaurant's "in use" china, silver, glassware and miscellaneous inventory depends on the seating capacity of the restaurant. Such inventory must not be left to guess work but must be calculated, taking into consideration peak periods and capacity of the dishwashing areas. When such calculations have been made, and the quantity on hand falls below the service par stock inventory, a requisition is made for the difference.

Whenever requisitioning, quantities should be rounded off to the nearest full dozen or half dozen. This inventory should be taken at a time other than when the monthly food and beverage inventory is taken, whenever possible. This should be done at least once a year.

MANAGEMENT POLICY

While various operational systems are being surveyed, management must also review broad overall policy to be sure that the restaurant is headed in the right direction. Markets and marketing techniques change in ways that may necessitate basic operational and strategical changes. Management must consider whether profit goals are realistic, and whether policies are consistent with objectives. Each principal assumption needs to be challenged and alternatives considered.

Management must consider whether the proportion of various market segments served has changed significantly enough to warrant some new directions. Does the public want more elaborate or more simple menus? Are they spending more or spending less on dining out? Is the neighborhood changing? Should promotional expenditures be increased or decreased? Are the decor or service style getting out of step with public taste?

A review of management policy is in reality a form of market analysis to assess long-range prospects in somewhat the same way that an initial analysis is used as the basis for the restaurant's original opening. Furthermore, the restaurant industry is perennially subject to various trends which can have substantial effects on continued profitability (see Chapter 11—Recent Industry Trends), therefore, periodic reviews of management policy are a necessary step in preserving profitability by responding quickly to changes.

FINANCIAL ANALYSIS

In addition to the review of basic accounting reports and annual financial statements, management needs to make periodic financial analyses to assess various critical ratios and to compare operations with the industry in general.

Particularly critical here is the ratio of fixed costs to revenues. Management must consider whether such fixed costs have been built into operations to a dangerous point in the event that revenues should turn downward. In addition to the stresses of inflation within the economy at large, the restaurant industry has built-in factors which drive up costs even more, therefore the break-even point continually escalates. With a sales decline, the restaurant could well reach that break-even point much earlier than management anticipated, thus precipitating both a profit crisis and a cash flow crisis.

In turn, the restaurant needs to examine various other ratios to exhibit relationships between various asset, income and expense values and to compare these with similar operations in the restaurant industry. For this purpose information on industry performance is published regularly, enabling management to consider how well they are doing. Significant differences from most comparable restaurants may be symptomatic of problems or inefficiencies (or a sign of superior performance!), and should be carefully and critically scrutinized. An important caution here is that the restaurant's own financial information must be compatible with industry figures. Without uniform reporting procedures, comparisons could well be misleading.

PLANT LAYOUT

The physical facilities and their layout play an important role in efficiency and, therefore, profitability and should accordingly be periodically scrutinized for their relative applicability to present conditions. The goal is prompt customer service and minimum cost; therefore, the layout should provide for a smooth one-way flow; ready accessibility of equipment, controls and supplies; adequate work space for employees and good working conditions.

The layout should be examined with particular care if new equipment has been installed within the past year; if the menu has been significantly changed, or if sales have increased notably. A quick clue to relative layout efficiency is to observe conditions in the kitchen and dining room during conditions of stress. The layout and facilities should be adequate to handle the sales volume during peak load periods without undue problems. Such problems are a warning signal, because with increased sales—always the objective—facilities will clearly be inadequate.

Example:

Our experience has demonstrated beyond any doubt that the seating arrangement can make a definite difference in attaining the goal of "optimum customer service." An alert restaurant general manager observed a table in his restaurant set up in a corner of the dining room with the place settings as follows:

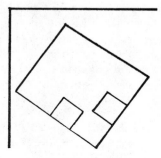

Figure 5-6

He immediately instructed the bus-boy to change the place setting to look like this:

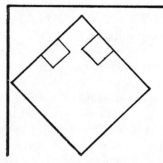

Figure 5-7

The restaurant general manager then explained that you should always empathize with the customer—put yourself in his place! Would you want to sit with your back to the rest of the dining room? Wouldn't you rather sit where you could see the action? The customer should always be seated, wherever possible, facing the dining room or looking out a window or facing a doorway—but *never* facing a blank wall!

Periodic operational surveys of the entire restaurant are a valuable management tool and a highly effective way of anticipating and avoiding problems. They can disclose opportunities for improvements which may be reflected directly in the profit and loss statement.

FOUR CASE STUDIES OF MBO APPLIED
TO RESTAURANT MANAGEMENT

The four illustrative case studies which follow have been adapted in part from the files of the National Institute for the Foodservice Industry and demonstrate situations where MBO has been successfully applied to restaurant management with profitable results.

Case Study No. 1

The owner of the restaurant was a 75-year old, retired army general. The restaurant manager found that the owner had begun giving orders to his workers without consulting the manager. In fact, several of the employees had begun to take advantage of the situation and were going over the manager's head directly to the owner. The manager was faced with a situation where he did not want to lose his job as restaurant manager, yet he felt it essential to stop this intolerable situation.

MBO As the Answer:

Utilizing one of the essential principles of MBO that a good manager informs his superior promptly of all unusual developments, the manager took the positive approach and went directly to the owner. He was able to convince the owner that it was essential that there be established lines of organizational responsibility in order for each level within the restaurant operation to properly perform. Consequently, as a result of his meeting with the owner they were able to clarify and review the areas of responsibility and organizational lines so that it was subtly made clear to the owner that his intervention undercut the very nature and function of the restaurant manager. Only after establishing such an understanding with the owner as to what the major activities and responsibilities of the manager were and should be, was the manager able to make the owner see the error of his ways in encouraging the employees to go around the manager. Since it was evident that the owner was acting in many respects out of boredom with his retirement, the restaurant manager was able to redirect his energies into the area of setting goals and objectives for the operation (a vital part of management by objectives), thereby allowing the manager to resume his previous responsibility and authority for day-to-day operating decisions and contact with all of the subordinates. This also serves to illustrate how MBO regards the successful manager as a "manager of situations." Most of these situations are best defined by identifying the purpose of the organization and the managerial behavior best calculated to achieve that purpose.

Case Study No. 2

A restaurant owner learned that the highway passing his restaurant and the adjacent service station owned by him was to be declared an exclusive truck route (with the exception of local car traffic). He roughly estimated that this development would increase traffic by about 30 percent and that this would begin in approximately six to nine months. He thought that he would have to increase his restaurant facilities by at least 30 percent prior to that date, and that he would have to hire someone to take charge of his kitchen after enlarging the facilities. Since most of his employees were from the farms and small towns surrounding the restaurant, and were motivated by factors such as hours, working conditions, and salary, as opposed to achievement, recognition, and more sophisticated motivational responses, the owner was confused as to the kind of a kitchen boss to hire so as to assure complete harmony and maximum work efficiency. complete harmony and maximum work efficiency.

MBO As the Answer:

One of the fundamental concepts inherent in MBO is that a basic responsibility of all managers is to coordinate the activities of their subordinates with each other and with other departments thereby developing and maintaining harmonious personnel relations. Similarly, a major premise of MBO recognizes that the environmental situation for an individual firm which changes dramatically imposes new requirements on both the company and on the individual managers within that company. Applying this learning to the facts of the case study—while it was easy to suggest that the new kitchen boss should be drawn from the same background as the present composition of the restaurant's employees thus assuring harmony and efficiency among a peer group,—would have been very shortsighted in the circumstances and would have ignored MBO. The more successful approach proved to be selecting a new kitchen boss who could best fulfill the leadership responsibilities to raise the performance standards of the kitchen employees, and one who could meet the needs reasonably anticipated to be imposed by the increased restaurant facility. True, some conflicts with present individual employees could be expected to arise. However, the departmental responsibility of the kitchen boss under the circumstances of an expanded facility was a far more important role to fill. Also, it could reasonably be anticipated that a strong achievement, recognition, and job-enrichment-oriented kitchen boss could raise the goals and objectives (and the values as well) of a good number of the present kitchen employees.

Case Study No. 3

A restaurant manager who was very concerned about improving service to his early morning breakfast customers, primarily golfers who wanted to eat quickly and be on their way, had been receiving numerous complaints about the slowness in getting food served. He suspected that the trouble resulted from his new hostess not knowing exactly what was expected of her, and he was confused about the right approach to take.

MBO As the Answer:

The manager decided, using MBO, to get together with his new hostess and jointly develop performance standards for her job. Similarly, he decided that it would be extremely useful for her to assist him in developing a "reporting system" so as to provide input on making his restaurant service more efficient. On a practical basis, he implemented his approach by requesting the hostess to outline what she thought were her major areas of responsibility in her job and how her performance in terms of results should periodically be measured. He then answered the same questions about her job himself and suggested that they compare their responses. This turned out to be extremely effective in helping the hostess understand what management expected of her. In addition, it gave her a sense of job enrichment by allowing her to feel that she had a hand in developing performance standards for her own job. Similarly, encouraging her participation in the development of an informal reporting system whereby her performance could be measured against the standards which she helped to develop gave her the needed sense of involvement and resulted in significant improvements in her performance and in the speed with which food got served. This also illustrates the MBO presumption that, while participating is highly desirable, its principal merit lies in those social and political values rather than its effect on production. Nevertheless, as seen in this case, MBO may have a favorable impact on production as well. In any case, it seldom hurts!

Case Study No. 4

For a period of three months a restaurant manager had been experiencing relatively poor business and, in response thereto, had been trying to increase his evening business. Suddenly he found himself booked solid with private parties, banquets and business dinners for the next two months. After the first such business dinner, he found that his chef and his hostess were not as well trained as he had come to believe, and guests were beginning to complain about both the quality of the food and service at the dinners. Since he did not want to lose this evenings business, which was salvaging his restaurant operation, he was almost in the dark about what to do.

MBO As the Answer:

The first step in resolving this quagmire is for the restaurant manager to make an objective determination whether the chef and hostess are trainable for the increased volume of work thrust upon them as a result of this evening business. If the manager decides the that the chef and/or hostess are not trainable, he has no alternative but to discharge them. If the manager decides that the chef and hostess are, in fact, trainable, MBO becomes an invaluable tool for his restaurant organization in terms of a fresh look (along with the participation of both the chef and hostess, respectively) at all of the following: objectives, teamwork, scheduling work and menu planning, recognized progress, and development of personnel. This should be best initiated by individual meetings with the chef and hostess and the manager might begin with a frank admission of some failure on his part in giving the employees the proper guidance and supervision. Further, MBO would dictate that an attempt be made to reach agreement on how the subordinate might be trained and exposed to better handling evening business, including frank examination of where he or she has fallen down in recent months. To the individual employee, the basic advantage of such an MBO approach is that the subordinate and his boss will establish a basic understanding in advance of the next two months' evening business which has already been booked. This mutual understanding should focus on the major areas of activity and responsibility, a definition of what constitutes a good job, and a bad one, and what conditions will exist at the end of the future period if results are to be considered either satisfactory or unsatisfactory in the interim. In addition, a vehicle should be established for having informal discussion between the manager and the chef and the hostess, respectively, of performance, progress, and results as often as possible during the months ahead.

CHAPTER 6

Long-Range Financial Planning for Restaurants

CHAPTER CAPSULE PREVIEW

In addition to all the other planning entailed in restaurant operations, finances must be carefully planned in both the short term and long term. The whole financial planning framework is established by the various initial operating decisions, thus, before any of those decisions are implemented, the restaurant operator needs to review his principal alternatives carefully. His choice will have substantial effects, and thus the tax, accounting, and economic implications of each alternative need to be developed clearly and in detail so that the financing approach most appropriate to the operator's circumstances can be identified.

When all basic decisions have been made as to site, building, major equipment items, furnishings, linens, flatware, china, and glassware, the major remaining question can be considered: how should the acquisition of these various capital items be financed?

The basic alternative is whether to buy or lease, but the restaurant operator not only may decide to purchase some capital items and lease others but he may also avail himself of various leasing alternatives which offer special advantages and considerable flexibility. Each approach has its advantages and limitations which must be reviewed both in the context of the proprietor's current circumstances and in the context of long range sales expectations. In addition, of course, expected financial and technological trends must be considered for the sake of their influence on operations.

In addition to all the other financial decisions, one major planning area for every restaurant in the years ahead is the prospect of investing in a computer.

LEASE OR BUY DECISIONS

For each category of assets, the restaurateurs must decide whether to buy or lease. Decisions are a function both of the operator's own circumstances and the prevailing tax and economic conditions.

Buying Assets Outright

Purchasing assets outright requires more substantial cash both initially and in subsequent operations, but it also entails advantages unavailable under leases. The owner has a greater command over assets and his broader tax options may result in significantly greater profitability over the years.

Thus, a major factor to consider in lease-buy decisions is the owner's own financial status and credit rating. It must be remembered that these must be more than merely initially adequate, since the investment of cash reduces the amount of funds that may be borrowed, and in turn, borrowing reduces the amount of cash that may be taken out of the business once it is developed and generates cash flow. Installment purchase may stretch out the payments and allow for tax deductions on interest payments, but the operator needs to allow for contingencies which may arise, either through saving or through preserving a credit line adequate for emergencies which may arise and for renovations, new equipment purchases, or other capital expenditure needs.

Investments and equipment replacement are a major source of tax deductions where property is owned outright, through allowances for depreciation and investment credit.

Depreciation is an allowable charge against income to accumulate a reserve over the life of the property sufficient to replace its original cost, but because the law allows the use of accelerated depreciation methods, annual deductions do not have to be uniform over the property's useful life. Thus, by using the sum-of-the-years-digits or double-declining-balance method, the owner can relate depreciation methods to the income and cash flow needs of starting a new business. Accelerated depreciation provides high deductions in the early years when the owner may need to keep taxes low and the retention of cash high. The result, of course, is lower deductions in later years, thus decisions on the depreciation method to be used should be based on carefully prepared projections of expected income and expenses over several years.

For example, accelerated depreciation methods may not be desirable for businesses which are expected to be slow to reach full profitability, both because income may be low—or nonexistent—in the initial years and because it reduces the deductions which would otherwise shelter income from taxes in later years. If high initial depreciation results in losses for tax purposes, the loss may be carried forward as a tax deduction could in later years, but loss carry forwards are limited, and in extreme cases, part of the tax deduction could be permanently lost.

The investment credit itself needs to be considered in deciding whether to use accelerated depreciation, because it is an additional deduction in the first year and is never offset against depreciation. Ranging from two percent to seven percent, depending on the nature of the property purchased, the investment credit can be a significant tax deduction factor in the first year of a new business. (Thereafter, of course, the fact that the investment credit is deductible all in one year can be important in tax planning, since the purchase of new property can to some extent be timed to fall in a year when the tax deductions will yield the most favorable results.

The rate at which property may be depreciated is established by Internal Revenue Service Regulations, which allow a fairly wide range for individual categories of property. No depreciation is allowed on land. Depreciation on buildings is slow, and on furniture and equipment, it is relatively rapid. Linen, flatware, china, and glassware may be treated as deductible expenses on the replacement method.

Leasing

A restaurant operator with limited cash resources may operate by leasing, or under some circumstances, it may be desirable to buy some property and lease others. Under a leasing arrangement, the restaurant operator may be somewhat less encumbered financially, but he also sacrifices some advantages. For example, if leased land gains in value over a period of years, the lessee cannot realize the gain as permitted if he owned the property outright. Offsetting the disadvantage, is a tax advantage: rental payments are fully tax deductible; whereas if the land is owned outright, the owner has no tax deduction (except for real estate taxes), because land is not depreciable.

Example:

We encountered a very successful, but financially unsophisticated, restaurant operator who developed a tremendous restaurant business but ignored long-range financial planning at the inception of his restaurant operation by entering into a five-year lease of the premises *without any option for lease renewal.* At the expiration of the initial term of the lease, the success of his operation turned out to be to his detriment because the landlord had him over the proverbial barrel and he was forced to submit a new lease providing for rental arrangements far in excess of those under the first lease. Prudence and shrewdness would have dictated an option for lease renewal (s) at predetermined intervals so that the landlord could never have had the restaurant operator at his economic mercy.

However, it must be noted that there is another side to this coin! The lessee-restaurant operator should exercise due diligence so as not to commit his operation for too long a lease term. This must properly be balanced against legitimate desire not to have frequent concern over renewing the lease at continuous short intervals. This is especially true if your site selection has been a sensible one and operations (and profits) are highly successful. No one can give you a foolproof guideline or answer to this problem—only the exercise of sound judgment, in light of all of the factors mentioned earlier applied to the particular facts and circumstances of the given individual case, will suffice. Nevertheless, don't overlook the travail encountered by the restaurant operator cited in our example above and the lesson to be learned therefrom.

It can sometimes be advantageous to buy major property items but lease individual items, such as particular pieces of equipment. For example, during a period of rapid innovation, improved equipment may be available before the useful life of existing equipment is exhausted. If the equipment is owned, the operator must seek to sell the old equipment before being able to take advantage of the new equipment. In such cases, leasing for short term periods may be preferable, because it provides great flexibility in capitalizing rapidly on technological improvements that become available. The lease period for land or buildings, however, should usually be long term in order to protect the lessee against arbitrary acts by the landlord. One leasing approach widely used in the restaurant industry is the "turnkey" operation, under which all assets from the building and land down to the glassware and china are owned by one party while operations are managed by another. Under this arrangement, the lessee is relieved of the major financial burden, yet he has complete control of the operation itself. The turnkey operation enables the two parties to run a business as a partnership yet remain completely separate for economic and tax purposes.

Another approach is the sale and leaseback transaction, in which the restaurant operator makes all arrangements such as buying the land and constructing the building and then sells it to an insurance company or other investment for lease-back on a long-term lease. Financing for the initial construction phase is borrowed, sometimes from the same investor who ultimately leases it back, and thus the operator does not have to have large cash assets of his own in order to enter into such an arrangement.

Frequently, an established restaurant can be acquired as a "bargain." In most instances, an established restaurant also can be acquired for much less of a cash outlay than would be required to begin a new restaurant business.

Example:

We were involved in the acquisition by one of our clients of a downtown Chicago restaurant for which the owner was asking $180,000. Our client wound up acquiring the restaurant for an aggregate $100,000 price, a $20,000 cash deposit with the remainder of $80,000 financed through a purchase money mortgage over eight years. What helped our client get such a "bargain," assuming the $180,000 was not intentionally overstated (which it wasn't)? It so happened that for personal health reasons, which our client found out about, the former owner was forced to move to Arizona as soon as he possibly could!

An astute businessman must make the effort to investigate carefully all phases of every potential business decision. We have witnessed the payoff in immediate dollars for such effort many times over.

ACCOUNTING ALTERNATIVES

Financial statements differ significantly from leased property to property owned outright, because of the accounting treatment. Accordingly, whether property is purchased or leased can have significant effects on lending sources' attitudes towards the amount of credit to be extended.

Accounting for Purchased Property

Where property has been purchased outright, fixed assets are shown at cost, and borrowings are reflected in liabilities in the full amount of the remaining loan principal. Portions of debt currently payable reduce working capital, and thus the working capital ratio.

Since assets are reported at cost, appreciation in the value of land and buildings is not reflected in financial statements until such time as it is actually realized by sale.

Interest and depreciation are changed as current expenses against income, and depreciation can be charged at a rate that is lower than the accelerated depreciation used for tax purposes. Straight-line depreciation is customarily used so that the depreciation deduction for each piece of property will be the same from year to year.

The applicable regulations promulgated under the Internal Revenue Code do not require that the same depreciation method be used for tax and accounting purposes. Consequently, accelerated methods of depreciation such as the double-declining balance method or the sum-of-the-years'-digits method, allow for a much larger tax depreciation deduction, up to twice as much as the straight-line method simultaneously used for financial accounting purposes, in the earlier years when the resultant tax savings can be used for the restaurant's working capital requirements and other financial purposes. This and other tax implications are presented in greater depth in Chapter 10.

Accounting For Leased Property

The restaurant operator can expect that he will have to capitalize leases and show the offsetting liability in all but the most exceptional circumstances. In such cases, he will, at a minimum, be required to make full disclosure of leases and related commitments in footnotes to the financial statements.

This is an opportune moment to touch briefly upon the peculiar accounting requirements relating to leases on the books and financial statements of the lessee. The Accounting Principles Board of the American Institute of CPA's in its Opinion No. 5, dated September 1964 and entitled "Reporting of Leases in Financial Statements of Lessee," concluded that "the nature of some lease agreements is such that an asset and a related liability should be shown in the balance sheet, and it is important to distinguish this type of lease from other leases." The opinion further concluded that "the distinction depends on the issue of whether or not the lease is in substance a purchase of the property rather than on the issue of whether or not a property right exists." In other words, it requires that a lease be capitalized as an asset on the lessee's accounting records and balance sheet (at an amount equal to the total lease payments discounted to present value over the term of the lease) when the lease is in economic reality a purchase.

Situations which lend themselves to this requirement are:

1. "Out-and-out installment purchases of property.

2. Leases with a short initial term with a lessee option to renew the lease for the remaining life of the property for substantially less than the fair rental value.

3. Where the lessee has a right at the end of the lease term to acquire the property at substantially less than the fair market value.

4. Where the property was acquired by lessor for a special need of the lessee and will probably be used only for this purpose and only by the lessee.

5. Where the lease terms correspond substantially to the estimated useful life of the property and also obligate the lessee to pay costs such as taxes, maintenance, etc., which are really ownership expenses.

6. Where the lessee guarantees the lessor's mortgage of the leased property.

7. Where the lessee treats the lease as a purchase for tax purposes.

8. Where the lessee is the parent corporation of the lessor or the lessee is a subsidiary of the same parent corporation.

9. Where the lessor and lessee have common officers, directors, or shareholders to a significant degree.

10. Where the lessor is a business entity, created by the lessee, and is dependent on the lessee for its operations.

11. Where the lessee has the option to acquire control of the lessor.

All rent payments are reported as current expenses, and where leases provide for the lessee to pay real estate taxes, insurance premiums, repairs and maintenance, or other costs, these are all chargeable to current expenses and, accordingly deductible for income tax purposes.

OPERATIONAL EFFECTS

The buy-lease decisions made at the beginning of a new restaurant can have a direct effect on subsequent operations and profits. In each case, these decisions must be carefully considered for a fairly long term and in relation to the various contingencies which may be expected to arise. Thus, for each major property item, the restaurant operator needs to define carefully the various effects of the investment of capital and then compare them with the financial consequences of leasing in order to select the pay-out schedule most suitable to the operator's circumstances.

Frequently, we have experienced how poor management in this regard can have disastrous consequences.

Example:

A restaurant operator who had plenty of cash, but a decided paucity of business acumen or sound advice, made an extremely poor selection of kitchen and dining room equipment (in which he also obviously excessively invested). As is many times the case, this was coupled with an extremely poor layout. Only the unlimited supply of his personal financial resources enabled extensive remodeling (about ten months after operations commenced), layout changes, and equipment replacements which were required to turn around a poor menu processing, low employee morale, slow foodservice, and poor food quality situation. Under ordinary circumstances, such an undertaking could not have been afforded and the operation would have failed within the first year.

REPLACEMENT DECISIONS

Since each category of property needs to be replaced sooner or later, the operator faces buy-lease decisions again and again throughout operations. In considering acquiring a new asset, the same considerations apply as for the asset being replaced.

This does not mean the decision will be the same as for the original asset, because circumstances differ, and special tax factors come into play. Furthermore, a major new consideration is timing: when should the old equipment be replaced? Which is most favorable, replacing old equipment when the first major repair or maintenance is needed or incurring that repair cost in order to postpone a new capital outlay, until a more favorable time?

Decisions should be based on the relative utility of the new and the old. Sometimes a history of high maintenance costs on owned equipment may make leasing replacement equipment more attractive than purchasing it.

Whatever method the restaurant operator used for making initial investment decisions should be used for replacement decisions, and where he decides to purchase rather than lease, his decision on timing needs to allow for return on investment on both the old and new equipment. Return on investment calculations should include the following:

New Equipment—all purchase and installation costs; also removal costs for old equipment, less salvage value that can be recovered, if any.

Old Equipment—major repairs that are needed or will be needed soon; also increased maintenance and replacement of parts that old equipment often requires.

Such computations provide a rational basis for comparing the economic alternatives objectively.

ASSET ACCOUNTING

Adequate records of capital asset costs are important to controlling and minimizing such costs. Records should include annual depreciation amounts, to support tax deductions, repair and maintenance expenses, as a basis for considering replacement, and, on major equipment items, some record of productivity as a standard for measuring whether the equipment continues to perform satisfactorily.

Such records are a basis for controlling assets and for clearly establishing book value in the event of property loss through fire or theft. Furthermore, the relatively modest effort entailed in record keeping is amply rewarded through the accumulation of data for informed decision-making whenever replacement needs to be considered for whatever reason.

DECISION FACTORS

Whether buying equipment the first time or replacing it, the major factors in buy-lease decisions are:

- The availability of funds and credit.
- The affect on financial statements and the affect thereafter on the operator's credit line.
- The affect on tax returns.
- The net return on investment over the property's expected life.

By considering all these factors for both the short and long term, the proprietor can trade off advantages and disadvantages so as to make the best ultimate buy-or-lease decision. Sometimes, of course, the decision is a combination: the most favorable results of all factors may be achieved by a sale-and leaseback transaction.

These considerations apply to all property and in recent years have come to be particularly important for a relatively new category of property: electronic data processing equipment, which we discuss separately because it will be an increasingly important operational tool for restaurants in the years ahead.

INVESTING IN A COMPUTER SYSTEM

During the first years of the electronic data processing industry, computers were of interest principally to large companies. Today, however, technological improvements and commercially available facilities have advanced to the point that even moderate-sized restaurants or small restaurant groups can benefit significantly from using computers. As a result of the various advances, typical options available are:

1. Purchase or lease of a minicomputer.
2. Rental of time on a computer.
3. The purchase of individual services from an EDP service bureau.

The options are graduated in the extent to which operations are computerized. The most ambitious option is the use of an in-house computer, since it entails the greatest investment, not merely in hardware but in time, effort, and related expenditures for developing computer programs.

To get the most from an in-house computer calls for relatively comprehensive use of the computer throughout all operational areas. Such use automatically entails significant expense and effort for software.

Renting computer time does not call for so ambitious an effort as does the installation of an in-house computer. The user is not only spared the outlay that can be involved in the purchase or lease of his own computer, but he is also spared the staff and space needs of an in-house installation. He needs only to develop (or purchase and adapt to his own needs) computer programs to perform those particular functions he feels will most benefit from automation.

Computers can be used on a still more modest scale through arrangements with an EDP service center. Such centers offer such specialized systems as payrolls, accounts payable, accounts receivable, inventory records, etc. One particularly useful system that can benefit restaurants is the maintenance of records on sales and cash receipts on a daily basis. The advantage of using such relatively routine systems is that they can be adapted individually at the user's convenience and with a minimum of effort.

With each passing year, computer capabilities become more and more practical and useful, and every restaurant operator should consider conducting feasibility studies to determine how those capabilities apply to his own operations. A feasibility study considers each of the three alternatives and establishes the benefits and costs each would entail. It establishes such operating costs as personnel, space, power, air conditioning, stationery and forms for an in-house installation, compared with the lesser costs—and lesser benefits—of the other two alternatives. At the other end of the scale, a feasibility study analyzes the existing manual system and determines how it might be improved and made more efficient without a computer. In some cases, the use of non-electronic office equipment and streamline systems can yield substantial benefits.

EDP BENEFITS

The computer-user can usually expect to need fewer office employees, thus lowering the payroll cost and reducing problems of turnover, absenteeism, etc. With the computer, reports for controlling operations are available much more rapidly and they can be designed to provide more and more useful information. In turn, they will be substantially more accurate.

The computer can provide valuable benefits, but cost reductions, *per se* should not be a principal motivation, because cost savings are seldom achieved overall. For example, lower clerical payroll is often offset by higher salaries for the technicians who run the computer system.

Operating costs before and after adopting a computer should not be the principal measure of its value, because the tangible and intangible benefits of EDP can be substantial. Not only can the computer do things faster and more efficiently, but it also can do things which are just not practical manually. Computers can be programmed to make analyses which could not be easily or regularly performed manually at a reasonable cost.

Even where no direct cost savings are achieved, intangible and indirect benefits can be significant. For example, audits may require less time if records are in good order and controls are effectively maintained. Auditors will review the EDP internal control system before determining the extent of their audit procedures, and where such control is deemed to be good, the scope of audit tests may well be smaller. For this reason, it is well to consult with the independent auditors during the selection, programming, and implementation stages described below.

For restaurants, computers can be used to develop information systems which not only portray operations overall, but also produce:

Sales forecasts for establishing optimally effective staffing levels.

Usage reports to assist timely purchasing in economic quantities which will avoid or minimize shortages or excess and waste.

Sales reports to assist in menu planning that will optimize customer satisfaction—and sales.

Among the three basic options, restaurants have the flexibility to automate their operations in individual modules, computerizing a single operation at a time. Beginning with the simplest "housekeeping" functions, the restaurant operator can gradually convert more and more of his systems from manual operation to computer operation.

This does not mean that the restaurant operator should begin with the simplest option and then shift to others as preliminary systems are installed. On the contrary, the initial consideration of EDP should begin with a feasibility study to determine which option will most effectively accomplish the overall goal.

The computerization process should proceed in carefully controlled stages. The feasibility study should evaluate overall system needs, identify the individual system components and consider each step at a time. In this way, a go/no-go decision can be made at the end of each step, thus cutting the cost of studies early, if a negative decision is indicated.

System specifications should be prepared in a way that fully identifies input that will be made available and the output that is desired. The structure and form of the output are critical since the crux of computer-produced information is integration: when suitably programmed, the computer can combine, analyze, and report information in the form needed for each separate use. Redundance in a manual system—the same information maintained in separate departments for separate purposes—is one of the keystones of economy of effort in computerized operations, because the computer retains the basic information centrally but produces separate reports for each separate use that will be made of the information.

For example, sales information is used for both short term and long term financial planning, but it is also used for cash control, for menu planning, for purchasing, for marketing, for staffing, etc. Similarly, cost information has many different valuable uses. Thus, system specifications need to provide for the kind of information storage required and the nature and frequency of reports to be rendered.

By submitting system specifications to manufacturers and EDP service centers, the operator can get competitive bids and consider which of the options will best suit his needs. An important part of the feasibility study, of course, is accurately rendering the two options comparable through determining the extra costs—and savings—entailed in installing an in-house computer, whether that computer be purchased or leased.

Once a selection is made, a major concern is preparing employees for the changes which will occur. These are likely to be substantial, and they can be exciting or upsetting to the staff, depending on how they are presented. An air of secrecy should be avoided, and employees should be actively involved in planning the parts of the new system which will affect them. This is a very practical matter, since a system designed in the abstract can all too easily omit important factors or result in producing information which is not really needed or is needed in a significantly different form.

The staff should be regularly informed of progress, and it is particularly important that they be educated to recognize that EDP imposes a stringent discipline. One of the most difficult adjustments employees have to make is to learn that the easy flexibility of manual systems is not possible with computers. What would be a minor, easily-corrected error in a manual system can be a much larger headache in a computerized system. Coding accuracy is essential and controls must be strictly observed, otherwise errors will either be run and produce unsatisfactory results or if input does not conform to requirements, the computer program may reject the run, thus delaying needed information. Similarly, employees must conform with rigid timing and cut-offs because individual transactions no longer have the independence they have in manual operations, and adjustments to include omitted transactions cannot be made as flexibly as in manual systems, because each additional run entails a cost, particularly where a service bureau is being used.

Because of the extra formality required for computerized operations, the new systems should be presented to employees in the implementation phase in a training program designed to educate all employees in how the system works in general and in what is expected of them as individuals.

Where an in-house computer is being used, the programming should be well developed before the computer arrives, at which point testing, debugging, and trial runs are needed before the systems can be installed. Even when the systems begin to operate, it is important to continue the manual system in operation for a period of time. By having parallel operations, the computer-user can compare and test the new system's output with information in the old system and thus check out the new system's effectiveness and observe any significant problems that may have occurred in programming. Without such a control frame of reference, a basic programming error could break the continuity of information and require a major reconstruction of information much more costly than the effort required in the parallel systems.

Each restaurant will differ in its potential for using computers, but as computers become more and more flexible and economical in handling the restaurant's data processing needs, the feasibility of computerizing should be considered and periodically reconsidered. At a minimum, many, if not most, restaurants will find that service centers can offer significant help. In some cases, the service center may prove to be a satisfactory long-term arrangement, and in many others it may prove to be either a temporary arrangement for the restaurant's staff to adapt to the computer discipline or a transitional stage towards the adoption of an in-house computer.

CHAPTER **7**

Streamlining Restaurant Accounting

CHAPTER CAPSULE PREVIEW

As a reflection of restaurant operations and financial operations, accounting is frequently regarded as a necessary but static historical record of how sales and profits are going. But, by streamlining restaurant accounting systems, management can convert accounting reports into a dynamic operational tool and financing vehicle.

Accounting systems are designed to gather financial data in a form that facilitates the preparation of financial statements for external purposes on the one hand and operating reports for internal management use on the other.

Financial Statements must reflect economic reality in two forms:

1. Balance sheets which show assets and liabilities and the owner's net status at the reporting date.
2. Income statements which show the profit and loss results of operations over a period of time.

These financial statements must comply with *Generally Accepted Accounting Principles,* a body of requirements established by the American Institute of CPA's for accountants to use in their audits and in expressing their opinion in an accountants' report which accompanies the published financial statements.

These principles, which must always be applied to the situation at hand, are highly pragmatic and highly useful. They are aimed at providing as realistic a picture as possible both of how the reporting company's finances stand at the reporting date and of what its earnings were during the reporting period. The result is lender or investor confidence in the reports and thus a willingness to advance funds for the business.

Internal Accounting Reports must report economic reality in a great variety

119

of forms. They provide operating details for each department and comparisons of those details either with predetermined standards or with previous results. Accordingly, internal reports are much more diverse than financial statements, and in some areas, are sometimes prepared for shorter reporting periods than financial statements.

DIFFERENCES BETWEEN FINANCIAL STATEMENTS AND INTERNAL REPORTS

Accounting used for financial statements and accounting used for internal reports serve significantly different purposes. Accordingly, the former is known as *Stewardship Accounting* (or *Custodial Accounting),* and the latter is known as *Managerial Accounting.*

Stewardship Accounting is aimed primarily at the interest of investors and lenders. It provides information which will inform them about how well enterprise assets have been protected—and enhanced—during the reporting period.

Both investors and lenders are concerned about the security of assets. Investors, however, are substantially concerned about the rate of earnings which management has generated on their investment, and prospects for earnings in subsequent years. Lenders, on the other hand, place a heavy emphasis on security and are concerned about earnings only to the extent that they reflect any ability to repay any loans that may be granted.

The objectives of investors and lenders are similar, but their emphases differ. Investors may accept a somewhat higher degree of risk than lenders for the sake of higher earnings. Lenders may be satisfied with a lower rate of earnings than investors for the sake of greater security.

Accordingly, accounting principles have evolved over the years to provide a judicious balance between security and earnings information.

The principal reporting period for financial statements is one year (although interim statements are issued regularly), and the principal foundation for confidence in the annual statement is the accountants' attestation that the report "fairly presents" the company's financial position. For stewardship accounting, basic information such as that shown in Exhibit VII A (Figure 7-1), which is taken from the Uniform Systems of Accounts for Restaurants, forms the basic financial statement for restaurants.

Managerial Accounting is aimed primarily at the interests of management in operating the business. Reports provide information which enables management to monitor results on a short-term basis, make decisions, and make necessary operating adjustments.

Like investors and lenders, management is also concerned about both security and earnings, but protecting them requires an almost constant finger on the pulse of how the business is going. Thus, internal reports are issued at much more frequent intervals than financial statements in order to provide management with the feedback needed for planning and control.

Internal reports represent period-to-period link to budgets. By comparing results shown in reports to results projected for the period by the budget, management has a measure of how well expectations are being met. Variances from budget are a signal that something has changed and requires attention.

By analyzing these variances, management may find that they grow from a larger-than-expected sales volume or some other acceptable operational change. But the analysis may also bring to light an operational problem which needs remedial measures.

Effective internal reports are based on the principles of *responsibility accounting,* with information classified by operating departments for which results can be directly measured and thus controlled.

Internal reports concentrate on controllable expenses, rather than fixed costs such as rent or occupation costs, depreciation, and income tax, which are either fixed or depend upon the total year's operations. The costs of food and beverages and payroll (so-called "prime costs"), direct operating expenses, music and entertainment, and other controllable expenses need to be watched closely. Internal reports at suitable intervals enable management to keep close tabs on whether costs are remaining within an acceptable range and thus to take prompt remedial action if unreasonable variances occur.

By applying principles of responsibility accounting, internal reports may be directed to different levels, with each report going to the supervisor responsible for the subject area. The supervisor then takes any necessary action or, where appropriate, consults with top management on alternative courses of action.

Internal reports can be used to implement and monitor a program of *management by objectives.* Breaking down data in terms of income and expense levels needed to meet management objectives provides standards against which report results can be compared.

The use of responsibility accounting and management by objectives is an important trend which all restaurant operators can use in one form or another to sharpen controls over operations. Internal reports can be used as a powerful device for tightening departmental responsibility and for incorporating objectives directly into day-to-day operations.

Responsibility accounting and management by objectives can relieve top management of a considerable amount of day-to-day work by permitting *exceptional reporting.* So long as individual departments have clear standards to meet, reports of operations in many areas need to be directed to management only on an exception basis, i.e. only when results differ significantly from the established standard.

THE UNIFORM SYSTEM OF ACCOUNTS FOR RESTAURANTS

The National Restaurant Association has issued a "Uniform System of Accounts for Restaurants," prepared by Laventhol Krekstein Horwath & Horwath,

NAME OF RESTAURANT OR COMPANY
DESCRIPTION OF PERIOD COVERED BY STATEMENT

	Amounts	Percentages
SALES		
Food	$	%
Beverages		
Total food and beverage sales	$	100.00%
COST OF SALES		
Food		
Beverages		
Total cost of sales	$	%
GROSS PROFIT		
Food	$	%
Beverages		
Total gross profit	$	%
SERVICE CHARGES		
OTHER INCOME		
TOTAL INCOME	$	%
CONTROLLABLE EXPENSES		
Payroll	$	%
Service charge distribution		
Reserved for bonuses, vacation pay,etc.		
Employee benefits		
Employees' meals		
Direct operating expenses		
Music and entertainment		
Advertising and sales promotion		
Utilities		
Administrative and general expenses		
Repairs and maintenance		
Total controllable expenses	$	%
PROFIT BEFORE RENT OR OCCUPATION COSTS	$	%
RENT OR OCCUPATION COSTS		
PROFIT BEFORE DEPRECIATION	$	%
DEPRECIATION		
RESTAURANT PROFIT	$	%
ADDITIONS TO OR DEDUCTIONS FROM		
RESTAURANT PROFIT		
NET PROFIT BEFORE INCOME TAX	$	%
INCOME TAX		
NET PROFIT	$	%

Figure 7-1. Summary Profit and Loss Statement.

which is important for every restaurant because it meets the needs of both stewardship accounting and management accounting.

The "Uniform System" is adaptable to the needs of both large and small restaurants. In addition to presenting the "Uniform System" in full detail, the NRA's book includes examples of financial statements, a system of recordkeeping and forms for the small restaurant, systems and report forms for food and beverage cost control, statistics of restaurant operations and a summary of how the Fair Labor Standards Act applies to restaurants.

The "Uniform System" is an adaptation of general accounting methods to the specific needs of the restaurant business. It simplifies recordkeeping, provides an audit trail and, through its widespread use in the industry, permits comparisons between similar units and with industry averages. Because common definitions are used in gathering and presenting data in annual summaries of industry performance, the individual restaurant using the "Uniform System" has a basis for determining how its performance compares, area by area, with the industry in general.

A further advantage of the "Uniform System" is that it provides data promptly for internal control, in the form of daily reports on sales, food and beverage costs, and cash as well as an analysis of payroll. Examination of these reports and a comparison of the results from one area to another help to identify problem areas and permit prompt action before deteriorating situations get out of hand and hence move into the "uncontrollable" category.

The "Uniform System of Accounts" and its various related reporting forms have been designed with ample flexibility to permit the individual unit to adapt the system to its own needs and, at the same time, maintain the needed degree of comparability with other restaurants utilizing the basic system.

CHARACTERISTICS OF MODERN INTERNAL MANAGEMENT REPORTS

An effective internal reporting system organizes operations by revenue centers and relates costs and income for each. Food sales and beverage sales are principal revenue centers, and accordingly, detailed daily reports analyzing sales are essential control devices. Schedules VII-A-1 and VII-A-2 (Figures 7-2-A and 7-2-B), "Uniform System of Accounts" book show basic daily report forms, with the additional analyses recommended where total sales are distributed over several dining rooms and bars.

Summarizing daily sales by meals permits the observation of trends over a period of time, not merely in the basic sales data but in supportive analyses of such factors as:

1. Customers served and average check, per meal, and in total.
2. Average food sales per seat and daily customer turnover.
3. Average sales per waitress and customers served per waitress.

FOOD SALES

	Meals Served	Amounts	Percentages
BY MEALS		$	%
Breakfast			
Lunch			
Dinner			
Supper			
TOTAL DINING ROOMS			
Banquets and Parties			
TOTAL MEALS SERVED		$	%
BAKERY COUNTER			
TAKE-OUT SALES			
OUTSIDE CATERING			
TOTAL FOOD SALES		$	%

	Meals Served	Amounts	Percentages
BY DINING ROOMS		$	%
Main Dining Room			
Coffee Shop			
Counter or Lunch Room			
Grill			
Cafeteria			
Patio			
Drive-in			
Banquet Rooms			
TOTAL MEALS SERVED		$	%

Figure 7-2-A. Schedule of Food Sales.

BEVERAGE SALES

	Amounts	Percentages
BY TYPES OF DRINKS		
Mixed Drinks and Cocktails	$	%
Beer and Ale		
Wines		
Soft Drinks		
Bottle Sales		
TOTAL BEVERAGE SALES	$	100.00%
BY BARS		
Main Bar	$	%
Service Bar		
Dining Room		
Grill		
Banquet and Parties		
Bottle Sales		
TOTAL BEVERAGE SALES	$	100.00%

Figure 7-2-B. Schedule of Beverage Sales.

These factors are important measures of productivity, and thus indicators of how the restaurant is faring. While they will obviously vary from day to day, variances from long-term patterns can be a sign that something is wrong and call for an investigation by management.

For adequate control, costs must also be reported, and a simple summary of food costs is as follows:

BEGINNING INVENTORY		$1,600.00
Add:		
Food Purchases	$6,750.00	
Express Delivery Charges	55.00	6,805.00
		$8,405.00
Deduct:		
Ending Inventory		1,755.00
Cost of Food Consumed		$6,650.00

Beverage cost reports follow approximately the same format. Where general storerooms for both food and beverages are maintained, a separate report for storeroom inventories, receipts, requisitions, and closing inventories must also be maintained. As a result, the summary of food costs shown above must be modified to include the value of storeroom receipts and disbursements.

An important food cost which must also be considered is the cost of employees' meals, part of which may be recorded on meal checks and part of which is unrecorded. Thus, total sales must be reduced by the value of officers' checks, in the amount of the checks, and by the amount of other employees' meals, which are usually priced on a relatively arbitrary average cost basis.

Internal reports emphasize operating statistics and ratios, providing item-by-item details of cost factors which are only summarized in financial statements. The frequency of reports depends upon the relative importance of the individual cost factors. Thus, prime costs, where the largest expenditures are, need to be reviewed almost constantly. Less significant cost factors, and costs which are not incurred on a day-to-day basis, may be reported less frequently.

The cost-of-sales ratios are the most important to control, since significant increases or decreases in these ratios can be an indication that something is not in order. The ratio of payroll to sales is among the most critical, because it commonly runs approximately one-third or more of sales.

But ratios in other areas are also important. The basic year-round accounting records just present all individual expenses by each area of controllable expenses (see Controllable Expenses listed in Exhibit VII-A (Figure 7-1). By reviewing periodic reports of cost of sales ratios during the year, management can keep its pulse on how the business is running and exercise continuing operating control, rather than waiting for data at the end of an accounting period.

Effective operating control depends upon timeliness. The system should be designed to provide flash reports on any unusual condition. Since top management cannot be burdened with a constant review of reports and records, the availability of reports when needed to take remedial action is critically dependent upon effective planning and the establishment of budgets which provide standards for recordkeepers to use in determining whether performance during the year requires a report to top management.

To illustrate major ratios and how they may vary, Figure 7-2, which has been taken from the "Uniform System of Accounts" book, shows a two-year comparative profit and loss statement for a large restaurant with beverage facilities. For the large restaurant in Exhibit VII-B (Figure 7-3), sales and ratios are presented for two years in order to illustrate the critical importance of such ratios. Sales declined in the current year, but the ratios to sales of both payroll costs and employee benefits increased-from a total of 36.62 percent in the prior year to a total of 38.10 percent in the current year.

This increase reflects the growing pressure of wages and salaries, and is, of course, a drain on profits. But it should also be noted that ratios for other expenses declined during the current year over the prior year.

This may reflect the decline in costs associated with reduced sales—or it could reflect marginal retrenchments undertaken by management as interim internal reports reflected declining sales, since the total decline in net profit from 3.04 percent to 2.08 percent is less than the decline in sales.

Still another interpretation that could be put upon these figures is that sales were lower because of reduced expenditures on Advertising and Promotion. While this is unlikely, because the reduction was comparatively small, an interim report reflecting the kind of sales reduction and cost-to-sales ratios shown here might well be a cue to management to *increase* its advertising and promotion expenditures, as a measure of increasing sales to a level that would preserve the profit margin.

The important thing:—with explicit standards, provisions for comparing performance with those standards, and provisions for interim flash reports to top management when variances occur, a restaurant has a valuable operating tool. Changes from budget or from past performance are an early warning that action may be needed and careful analysis of the ratios and detailed exploration of individual cost areas can suggest the kinds of action which might be desirable.

Thus, the standard or budget established at the beginning of the year is an important game plan for the year. For increased sales of any given level, the associated increases in costs can be computed based upon historical experience in order to establish standards which can be used for internal reports to monitor how well the restaurant is actually performing during the year.

The use of well-designed budgets and such techniques as responsibility accounting and management by objectives can be particularly important in the face of industry trends. Rising minimum wages and recruitment difficulties have been putting considerable pressure on payroll costs. With other costs on the upgrade also,

| | Amounts | | Percentages | |
	Current Year	Prior Year	Current Year	Prior Year
SALES				
Food	$2,025,000	$2,065,000	75.00%	74.41%
Beverages	675,000	710,000	25.00	25.59
Total Sales	$2,700,000	$2,775,000	100.00%	100.00%
COST OF SALES				
Food	$ 765,500	$ 775,000	37.80%	37.53%
Beverages	202,500	215,000	30.00	30.28
Total Cost of Sales	$ 968,000	$ 990,000	35.85%	35.68%
GROSS PROFIT	$1,732,000	$1,785,000	64.15%	64.32%
OTHER INCOME	20,500	22,200	.76	.80
TOTAL INCOME	$1,752,500	$1,807,200	64.91%	65.12%
CONTROLLABLE EXPENSES				
Payroll	$ 920,700	$ 888,775	34.10%	32.03%
Employee Benefits	108,000	99,525	4.00	3.59
Employees' Meals	63,450	64,100	2.35	2.31
Direct Operating Expenses	165,000	171,500	6.11	6.18
Music and Entertainment	13,500	15,600	.50	.56
Advertising and Promotion	47,250	58,275	1.75	2.10
Utilities	48,750	47,175	1.81	1.70
Administrative and General	94,500	104,150	3.50	3.75
Repairs and Maintenance	46,150	58,850	1.71	2.12
Total Controllable Expenses	$1,507,300	$1,507,950	55.83%	54.34%
PROFIT BEFORE RENT AND OCCUPATION COSTS	$ 245,200	$ 299,250	9.08%	10.78%
RENT AND OCCUPATION EXPENSES	105,250	104,000	3.90	3.75
PROFIT BEFORE DEPRECIATION	$ 139,950	$ 195,250	5.18%	7.03%
DEPRECIATION	44,350	44,675	1.64	1.61
PROFIT BEFORE INCOME TAX	$ 95,600	$ 150,575	3.54%	5.42%
INCOME TAX PROVISION	39,400	66,175	1.46	2.38
NET PROFIT	$ 56,200	$ 84,400	2.08%	3.04%

Figure 7-3. Comparative Profit and Loss
Statement (Large Restaurant with Beverage Facilities)

restaurants are subject to a profit squeeze which obliges them to use every available resource and management tool to hold the line on controllable costs.

CASH CONTROL AND SALES CONTROL

For any business dependent upon cash transactions, stringent control of cash receipts and disbursements is essential. Accordingly, restaurants need a well-designed form and related control system for ensuring that cash received is adequately recorded and retained.

The system must control cash both before and after receipt since the adequacy of controls over receipts can be defeated if necessary disbursements are not also adequately controlled.

Guest checks and cash register tapes are the principal beginning elements of a control system. By using guest checks with a controlled numerical sequence, a daily audit of guest checks can provide a comparison with total cash receipts and an immediate indication if any sales were not paid. Sequenced guest checks can also be useful when duplicates are used as a food order for the chef—saving time in transmitting the order to the kitchen and providing an extra measure of control.

Cash register receipts are the critical second measure of control. They are reconciled on the one hand with guest checks in total, and on the other hand they can be the basis for separating cash and charge sales, thus identifying the amount of cash that should be on hand after any disbursements and the amount of accounts receivable which must be collected.

Cash disbursements from the cash register must also be carefully controlled in order for food checks and cash remaining at the end of the day to balance. Cash paid out of the drawer includes payments for tips, customer accounts charged, and payments for deliveries of food, beverages, services, supplies, and bank deposits.

Guest checks and cash register tapes are thus the raw material for a daily sales and cash report to provide a posting medium for accounting purposes. This daily posting creates a cumulative record which at the same time perpetuates the needed control and provides management with a useful planning tool. The former occurs through self-liquidating receipt and disbursement amounts. The latter occurs through the accumulative observation of sales.

The Cash and Sales Receipts Form should provide separate space for each principal category of receipts and disbursements and should be organized to provide for totaling at the end of each month. Major categories for many restaurants would be as follows:

CREDITS	DEBITS
Food Sales	Cash Paid Out of Drawer
Beverage Sales	Tips Paid
Cigar Counter Sales	Other Payments

Sales Taxes	Customers' Accounts Charged
Tips Charged by Customers	Bank Deposits
Customers' Accounts Collected	
Miscellaneous Receipts	
Cash Over (and Short)	

A Sales and Receipts Form using these categories would appear as shown in Exhibit VII-C (Figure 7-4). Clearly, the individual restaurant would alter this form with variations in its own practices and informational needs. Smaller restaurants and restaurants with a negligible charge account business might omit the Sales Tax and Customers' Accounts Collected column. In doing so, however, they would have to allow for these factors in computing cost-to-sales ratios and in allowing for noncash sales in making monthly analyses of sales, cash receipts, and disbursements.

With the use of such a Sales and Receipts Form, management has a valuable overview of how the business is doing and of how well controls are working. Comparing actual sales with sales expected for the month and for the year to date, management can analyze how close to target sales are coming and can take any necessary actions to insure the business's continued operating health.

Cash disbursements need similarly detailed control, and a separate Cash Disbursement Form should be maintained in order to insure that outlays are in order. Exhibit VII-D. (Figure 7-5), shows a recommended form for recording and summarizing daily and monthly disbursements.

A third record needed to complete the picture is a Record of Unpaid Bills to give management a picture of liabilities against the net cash and bank account assets, as shown in Exhibit VII-E (Figure 7-6).

Daily reports are an important part of restaurant operations, and in addition to the forms cited here, the restaurant may find it desirable to supplement the basic forms with such forms as weekly payroll sheets and quarterly payroll summaries, as a reconciliation and control of other records, as well as a reconciliation and accounting for cash deposited in banks.

For control of beverage sales, and disbursements, similar records are usually needed, following similar principles as those described above but with added measure to insure that slippage is not occuring in dispensing drinks. For this purpose, restaurants now have available automatic bartender devices to control the size of drinks (a fairly well-established practice by now), equipment to mix and tally drinks and automatic equipment to tally drinks electronically.

Since the dispensation of beverages is harder to control, restaurants should avail themselves of these various devices in order to assure that the disbursement of beverages is adequately matched with sales receipts.

Restaurant owners need to keep current with new developments in restaurant management, since punch card systems are already being tested and refined to allow cashiers to record the consumption of food and thus add an extra measure of control over disbursements and cash receipts.

	INITIALS	DATE
PREPARED BY		
APPROVED BY		

FOR MONTH OF ____________, 19__

	(1)	(2)	(3)	(4)	(5)	(6)	(7)	(8)	(9)	(10)	(11)	(12)	(13)	(14)	(15)	(16)	
		CREDITS										DEBITS					
							Customers'	Miscellaneous Receipts					Other Payments		Customers'		
LINE No.	Date	Food Sales	Beverage Sales	Cigar Counter	Sales Tax	Tips Charged	Accounts Collected	Amount	Explanation	Cash Over or Short	Daily Totals	Tips Paid	Amount	Explanation	Accounts Collected	Bank Deposit	LINE No.
1																	1
2																	2
3																	3
4																	4
5																	5
6																	6
7																	7
8																	8
9																	9
10																	10
11																	11
12																	12
13																	13
14																	14
15																	15
16																	16
17																	17
18																	18
19																	19
20																	20
21																	21
22																	22
23																	23
24																	24
25																	25
26																	26
27																	27
28																	28
29																	29
30																	30
31																	31
32																	32
33																	33
34																	34
35																	35
36																	36
37																	37
38																	38
39																	39
40																	40
	1	2	3	4	5	6	7	8	9	10	11	12	13	14	15	16	

Figure 7-4. Sales and Cash Receipts

Figure 7-5. Cash Disbursements.

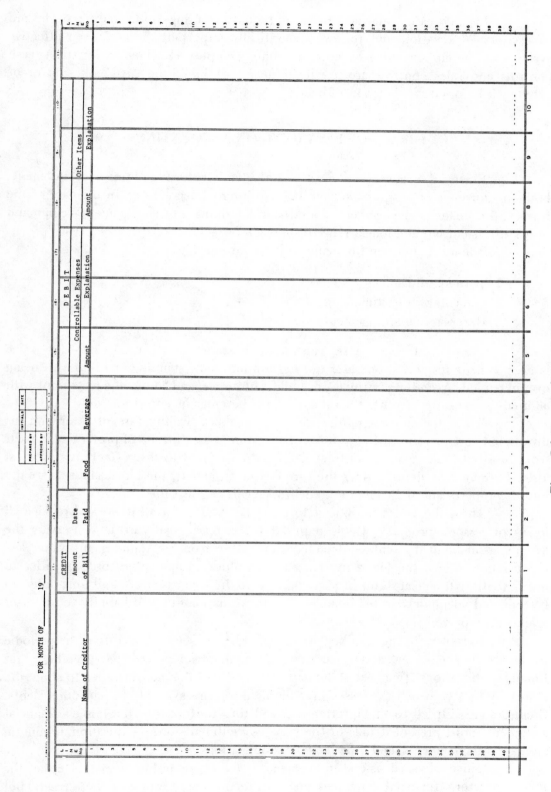

Figure 7-6. Record of Unpaid Bills.

In any case, internal check and control, using both daily reports and supervisory observation and review, are critically important, because even effective systems can be circumvented by collusion among employees. Thus, having strong cash controls and sales controls are a critical means of inhibiting such collusion or of catching it before it gets gets out of hand.

IMPACT OF FINANCING ON ACCOUNTING

Financial arrangements must be reflected in records and financial statements both for purposes of custodial accounting and internal accounting. In the case of the former, the financial arrangement is a critical determinant of management's command over both its current and longer range resources.

The most common financing arrangements are:

1. Turn-key financing.
2. Percentage lease financing.
3. Excess rental arrangements.

Turn-key Arrangements. The turn-key arrangement is used where the lessee is an excellent restaurant-operator but has a poor credit standing or is close to being over-extended. Accordingly, the lessor builds, furnishes, and equips the restaurant with all utensils and supplies other than the food and beverage inventories.

While the lessor's motivation is to make a healthy rate of return on his investment, he uses the turn-key form of investment as a means of protecting himself from having to take over a bad financial situation later with the restaurant's physical assets burdened by debts. Under the turn-key arrangement, the physical assets are the lessor's property and thus immune to debtors' claims against the lessee.

Thus, the lessee is obliged to make restitution for all items and replace all losses of lessor's property. He is required to exercise great care in conserving the lessor's assets and to replace depleted items at reasonable replacement value less depreciation. Thus, the lessee must keep meticulous equipment records in order to insure that the financial status of his obligation to the lessor is clear at all times and can be reflected adequately in his financial statements as a contingent liability to be offset against his reported assets.

In return for the turn-key arrangement, the lessee is obliged to make periodic payments to the lessor, and since these payments take precedence over his other financial obligations, financial statements must reflect this fact in order to show the relative extent to which the lessee's remaining assets are available to pay other debts. Creditors are entitled to this information, and thus footnotes to the lessee's financial statements must present details of the lease commitment—term, expiration, minimum annual rental payments, and other collateral obligations.

Since physical assets are owned by the lessor rather than the lessee, the lessee-operator's financial statement may not record depreciation of these assets, but rather reports his rent expense instead. In turn, replacement by the lessee of flatware, china, glassware, linens and utensils is treated as a current operating expense. Only leasehold improvements paid for by the lessee may be amortized over future periods' operations in his financial statements.

Percentage Leases are a second form of lease. In such leases, the lessee may or may not purchase and own the restaurant's physical assets. The lessee pays a minimum rent (theoretically to compensate the lessor for amortization, depreciation, and return on investment), plus a percentage of food and beverage sales, and sometimes of other income.

The rate of the override percentage above the minimum rent depends to some extend upon which party to the lease provides the furniture and equipment. Rates prevailing at this writing are from 8 percent to 10 percent on food and 10 percent to 12 percent on beverages where the lessee provides no furniture or equipment. Where he provides furniture and equipment and the lessor provides only the building, the rates range from 5 percent to 7 percent on food and from 8 percent to 10 percent on beverages. Although a single rate for both food and beverages is sometimes used, this is exceptional.

The emphasis in accounting records under a percentage lease arrangement differs significantly from turn-key arrangements. Accurate and complete sales records are essential and must be held available for audit by the lessor's representatives at all times.

While the lessor's interest in the lessee's ability to pay is a matter of concern under any financing arrangement, his incentive for the lessee to do well is substantially greater under the percentage lease arrangement, and thus such arrangements are usually preceded by relatively detailed investigations of the lessee's prospective ability to pay through successful operations.

The advance investigations usually include a feasibility study to determine markets, volume that can be expected to be realized from those markets, estimated expenses required to achieve the expected degree of realization and the operator's remuneration for his time and investment. Furthermore, the results of these advance investigations are carefully recast in the form of cash flow projections as a further evaluation of the lessee's ability to make payments of both the minimum rent and the percentages of sales to which the lessor is entitled. Needless to say, the lessee's prior track record is also of substantial importance in such an investigation.

Excess Rental Arrangements are a third common financing device for restaurants. Under this arrangement, lessees are also obliged to pay a percentage of all sales, but not irrespective of the level of operations. Rather, the lessee is obligated to pay an override only when sales have exceeded an agreed-upon level.

As in percentage leases, the lessor is obligated to pay a fixed minimum amount, but he is free of extra payments until the total sales have reached the stipulated level. For example, he may be required to pay $50,000 a year, plus 5 percent of sales in excess of $1,000,000.

Rental terms are settled by the relative bargaining strength of the two negotiating parties, and the override percentage is frequently progressively reduced with increases in sales volume.

Excess rental arrangements are highly flexible in that rates may apply only to food and beverage sales or to all sales, including cigar stand, vending machines, telephones, etc. Payments may be made monthly or quarterly, depending upon the pattern of income and the assurance that income will, indeed, exceed the stipulated level.

In accounting for excess rental arrangements, the liability must be accrued and shown on the lessee's financial statements in order to avoid over-statement of the lessee's income. Similarly, interim financial statements must adequately provide accruals which reflect seasonal factors. This is particularly important for resorts and highly seasonal restaurants in order to avoid material overstatements or understatements of what the net financial position will be after fulfilling the financial obligation to the lessor under the excess rental agreement.

The three financing alternatives described above are not only crucial to financial statements which meet the requirements of stewardship accounting, but they are also critically important considerations in the period preceding the launching of a new restaurant. Businessmen contemplating the establishment of a restaurant must carefully evaluate each of the three alternatives means of lease financing in order to determine which will best suit their particular circumstances, the market they will seek to exploit and the long-term profit objectives they can realistically set for themselves under each.

Brief mention should also be made at this point of the use of security deposits as an additional financing cost in connection with lease arrangements. Frequently, when the landlord has not included a restriction against chattel mortgages and other borrowings collateralized by the equipment covered under a lease, he will require a deposit from the lessee as an additional measure of security for the lessee's obligations under the lease agreement. Under such circumstances, the interest lost by the lessee on the security deposit is, in effect, a true financing cost because he has relinquished the use of those funds for the period of the lease.

Accounting begins to play a critical role even before the prospective operator has turned the first spade of sod—or even narrowed down his choice among alternative sites for the location of his restaurant. His net profit—both short-term and long-term—depends substantially upon the financing arrangement he negotiates.

Accordingly, the financial consequences of the various courses of action open to him should be spelled out in pro-forma or projected accounting statements which reflect the sales, cost, income or loss, and other operational factors of operations in each of several years ahead.

Ideally, pro-forma or projected financial statements should reflect expectations at pessimistic, realistic, and optimistic levels in order to provide the operator with as clear a picture as possible of the strength of his bargaining position before he begins his negotiations with a prospective lessor.

Clearly, the alternative financing arrangements call for significant differences in accounting records and the financial statements that grow from them. These financial statements inevitably serve a dual purpose:

1. They inform financing sources of how well obligations are being met.
2. They provide a basis for external financing to enable the lessee to obtain further funds on his own right as a means of enhancing his own profitability when expansion possibilities could permit growth and even greater profitability.

Thus, such financial statements are a part of stewardship accounting. But the accounting used for financial statements, and thus primarily for external purposes, is only part of the story.

Managerial accounting is the cornerstone of day-to-day, week-to-week and month-to-month operations. Unless the related multitude of interim operational decisions is resolved in favor of maximizing profitability, the year-end financial statements will not reflect the conditions most favorable for external purposes.

Therefore, internal accounting reports are the key tool available to management in making the decisions that will continually tip the scales in favor of preserving and enhancing profitability.

CHAPTER 8

Establishing and Implementing the Profit Planning Program

CHAPTER CAPSULE PREVIEW

Profit planning involves more than mere prediction. In its entirety, it involves a reconsideration of assumptions, alternatives, modes of operation, markets, potentials, allocation of recources, and much more. *Every* aspect of operations should come under someone's review in detail before the planning exercise is over!

Futhermore, preliminary budgets, derived from initial determinations, serve often to alert management personnel to a need to change their thinking. Budgets can point out developing problems before they get out of hand. And when such problems are uncovered, the restaurateur has time to solve them methodically, without resort to crisis management and repeated fire-fighting.

In this chapter, we will review methods for improving earnings by increasing revenues and by reducing expenses, both fixed and variable. And we will hopefully demonstrate the need to recognize and resolve developing cash problems as well. Of all the prerogatives of management, planning is perhaps the one most directly associated with peace of mind.

WHAT IS PROFIT PLANNING FOR RESTAURANTS?

Every year, new restaurants open their doors to compete with each other and with older, established restaurants. And every year, a substantial number of restaurants close their doors permanently! The difference between success and failure is often attributable to the adequacy of planning. Or more precisely, profit planning.

Profit planning is the process by which all aspects of the operation are coordinated to achieve established objectives. The need for coordination is obvious.

There is no point in hiring or training waiters to serve five hundred people if the dining room can seat only one hundred. Nor should advertising stress roast beef if the kitchen's roasting capacity is severely limited. There has to be a uniform plan that balances and coordinates activities while remaining within the capacity of each activity.

Moreover, the profit plan must have direction; it must head toward objectives that have been agreed upon. Objectives may be expressed in many different ways. One restaurant may have a goal of reaching a specified volume in five years. Another may seek to be the most prestigious meeting place for businessmen in its area. A third may go after a preeminent place in attracting families for dinner.

Other restaurants may set their objectives in terms of community service. Some may want to be known primarily for their helpfulness to clubs, societies, and local organizations. Others may want to establish a reputation for cooperating fully with all efforts to cope with their communities' ecological problems. And still others may want to be regarded as good employers.

Financial considerations are generally present among the objectives of a business. The owners may want a specified return on their investment. They may plan to reinvest earnings so as to reach a certain size in a given period. They may want to acquire other restaurants. They may want to "go public."

There are many kinds of objectives to choose from, and a restaurant may pursue several at the same time, so long as they are not in conflict with each other. The main thing is to establish goals and then lay plans to achieve them. At this point, it will be well to distinguish between long-range plans and short-range plans, and how they intermesh.

Long-range plans run for five years or more. Characteristically, they include plans for committing resources over long periods; for example, the purchase of major items of equipment that last a number of years. Such capital budgets generally adopt as their objective a satisfactory return on investment at an acceptable risk.

Intermediate plans bridge the gap between long-range and short-range plans. For our purposes, they may be regarded as sufficiently similar to long-range plans so as to require no additional discussion in and of themselves.

Short-range plans, running up to one year, guide current operations along the way to the achievement of long-range plans and objectives. Conformity with long-range objectives is itself an objective of short-term planning. Survival may be another objective over the short run. In addition to these and other objectives, short-range planning comprises sales forecasts and predictions of expenses set forth in operating budgets and cash budgets.

HOW TO IMPLEMENT PROFIT PLANNING AND BUDGETING

A profit plan, then, is a conceptual set of objectives and proposals, dynamic because it covers a period during which external and internal conditions may change. The profit planning process calls for questioning of assumptions, aims, methods, and expectations. It calls for delving into operations, looking for improvements, and making decisions on many matters in a very definitive fashion.

A budget is only a part of the profit planning process. It is practical rather than conceptual, a device for spelling out for the financial details of the profit plan, while providing, at the same time, a handle for managerial control. Actually, there are several kinds of budgets, and it will be useful to begin by reviewing some of the distinctions.

Capital budgets provide for long-term investments in land, buildings, equipment, and furnishings. They project both expenditures and returns on specific investments. In capital budgeting, proposals for alternative investments are evaluated in terms of return on investment or discounted cash flow as an aid in making decisions. While a full discussion of discounted cash flow is beyond the scope of this chapter, the concept may be described briefly. If an investment generates a cash return over a period of years, the aggregate future return has a present value, just as an annuity has a present value. This present value of aggregate future returns may be compared with the outlay that is required for each alternative investment proposal. Other comparisons, including the probabilities of the expected returns and the risk of loss, are also accumulated for consideration in the decision making process.

A cash budget predicts receipts, disbursements, and cash balances, usually for short periods, so that management may have time to get ready to meet obligations when they come due. Techniques of cash budgeting, or cash flow forecasting, will be discussed later in this chapter.

Operating budgets are designed to coordinate and control operations over the short term. A specialized field of knowledge has been built up concerning the mechanics of budgeting in various kinds of situations and applications. Our discussion will cover those aspects of budgeting that are particularly appropriate to the restaurant business.

Flexible budgets are operating budgets that provide control information at several volume levels. Thus, a flexible budget might show revenues, expenses, and profit margins at the expected level of sales, at 10 percent and 20 percent above that level, and at 10 percent and 20 percent below it. This means that budgeted expenses are shown at five different levels of operation to facilitate control by management.

Before a flexible budget can be completed, a special kind of analysis must be undertaken of all expenses: they must be analyzed into fixed components that remain constant at all volume levels, and variable components that increase proportionately as the volume increases. Thus, property taxes or rent are fixed expenses, while food costs are variable. Many expenses, even those often spoken of loosely as variable, are in reality semi-fixed, with a fixed component and a variable component within a given operating range. For example, labor costs show a tendency toward two components, even though they are widely thought of as variable.

Another planning tool, akin to budgeting, that depends upon analysis of expenses into fixed and variable components, is break-even analysis. The usual form of presentation, the break-even chart, graphically displays the relationships between revenues and expenses over a broad range. Fixed expenses, being constant, are represented by a horizontal line. Above the level of fixed expense, variable expenses slope upward. Revenues form a sloping line that intersects the total expense line at the break-even point. Below this point, expenses exceed revenues, and there is a loss; above the break-even point, revenues exceed expenses, and the restaurant earns a profit.

Out of the concern of management for some means to learn the exact sales volume that must be attained so that total costs just equal the inflow of sales revenue came the break-even analysis. The first step, of course, in preparing such an analysis is a comprehension of the distinction between *fixed* and *variable* costs. While economists will give cognizance to the law of diminishing returns and the concept of marginal utility, thereby realizing that the variable costs will not vary in direct proportion to changes in the level of productive activity, the break-even analysis ignores (for simplification purposes) this crucial fact and assumes that variable costs do vary in direct proportion with changes in volume, i.e., that variable costs are exactly three times as great at full activity as at one-third activity. With this fixed variable distinction in mind, we can then move to the latest year's income statement. Let us consider the following income statement of the Triple H Restaurant, Inc.:

Triple H Restaurant, Inc.
Income Statement
Year Ended December 31, 1971

Net Sales		$1,000,000
Less Cost of Goods Sold		400,000
Gross Margin		$ 600,000
Operating Expenses:		
Direct Expenses	$200,000	
Planning and Control Expenses	50,000	
Administrative Expenses	150,000	400,000
Net Income from Operations		$ 200,000

Our first task is to split the $800,000 of total costs into the fixed portion and the variable portion. The accounting methodology for making this dichotomy has always struck us as somewhat arbitrary, considering the facts that there exist within any restaurant operation a large category of so-called semi-fixed costs, as mentioned earlier, which may remain constant up to some level of activity and then commence to vary, usually in no direct or even predictable manner. But, for safety sake, let us avoid these knotty problems and assume that $200,000 of the $800,000 costs are fixed. The variable costs, then must be $600,000, or 60 percent of the sales volume at this level of activity *and at every other level of activity*. Since for break-even analysis purposes we identify those costs which are directly variable with sales volume, the variable cost percentage of net sales must be the same at all levels of activity. Consequently, 60 cents out of every dollar of restaurant sales must be used to cover variable costs; and that level at which the combined total of 60 percent of the sales volume plus the fixed costs, $200,000, are equal to the sales volume will represent the point where sales volume and total costs are equal, i.e., the "break-even" point. This analysis can be presented in the following manner, with X representing the unknown sales volume:

$$X = \$200,000 + .60X$$
$$X - .60X = \$200,000$$
$$.40X = \$200,000$$
$$X = \$500,000$$

Thus, the break-even point is the level of activity which produces a sales volume of $500,000. This result can be proved as follows:

Sales		$500,000
Costs:		
Fixed	$200,000	
Variable (60% of $500,000)	300,000	500,000
Net Income from Operations		-0-

Illustration:

As previously indicated, the entire break-even analysis is also subject to graphic presentation in the form of a break-even chart. The chart (Figure 8-1) depicts the Triple H Restaurant break-even analysis.

To sum up, profit planning includes budgeting of different types involving different time frames: capital budgeting for the long term, cash budgeting and operational budgeting for the short term. Analysis of expenses into fixed and variable components is essential to good planning, because it provides essential ingredients of both flexible budgeting and break-even analysis.

THE STAGES OF PLANNING AND BUDGETING

The annual preparation of a profit plan and budget for a year ahead follows a definite pattern or sequence of events. Let us assume that the restaurant's objectives have been established; the restaurant is in operation, so that all its equipment and furnishings carry over into the coming year; and its market strategy is agreed upon, at least temporarily. The preparation of the budget will require schedules and worksheets, which should be set up in advance.

The budget exercise will lead up to summary schedules similar in format to a set of financial statements. There will be a projected annual profit and loss statement and a projected balance sheet as at year end. There will also be monthly projections in support of the annual ones, but these monthly statements will be prepared after the annual budget will entail many schedules projecting the requirements of various

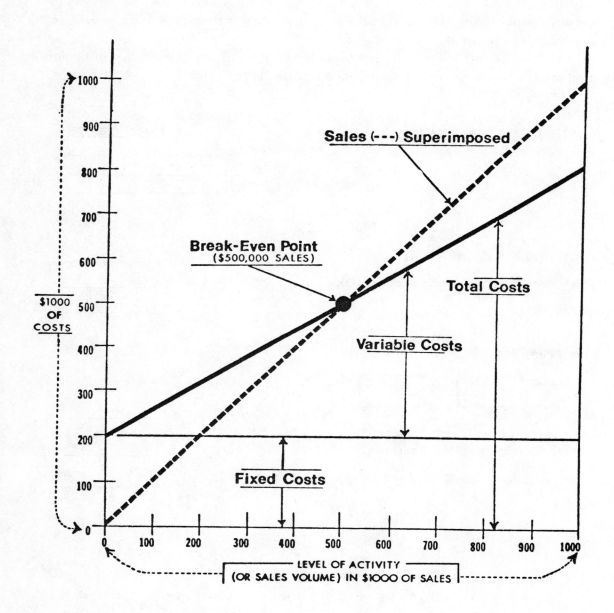

Figure 8-1.

activities for staff, materials, and services. These schedules will all have to conform to the anticipated volume levels, so that the summary schedules present uniform data for a coordinated operation.

The forms which follow provide a handy set of budgeting and profit-planning worksheets usable for any restaurant operation, large or small.

BUDGETING AND PROFIT PLANNING   BUDGET WORKSHEET

Restaurant_____

Period_____

Prep. by_____

INCOME SUMMARY

Sales (From Detail Worksheet A) $ _____

Other Income (From Detail Worksheet B)   _____

  Total   _____

Variable Expenses

Sales [   ] x [   ]

      Amount   Ratio (From Detail Worksheet C) _____

Total Fixed Costs (From Detail Worksheet D) _____

Net Income or (loss) before income tax _____

This worksheet is supported by four detail budget worksheets, labeled A through D as follows, providing vehicles for calculating total sales (food and beverage), other income, variable expense ratio, and total fixed costs, respectively.

Figure 8-2.

When budgets and financial statements are made to adhere to similar formats, comparison between budget and actual are facilitated. There is no need to juggle figures, break the details out of grouped totals, or recalculate projections, when

BUDGETING AND PROFIT PLANNING   DETAIL BUDGET WORKSHEET-A

Restaurant _____

Period _____

Prep. by _____

INCOME STATEMENT

FOOD SALES

Formula:

Number of persons served _____

X Average check   _____   = $ _____

Calculations:

	This Year	Adj.	Next Year
Persons served			
Average check			

Explain adjustments

_____

_____

BEVERAGE SALES

Formula:

Number of persons served _____

X Average check   _____   = $ _____

Calculations:

	This Year	Adj.	Next Year
Persons served			
Average check			

Explain adjustments

_____

_____

TOTAL SALES $ _____

Figure 8-3.

BUDGETING AND PROFIT PLANNING

Restaurant_____

Period_____

Prepared by_____

$

OTHER INCOME

Calculations:

Source	This Year	Adj.	Next Year

Explain Adjustments

_____

_____

_____

_____

VARIABLE EXPENSES   DETAIL BUDGET WORKSHEET-C

1. Cost of Sales - ratio   Food   Beverage

   Last Period Cost Ratio
   x Ratio of New Cost to Old Cost   _____   _____

   + Ratio of New Price to
              Old Price   _____   _____

   New Cost Ratios   _____   _____

New Food Cost Ratio _____ x Ratio of Food Sales to Total Sales _____ =   %

+New Beverage Cost Ratio _____ x Ratio of Beverage Sales to Total Sales _____=_____

              Total Cost of Sales Ratio=   %

Figure 8-4.

VARIABLE EXPENSES (cont'd)

  2. Payroll-Ratio

	Payroll	Related Expenses
Last Period Cost Ratio x Ratio of New Cost to Old Cost	_____	_____
+ Ratio of New Price to Old Price	_____	_____
New Cost Ratios	_____	_____

Payroll Ratio _____ % + Related Expense Ratio _____ % = [_____ %]

3. Other Variable Expenses _____ _____ _____ _____ _____

    Last Period Cost Ratio
x Ratio of New Cost to
    Old Cost _____ _____ _____ _____ _____

+ Ratio of New Price to
    Old Price _____ _____ _____ _____ _____

New Cost Ratios _____ % + _____ % + _____ % + _____ % + _____ %

    = Total Other Variable Expense Ratio [_____ %]

TOTAL VARIABLE EXPENSE RATIO

[_____ %]

FIXED EXPENSES   DETAIL BUDGET WORKSHEET-D

1. Payroll (Fixed portion) _____
   and related expenses   _____ = [$ _____]

Calculations:

	This Year	Adj.	Next Year
Payroll			
Related Expenses			

    Explain adjustments _____

_____

Figure 8-5.

FIXED EXPENSES   (cont'd)

2. Operating expenses
Calculations: $ [   ]

	This Year	Adj.(A)	Next Year
Direct			
Advertising			
Utilities			
Administrative			
Repairs			

(A) Explain adjustments _____

_____

2. Occupancy costs
Calculations: $ [   ]

	This Year	Adj.(A)	Next Year
Rent			
Property tax			
Insurance			
Interest			
Depreciation			

(A) Explain adjustments _____

_____

TOTAL FIXED COSTS

$ [   ]

Figure 8-6.

the reporting basis is the same throughout. This advantage is so great that a restaurant contemplating changes in its financial reporting format must first incorporate the same changes in its budget, in order to retain the similarity in presentation essential to an evaluation of actual results as measured against the budget.

The advance preparation of budget worksheets includes more than just format. Formulas are used for many calculations, and these should be inserted beforehand. For example, vacation pay, holiday pay, payroll taxes, and fringe benefits are generally estimated by applying percentages to wages and salaries, respectively. Hourly pay rates for various jobs and other parameters should be inserted early, too.

The degree of sophistication that is brought to the budget varies from one business to another. Some companies refine their estimating formulas on the basis of precise studies that may include statistical correlations and keep knowledge of the relationships between activities, while others settle for crude measures of superficial understanding. Where only small amounts are involved, there is little risk in using crude estimates; but where the sums are larger, the benefits are likely to support analysis and refinement to produce a more accurate budget.

On the basis of the restaurant's proposed operations for the budget year, volumes are forecast. Here, again, there is considerable variation in the degree of sophistication that individual restaurant businesses employ, ranging from guesswork to estimating by computer programs.

The forecasted volumes are inserted in the worksheets and a tentative budget is completed, using all the formulas and parameters that have been inserted in advance. In a computerized system, the pertinent information is fed to a computer, and the schedules are derived as output.

The tentative budget is then subjected to management review. Having arrived at a decision point, management must then decide whether the indicated results are to be accepted as satisfactory. It is not too late to consider alternatives and to contemplate the effects of changes in concept. In fact, if the indicated results of the preliminary budget fall below what is deemed to be an adequate expectation, then the restaurateur has no choice but to consider how he might go about improving the outlook for his restaurant operation.

Each change in concept results in a different pattern of operation, so that for each change there must be, not only a revised forecast of volume, but a reconstructed budget that takes into account all the changes in expenditures that a new operating mode implies. Every change in concept, of necessity, involves preparation of a new budget. Since this process can become quite burdensome, managements try to spare themselves grief by planning accurately in advance and by using computers to produce budgets quickly and accurately. This may frequently involve the use of an outside computer service bureau.

Finally, management's efforts are rewarded by the completion of a satisfactory budget, one that its personnel can operate with in the expectation that they will and can achieve suitable goals. The adoption of the final budget is not the end of it, however! It marks the beginning of the operating phase.

During the year for which the budget is in operation, it is the primary instrument of control. Operating reports are regularly compared in detail with budgeted figures, and variances are analyzed to seek out causes and correct problems promptly. Even before formal variance reports are available, operating people should be guided by the budget in directing and controlling their activities. The insights gained in the budget process should not be allowed to go unused the rest of the year. The importance of this warning cannot be overemphasized.

Variances are not always an indication that something is wrong. They may disclose a previously unrecognized change in conditions, sometimes caused by a slow drift in external factors. It is conceivable, for instance, that a diet fad could cause a shift away from certain foods and desserts that might alter a restaurant's profit picture significantly. Accordingly, variance analysis provides feedback concerning assumptions and standards built into the budget, as well as notification that operating results are straying from preconceived plans. Such feedback is valuable when the next planning cycle commences, and management considers the current status of operations in order to plan ahead once more.

We have now come full cycle through planning and budgeting. Advance preparation includes the establishment of objectives, a review of operations, determination of marketing strategy, and definition of relationships, formulas, and parameters. Then forecasts are made, and a tentative budget is prepared. This tentative budget is scrutinized and revised, if necessary, until a workable plan and budget are devised that offer acceptable results. Once adopted, the final budget becomes an effective instrument of control, in part through variance analysis, which in turn provides feedback and improved information for the succeeding budget cycle.

Options for Decision-Making

Let us pause for a moment at the stage in the planning cycle where a tentative budget has been prepared for management's scrutiny. And let us ask: What if the projected results are unacceptable? We have said that other plans, new alternatives, must be considered. Now we will discuss some of the options available to a restaurant management that is faced with the necessity of having to plan its operations differently for improved results. Basically, the restaurateur in these circumstances may look for ways to cut expenses or increase revenues. In doing so, he is likely to scrutinize his variable expenses first, for these are the most obvious targets for control.

CONTROLLING VARIABLE EXPENSES

Variable expenses are those that increase with expanding volume. One way to hold them down is by instituting tighter control. When volume falls, it may be possible to lay off superfluous people more promply. Wasteful practices can be ferreted out and discontinued. Variances themselves can be watched more closely, with less willingness to tolerate minor deviations.

Reporting can be speeded up. The more promptly reports are issued, and the more promptly action is taken to correct situations before they develop, the more effective will a cost reduction program be.

Daily planning of activities can be improved. Perhaps, work loads can be leveled so that fewer people are required to handle peak loads. Or, tighter scheduling and shifting of duties may provide an answer. All these methods have been used successfully to "turn around" unfavorable restaurant operations that we have observed.

A full scale cost reduction study would include job analysis, methods-time-motion studies, and perhaps work sampling, to bring down the cost of labor. Food handling would also be studied to eliminate waste of all kinds. And the results of all these efforts at lowering variable expense would then be incorporated in the budget. Frequently, outside expert assistance is required to conduct such studies for a variety of reasons.

Although cost reduction methods applied to variable expenses have certainly produced savings in many restaurant businesses, it must be conceded that such studies alone are no longer enough. There has been a steady trend in all industry away from variable expense to fixed expense. When a machine is purchased to replace labor, perhaps a dishwashing machine that does the work of several men, a fixed expense is replacing a larger variable expense. Future opportunities to reduce variable expense will be limited because a great reduction has already been achieved in one stroke. From then on, opportunities for cost reduction are more likely to be found in improved machines and better machine productivity.

Mechanization has not been the *only* trend that increases fixed expenses. There has been a tendency for occupancy charges to move upward over the years as the costs of rent, services, furnishings, and equipment have increased. On the other hand, demand for services on the part of customers has tended downward, so that less labor is required.

Moreover, the fixed component of labor cost has itself become more significant, due in part to specialization. All in all, fixed expense has grown in significance to such an extent that ways to hold it down must be considered in any effort to make a restaurant profitable. In the "old days," cost reduction was much simpler since focus had to be directed only toward variable expense, as a practical matter.

WATCHDOGGING FIXED EXPENSES

Since many fixed costs are the result of long-term investment, the time to begin holding fixed costs down is when such investments are being planned and not when the cash is being disbursed. Expensive furnishings may have a stronger appeal to some people than less costly items, but unless that appeal is translated eventually into sales dollars, the additional expenditure will constitute a drain on the profits of many accounting periods.

Other long-term commitments also ultimately create fixed expenses, Leases and rental agreements should be viewed realistically, and not with the kind of unbounded optimism that leads to financial straits. Here, again, high cost premises may have greater appeal or more traffic, but is the traffic of the right kind for the contemplated operation, and is the edge in attractiveness convertible into additional revenues? This basic question must always be confronted honestly and *at the planning stage.*

A restaurant that is operating has sunk costs to recover. If its outlook is unsatisfactory, its budget projects insufficient profits (perhaps a loss), and its management is forced to seek ways to cut costs, it must distinguish between those fixed costs that are escapable and those that are not. For there may still be ways to avoid or reduce some of the fixed expenses.

For instance, a maintenance contract may be too costly; perhaps it ought not to be renewed. Or perhaps a different type of display is available at lower cost. A program of preventive maintenance may be able to save money for the restaurant by avoiding breakdowns of equipment with their attendant losses. In other words, even a "non-controllable" fixed cost may be able to be eliminated *in toto.*

We have mentioned that part of labor cost is ordinarily fixed. Various activities require one or more people as a minimum number regardless of the volume level. This expense is indeed "fixed" for a given day, or so long as operations continue exactly as they are. But over the long term, planning may be able to accomplish changes in operation that effectively reduce the minimum staff requirement. This may require training people and adjusting the specific content of jobs, and it may not result in any reduction of labor needs at high volumes; but at low volumes, such flexibility may succeed in holding down the restaurant's fixed cost.

Long-range plans to reduce expenses, whether they are considered to be fixed or variable, must be worked out carefully if the anticipated gains in the bottom line are to be realized. For instance, a restaurant may decide to seek relief from labor shortages and other problems by turning to convenience foods. This is a reasonable alternative; but the desired results can be accomplished only by an actual reduction in staff. Now the question arises: Can this be done? Can staff be reduced under the terms of a union contract? If so, would such reductions be practicable under the new operation? These questions must be answered before a final decision can be made. At least, the kind of intelligent restaurant management judgment we would recommend based on our knowledge and experience in this field.

REVENUES

Cost reduction is not the only way to improve earnings. In many situations, it is not even the best way. Efforts to improve earnings by bringing in more revenue may be far more successful, provided that these efforts are real, and that the planning behind them is specific and concrete. Vagueness in these matters is hardly better than idle dreaming, for imaginary revenue increments hardly materialize on the actual financial statements and rarely bring a ring to the cash register.

One way to increase revenues is to increase the number of customers. If the market segments that the restaurant is catering to have been changing in size or in their wants and needs, investigation may disclose ways of capitalizing on these shifts, or of moderating the loss of clientele. The restaurant may be catering to an evening market that demands white table cloths, and this market may have been moving away from the neighborhood. On the other hand, the prospects may have been improving substantially for a luncheon market that deserves to be explored. Relative customer composition must, in any case, be constantly and carefully analyzed.

These are but two examples of situations where expansion into new markets, perhaps into new areas, could be beneficial. In some cases, a redirected advertising and promotion program may be sufficient to bring back lost sales; while in other cases nothing less than a revamped marketing strategy will suffice. The new market strategy may broaden the appeal of the restaurant or change its emphasis. For example, it may be found to be advantageous to switch to cafeteria style service or a limited menu or lower priced items or a combination of these things to improve volume levels and the size of margins (although perhaps not the percentage of gross margin).

A market study may disclose that the restaurant is suffering because of inroads made by the competition. There are no easy answers to such a situation, but this much is certain: competitive strategy is not solely a matter of analyzing what the competitors are doing and then planning counter strategies. It is necessary to keep one eye on the market, actual and potential, and to understand its wants and needs. If there are too many restaurants competing for a limited market segment, it may even be wise to retire from that field and enter another with more favorable prospects for successful operation. Too often, restaurateurs are found to be over-reluctant even to consider the latter alternative.

New markets may be developing locally. If people are being brought into the area by new industries or new construction, and the restaurant intends to go after the new sources of potential revenue, it must not neglect to make all the preparations that are necessary to attract and serve an influx of customers. There may be a need for additional seating, equipment and trained personnel, as well as increased advertising and other promotional expenditures.

Increasing the number of prospective customers who come to a restaurant may not be a sufficient answer, especially if people are being turned away. If queuing exists, or if it can be expected, then revenues can be helped by exploring methods for increasing the turnover per seat. Methods must be adaptable to the restaurant's basic mode of operation.

To illustrate, in some restaurants it would be permissible to reduce waiting between courses as a means to improving turnover; but where relaxed or elegant dining is the very attraction that draws customers, faster service may be a marketing blunder. At the other extreme, counter service is expected to be fast, and a further speed-up depends on the capabilities of the staff rather than the tolerance of the customers. In some situations, increased turnover can be achieved by extending the hours of operation. Costs will ordinarily rise along with revenues when the restaurant keeps its doors open longer, and such a decision should be made on the basis of incremental margins rather than incremental sales.

Perhaps the most obvious method for increasing revenues is to increase prices. It need hardly be pointed out that competition and consumer resistance set limits on the usefulness of this approach. When costs have increased for a particular restaurant, they have generally increased for other restaurants of the same kind. If beef prices go up, all steak houses are affected. But seafood prices may not move the same way: they may hold, or even go down. The implications for a steak house are plain. In passing their increased costs on to their customers, they are weakening their competitive position as against seafood restaurants.

Likewise, food costs in the home become a competitive factor. If, for one reason or another, they fail to keep pace with wholesale food costs in an area for a period, the restaurateur has to be careful in adjusting his prices, especially if he draws heavily on the family market. Poor timing may cost him part of his following, and on a *permanent* basis.

That increased prices may result in lower earnings may be seen from the following tabulation. Food cost is assumed to be 40 percent of sales, initially, and approximately 28 percent of sales after the price increase. The first column shows the contribution margin before a price change; the other columns include price increases of 5 percent. In the second column, there is no loss of volume; in the third column, there is a 5 percent decline; and in the fourth column, a 10 percent decline in sales volume.

	Before Price Change	5% Increase in Prices		
		No Volume Decline	5% Volume Decline	10% Volume Decline
Sales	$100.00	$105.00	$ 99.75	$ 94.50
Food Cost	40.00	40.00	38.00	36.00
Contribution Margin	$ 60.00	$ 65.00	$ 61.75	$ 58.50

A 5 percent increase in prices accompanied by a 5 percent decline in volume produces a higher dollar amount of margin than we started with; but a 10 percent decline in volume will reduce the dollar amount of margins.

Such considerations as these sometimes lead restaurateurs to think in terms of reducing prices to increase volumes and margins. Aside from retaliation by competitors, there is another factor that must not be over-looked: the interaction between price and volume. Economists refer to this phenomenon as "elasticity" of demand. If the demand in a particular situation is relatively inelastic, that is to say, if volume responds but little to price reductions, these cuts can serve no useful purpose to management.

Coming back to price increases as a means of increasing revenues, let us, this time, consider selective increases. We have often found it advisable to increase prices on selected menu items only, with a view to obtaining a constant dollar margin per cover instead of a constant percentage of gross margin to sales. Since it costs the restaurateur a fixed amount of money to maintain a place for a customer to have his meal, perhaps the restaurant should seek to recover a fixed margin over food cost from each meal that is served. This is a different concept from the idea of earning a contribution margin of 60 percent or 65 percent.

An objective, or at least a concomitant, of price increases is to raise the average check. This end may also be accomplished in other ways. It is often advisable to reduce the spread of prices on the menu by removing the least expensive items. The effect, of course, is to raise the average meal price. Similarly, the average check can be raised by replacing lower-priced items with items that carry a higher price. This may be done at any level in the menu.

One approach to such menu pricing is "prime costing." Prime costing entails adding an increment to the food cost for the cost of labor, and then marking up the combined total to arrive at a menu price. In many operations, it is both practical and realistic to determine the average amount of effort, and hence labor cost per meal served, and use this increment for pricing all entrees. It is practical because it is not difficult to implement, and realistic because service labor, warewashing labor, and preparation of surrounding courses will be virtually identical for all entrees. With few exceptions, average labor time in the preparation of many entrees themselves is likely to be quite close for the various entrees served.

Example:

Assume a chicken dish is sold for $2.50 and a steak dish is sold for $6.00 by the same restaurant. Both items have a 40 percent food cost. Assume that average labor cost per meal happens to be $1.35. Further, assume that the operator desires to change a menu price which is 40 percent more than the total of the combined food and labor cost. The following would result:

Food Cost + Labor

      Cost) X 140% = Menu Price

    or

(Food Cost + $1.35 X

          140% = Menu Price

Pricing steak and chicken on this basis, we arrive at the following prices:

Chicken

      (1.00 + $1.35) X 140% = $3.30

Steak

      ($2.40 + $1.35) X 140% = $5.25

This prime costing approach leads to a smaller price spread than marking on the basis of food cost alone. If food cost is marked up 250 percent (2½ times) to arrive at the menu price, any food cost differential will lead to 2½ times the price difference. Thus the $1.40 assumed cost difference between chicken and steak is magnified into a $3.50 menu price difference. Under a prime cost approach the multiple is much less. The $1.40 cost difference under our prime costing example would only be magnified 140 percent, thus resulting in a price difference of $1.95 as compared to $3.50 under the more conventional "food cost only" approach.

Under both types of pricing, the average price would be approximately $4.25. However, as demonstrated previously, the prime cost approach would be likely to yield an appreciably higher profit.

Prime costing has two further benefits for the operator. First, since it tends to increase check average, it also tends to increase service employees' tips. This should improve retention of more desirable employees. Second, although food cost and labor cost can be expected to vary greatly between specific restaurants, in our experience, the combination of the two, namely the prime cost, does not vary as much. Thus, it may be possible to compare a well-operated cafeteria with a first class restaurant on the basis of prime costs and arrive at a meaningful comparison.

Another method for improving the average check is by dressing up the menu to enhance the attractiveness of higher-priced items, This is sometimes done with words, sometimes with better layout, and sometimes with pictures in color.

The waiters can also contribute to the effort to increase the average check by their suggestions to diners. Cocktails, wines and desserts are often neglected by customers simply because the waiters failed to suggest them. This part of a waiter's job should be included in his training. Beyond training, occasional reminders and genuine efforts to maintain high morale among waiters are important to this part of the effort to raise the average check.

A Practical Illustration

The February 1973 issue of *Restaurant World* (Vol. 2. No. 5) sets forth the case of the Green Derby restaurant whose owner believes firmly that salesmanship and a thorough knowledge by employees of the items served are essential to increasing the size of the average guest check and the resultant gratuity of the service employee. Examine the story yourself: "If the check is only $5, you can expect as little as 75 cents, but if the check is $20, you can expect from $3 to $6," service employees are advised in a training manual.

Items to suggest to increase the check are listed . . .

Beverages from the bar
Oysters on the half shell
Crab fingers
Shrimp cocktails
Oysters "á la Abood"
Charcoal shrimp on a skewer
Relish trays
French fried onion rings
Wine with dinner
Desserts
After-dinner liqueurs

"In order to sell, you must know your product," employees are advised. "In your case, the product is the food, dessert, etc., listed on the menu. Know your menu. Know all à la carte items, know all extra items such as French fried onions, shrimp cocktails, wines, and desserts. Know your food accompaniment, such as mustard with corned beef and soy sauce with chop suey. Know the soup of the day, know your vegetables, know the entrees and how they are made."

Readings of the luncheon menu are held daily by the dining room manager. New items are explained and samples provided so employees will know what they are selling. Employees are urged, when they do not understand a new dish, to ask the chef or Mr. Abood (the owner) to explain, how it is made and what the ingredients are.

"The more you understand, the better job you can do in selling the customer," employees are told.

In summary, a drive to increase revenues may be directed at attracting more customers from old markets or new markets, increasing turnover by faster service or extended meal periods, raising prices generally or selectively, and improving the average check by changing the menu or selling wines and desserts.

Techniques of Forecasting

We have stressed the decision-making aspects of planning rather than the techniques, because decision-making is a major management function. At this point, it is appropriate to discuss briefly some fundamental matters in forecasting, again because management is likely to be involved in the process.

It is helpful to approach the subject of forecasting from two viewpoints: the history of the business itself, and the impact of external forces. Both are valid starting points; they complement each other; and they should be considered jointly in putting together a final forecast.

When the history of the business is used as a basis for a forecast, past trends are usually projected, or extrapolated, forward. Simple as this statements sounds, in a growth situation it may have one or two meanings. If the business is thought to be growing in constant increments, then the extrapolation will be along a straight line. But if growth is considered to be at a rate that is constant, as 20 percent each year, compounded, then the extrapolation follows an exponential curve, or growth curve, as it is sometimes called. A business cannot grow at a constant rate forever, but it may follow such a pattern for several years before tapering off.

The mere fact that sales have followed a certain trend in the past gives no assurance that they will continue to follow the same trend in the future. In extrapolating a trend, we make the implicit assumption that a causal system has been operative in the past, and that the same causal system will continue to operate unchanged. This may often be a dangerous assumption. Some changes may have a diminishing effect. others may be altered, and still others may cease to operate altogether.

Hence the need to examine carefully the markets that the restaurant serves, the competition, and all other factors relevant to the operation. In analyzing the situation for portents of the future, all indications of change should be scrutinized for their possible bearing on future results.

External factors may be national or local. The general level of the economy affects all sectors, and projections of the gross national product are of interest to all businesses. In situations where one industry, or even a few industries, dominate the local scene, the restaurateur should be concerned about the outlook for those industries when he projects his own level of operation. And he should consider the prospect of unemployment in his locality. He cannot expect to fare well when his customers are caught up in an economic squeeze.

All activity in the community has a potential for affecting the volume and earnings of a restaurant. Housing developments bring in residents; shopping centers not only attract people but also change patterns of local travel and movement; roads can redirect traffic, favoring some locations while hurting others; a population influx can upgrade or downgrade a neighborhood as a market. These are among the things to consider in preparing a forecast.

Finally, a realistic forecast must observe certain constraints. No matter how rosy the prospects may look for making gigantic strides and capturing huge new markets, a restaurant's own capacity to prepare and serve meals will set an upper limit that may be approached, but it cannot be exceeded. On the other hand, increased capacity from acquisition of new equipment, method changes, improved turnover, or any other reasonable expectation, should be reflected in the budget.

CASH BUDGETS

Cash budgets, or cash flow forecasts, are specialized projections which aim to avoid embarrassment by helping management to prepare to pay its bills and meet all its financial obligations as they come due. Thus, cash budgets are essentially short-term projections. It is useful to project cash balances week-by-week for 12 weeks, and to revise these projections monthly. In addition, a monthly cash forecast for six months is also useful.

At this point, we should mention briefly the increasingly popular use of a four-week accounting period by restaurants, as opposed to the standard calendar month reporting basis. The major benefit of this system, also called the 52-53 week year, is that there is a better comparability, or basis for comparison from one month to another. This gives the management a better yardstick to measure the results of its operation, mainly because each week of operations contains the same numbers of days. This avoids distortion by vacation periods or extended weeks due to variations in the calendar months.

Another benefit of such a four-week accounting period system is that it provides a means of coordinating weekly operating reports with financial reports, as the financial report ends with the end of the week. This also results in faster year-end reports to management, since there are fewer year-end adjustments to bring the actual weekly reports in line with the year-end report as is the case under the calendar month accounting system. Also, the auditor's year-end work is made easier, since there should be fewer adjustments due to incomplete operating transactions.

The final benefit is one of easier budgeting capabilities, since each week will contain the same number of days. This type of an accounting and financial reporting basis can be of great value to a restaurant in providing a handy device for comparison of operating results from one week to another and, in addition, may have the very practical effect of making financial and operating reports more meaningful to the restaurateur.

The construction of a cash budget requires that cash receipts and disbursements be predicted in some detail. On the receipts side, seasonal patterns should be analyzed for the help they provide. On the disbursements side, liabilities already incurred (including repayment of loans) and tax liabilities due on fixed dates are recorded first; then come liabilities arising from commitments to purchase that have already been made. After that, both normal expenditures and unusual items are estimated.

When all this information has been inserted, and the arithmetic is done, the tentative cash budget is reviewed for problem periods: low bank balances or cash deficits. If loans have to be extended or new loans made, it is much easier to make these arrangements in advance, while you can show a cash balance that is presently adequate and a planning system that alerts you to future developments before they occur. Scurrying around for cash at the last minute is no way to instill confidence in a banker, creditor, or other lender.

CHAPTER 9

Using Restaurant Financial Ratios and Analysis

CHAPTER CAPSULE PREVIEW

Interpretation of financial statements involves three things:

—An understanding of what each caption represents and its significance.
—Insight into the relationships between items and the manner in which they are interacted within the dynamic pattern of operations.
—A grasp of the significance of changing relationships and patterns as they emerge.

Consequently, a complete analytical study of the financial statements of a business involves, among other things, interpretations of a number of ratios and of trends associated with them. However, each ratio should express a genuine relationship that has particular significance to investors, lenders, or managers. The examples which will be offered in this chapter have been selected for their relevancy to the restaurant business.

As an overall warning, before undertaking the topic of financial statement analysis for restaurants, mention of its connection with the need for greater uniformity in accounting principles and procedures and the objective of standardized financial statements must be in order. The determination and evaluation of significant financial relationships are greatly facilitated when there exists uniformity in accounting theory and methodology. Conversely, this may be seriously hampered where some minimal degree of standardization (at least within the industry) of financial statement organization and presentation is lacking. It should be admitted frankly that the organized practice of accounting in this country still has a long way to go before the maximum feasible degree of uniformity and financial statement standardization is attained, so that financial statement analysis from one entity to another within an industry, such as the restaurant industry, may reach its full utilitarian potential.

Financial statements tell a story. Reading a financial statement is a matter of extracting from it the meaning that lies behind the figures. For every figure reflects s specific fact about the business.

The Balance Sheet, or Statement of Financial Condition, presents a picture of the business at a single point in time. It proclaims "This is how things stood at such-and-such a date. The assets owned by the business were such. The liabilities owed by the business were such. And the difference was the ownership equity."

The Profit and Loss Statement, or Income Statement or Statement of Operations, summarizes the results of operations for a stated period—a week, a month, a year. It shows revenues (sales, income) and expenses, classified and grouped to make interpretation easier. It shows profit margins at various levels (after certain expenses, but before others) and net earnings on the bottom line.

THE BALANCE SHEET

Within each section of the balance sheet, items are grouped into sub-sections: assets into current and fixed; liabilities into current and long-term. The obvious purpose is to permit evaluation of short-term prospects for meeting obligations as they become due.

Current assets comprise cash and those items that are readily convertible into cash, such as accounts receivable and temporary investments in marketable securities. Inventories are converted into cash in the normal course of business; therefore, inventories are included in current assets. In the restaurant business, inventories tend to be small, implying that their conversion through sales into receivables or cash is expected to occur quickly. The significance of this characteristic of restaurant inventories should not be overlooked in evaluating current position.

Fixed assets, or capital assets, may include land and building (if they are owned by the restaurant), furniture, fixtures, and equipment. These are reported at original cost less accumulated depreciation (or amortization). This method of evalua-tion has certain drawbacks: original cost may be quite different from current replacement value, and equipment bought in different years with different dollars is evaluated at a total dollar amount that is difficult to define accurately. Furthermore, accumulated depreciation does not represent a replacement reserve that will automat-ically become available to purchase new equipment as the old wears out. Obviously, balance sheet valuation of fixed assets can be misleading to the unwary.

From the standpoint of management, it would certainly appear that, within the context of present generally accepted historical cost accounting, the net income figure and the income statement are of far greater value in appraising the worth of an enterprise than the balance sheet.

Sophisticated observers have criticized the balance sheet on other grounds as well. They point, for example, to the assets of a business that go unrecorded either because they are considered to be acquired without payment or because measurement of their value is not agreed on. Thus, human assets, the aggregate skills of the managers and key personnel, are never reported although they contribute substantially to the restaurant's ability to make a profit.

Current liabilities comprise accounts payable, notes payable, accrued expenses and taxes payable or accured. If a debt is to be paid over a number of years, the portion that becomes due within one year is reported as a current liability. All other long-term debt is shown in a subsection of its own, separate from current liabilities.

The presentation of net worth reflects the type of business organization: capital accounts for individual proprietorships and partnerships, capital stock for corporations. Accumulated (retained) earnings add to net worth.

THE PROFIT AND LOSS STATEMENT

The profit and loss statement and its supporting schedules should present both sales and cost of sales by department (dining room, banquets, bar, cigar counter). Controllable expenses should also be reported by department. These include payroll and associated taxes and fringe benefits; such operating expenses as supplies, uniforms, and laundry; and such overhead items as utilities, repairs, and maintenance. departmental contribution margins are the results of revenues and expenses to this point; the total represents restaurant income before administrative overhead, advertising, depreciation, interest, and income taxes. Net earnings are customarily shown before taxes and after taxes.

There are several points at which balance sheet and income statement relate to each other. When assets are used up, they become expenses; inventories become part of the cost of sales; fixed assets are depreciated or amortized and expenses are recorded; and prepayments are charged to expense as they expire. On the other hand, assets are built up by revenues: sales generate receivables or bring in cash. And earnings increase net worth.

There are, in fact, many relationships between individual items in financial statements that are worth exploring for the insight they can provide to the workings of the enterprise. Let us now describe some of these relationships.

FINANCIAL STATEMENT RELATIONSHIPS

The geometric axiom that "the whole is equal to the sum of its parts" is extremely inapplicable to financial statements, for restaurants or otherwise. Invariably, financial statement analysis, wherein the component parts are scrutinized in themselves apart from the total picture of financial position and periodic operating results, will yield to the analyst additional useful information for evaluating the enterprise and its operating success or failure. Financial statement analysis is far more than a purely clerical task when properly performed. It is employed as a useful tool by both "insiders" (management) and "outsiders" (creditors, prospective and present investors, representatives of labor, investment bankers, and others).

Financial analysis, which is sometimes labeled as "historical," concerns a comparison of the relevant financial data for the present year with similarly compiled data for the previous year or a large number of prior years. The justification for this type of analysis seems to be the current accountancy craze for "trends" and period comparability, both as indicators of managerial efficiency and as guides to future decision-making. Every restaurateur must be aware that such comparative or historical analyses are multi-phased in that the present-year-previous-year analysis may be made for the entire enterprise; among the various departments within the restaurant enterprise, on either a current year or combined current-previous year basis with an eye toward ascertaining relative financial success, and within each department on a similar past-present comparison.

We have already noted that current assets are set out separately in the balance sheet, and that similar treatment is accorded current liabilities. Relationships between these two groups of items are important because current liabilities will have to be paid in the near term and that means they must be paid out of current assets in the main. Working capital, or net working capital, is the name given to the excess of current assets over current liabilities.

There is a special relationship between equity and debt (between net worth and liabilities). All the assets of a business are acquired in exchange for funds provided by the owners or loaned by banks and other lenders or loaned, in effect, by creditors who are willing to extend terms and wait for payment. What the owners do not put up, they must borrow. Frequently, there is an option. An owner may raise money for his business by making additional contributions of his own, by inviting a partner to join him or by selling stock, thereby increasing the equity in each case. Or he may increase the debt by borrowing.

If the owner chooses to borrow, he increases his leverage, assuming that the interest rate he pays is lower than the return that his restaurant earns. To illustrate, if a restaurateur borrows to increase his capacity, and the return on this increased volume is sufficient to pay the interest on the loan and leave something over as additional earnings, then the new earnings level, being higher than the old, is also a higher percentage of the owner's equity. This is the principle of leverage, and it results from a differential between the rate of return on assets and the cost of borrowed capital.

While debt financing has a potential for providing leverage, it also increases the owner's risk. Interest must be paid when due and so must instalments on loans. If earnings fall short of expectations, it may be difficult to make these payments. If earnings fall below the rate of interest on borrowings, then leverage operates in reverse, and the owner begins to suffer losses on the borrowed capital. If the owner were to sell stock in his enterprise instead, the exposure to risk would be accepted by the new stockholders. If earnings fall, dividends can be cut, and the restaurant's cash position need not be jeopardized.

These observations make it plain that the relationship between debt and equity is important to the owner because it determines his leverage and it exerts a strong influence on his exposure to risk. But the owner is not alone in his concerns. Prospective lenders will want to satisfy themselves that interest charges on proposed loans, added to interest charges on outstanding loans, will not be so burdensome as to create financial difficulties at the first slackening of business. Fixed charges, including interest payments, can impair the ability of the business to withstand cyclical downturns, stringent competitive conditions, unforeseen emergencies, or other adverse contingencies. In extreme cases, exceptionally sanguine operators with a speculative bent may concentrate their attention so narrowly on the advantages of leverage, ignoring the drawbacks, that they are quite prepared to borrow far beyond the limits of prudence. At some point, excessive borrowing serves to transfer a portion of the owner's risk to the lenders. For, if things go wrong, not only will the owner be wiped out, but the creditors will suffer substantial losses as well, Accordingly, the larger the debt, in proportion to the equity investment, the more difficult it becomes to persuade lenders to provide new money and, of course, the higher the interest they will demand.

Part of our discussion of the relationship between debt and equity turned on another relationship, that between earnings and assets. As we have seen earlier, the total investment in assets is provided by the sum of the owner's investment and borrowings from other sources. The return on invested funds from all sources is a significant measure of the restaurant's ability to meet its obligations to outsiders and provide a fair return to the owners. Both lenders and investors, therefore, are interested in the business's return on investment in the broadest sense. That is to say, the relationship between earnings and total assets has a definite significance of its own, regardless of the source of invested funds.

We have been considering relationships between two individual items or two groups of items: current assets and current liabilities; equity and debt; earnings and investment. Now let us examine a series of sequential relationships known as the cash cycle.

In the ordinary course of business, cash is converted into inventories through the purchase of foods and beverages, the inventories are consumed in preparing meals and drinks that are sold to customers, and these sales produce cash receipts or receivables that are ultimately collected in cash. Thus, a complete cycle takes the business from cash through purchases to inventories, through consumption and sale to receivables, through collection to cash once again. Significant relationships exist at several points in this cycle: There is an interesting relationship between inventories and consumption and another between receivables and sales.

An understanding of a relationship between two things requires that they be subjected to joint consideration, and where the items are quantified, as accounting data are, it is often possible to gain insight by comparing numbers and expressing the comparisons in terms of ratios. These ratios may then be subjected to further analysis by observing their behavior through time. The last part of this chapter will be dedicated to ratio analysis. Before turning to specific ratios, however, let us first examine the specific wants and needs of various interested parties who might be expected to analyze financial statements and to use the ratios we will discuss.

ANALYTICAL OBJECTIVES

What do people look for when they analyze financial statements? That will depend on who they are and where their interests lie. Perhaps a better first question would be: What kinds or groups of people are to be found analyzing financial statements? For our purposes, it is sufficient to identify investors, lenders, and managers and to distinguish between two outlooks: the long-term and the short.

Long-term lenders and investors have much in common. They are both interested in the ability of the business to survive as a profitable venture into the future. Therefore, they will want to assess the profitability of the business, the use it makes of its assets as indicated by the adequacy of its return on investment. They will also want to scrutinize the relationship between equity and debt, as an indication of the manner in which risks are spread. Moreover, they will be interested in long-term trends.

Short-term lenders and trade creditors may be forgiven if they take a more limited view. It may be sufficient for them to be satisfied that the current position of the business is adequate to meet current obligations. They will want to look closely at current assets, and particularly at quick assets (those that are immediately convertible into cash and therefore quickly available to pay off debts). But long-term profit potentials are of less interest, except insofar as they may affect continuing relations and renewing credit.

Management has responsibilities to both long-term and short-term creditors, and to the owners as well. Accordingly, its interests include the kinds of analysis that the other groups need. In addition, the management functions of planning and control impose an emphasis on the future, an orientation on where the business is headed and how it proposes to get there and an interest in financial statements as feedback that provides information as to how well the restaurant is keeping on course.

With this background concerning the needs of various groups and the basic concepts for interpreting financial statements, let us proceed to a detailed description of helpful ratios.

RATIO ANALYSIS

The ratio of debt to equity may be calculated by dividing net worth into total liabilities. This ratio indicates the strength of the capitalization. It answers such questions as these: Is the owner's stake so small that he is encouraged to speculate with outsiders' money? Will an issue of common stock still permit reasonable leverage? Would obligations to repay debts prove burdensome if the business suffered reverses?

If current liabilities fluctuate, those who prefer a more stable ratio may divide net worth into long-term debt instead of total liabilities. The interpretation of such a ratio will be similar to the ratio described above, except that the numbers will be smaller.

The ratio of earnings to assets requires some explanation. For this calculation, earnings should be taken before deductions for interest and income taxes. These two items are extraneous to the purpose of the ratio, and they can confuse the basic issue. We are looking for a measure of management's effectiveness in employing assets to produce profits. Interest is not a charge against operations, but rather a charge associated with a particular method for raising capital, that is, by borrowing. An evaluation of the effective use of assets should not be confused by charges related to the sources of funds for acquiring the assets. Income taxes need not be considered in evaluating the relationship between earnings and assets because changes in tax rates merely introduce variations that obscure the trends that are sought.

Similarly, total assets are used in the calculation, instead of net worth, because the sources of funds—whether equity or debt—are of no consequence in evaluating the use that is made of the assets themselves. Dividing earnings by assets, as we have now defined both terms, yields a ratio that is capable of measuring return on investment for those who must decide whether to invest in the business or to lend money to it.

The current ratio is obtained by dividing liabilities into current assets. This is a measure of the restaurant's solvency. In the restaurant business, a ratio of 1:1 is considered acceptable in recognition of the fact that inventories are low enough to be of little concern and also low enough to be converted into cash in the normal course in a short time. In other businesses, where inventories are a much larger part of current assets, the 1:1 ratio is held acceptable for the quick ratio rather than the current ratio. The quick ratio, of course, excludes inventories so that only cash, marketable securities and receivables, in total, are divided by current liabilities. The distinction between quick ratio (sometimes the term "acid test" is encountered in pedantic usage) and current ratio is of little consequence to restaurants generally.

The increased emphasis upon the use of the quick-asset ratio has resulted from the frequent clamor for cash or its practical equivalent in our modern monetary economy. In other words, a demand has been created for some device to measure the "liquidity" of an enterprise. By liquidity, financial analysts mean the ease of convertibility of assets into cash, and in a practical context the quick-asset ratio measuring such liquidity serves as a safeguard to detect a current ratio which may hide a condition known as "over-loaded inventories." In effect, a current ratio appearing quite feasible because of exessively high inventories would in reality be a distortion of a seriously impaired current condition and would go unnoticed but for the quick-asset ratio.

Income statements often show a large number of ratios simply by presenting alongside each dollar figure its *percentage to sales*. Thus, individual revenue items are shown as percentages of total revenues; individual expenses and grouped expenses are also related directly to net sales; and margins at various levels are treated similarly. The trends disclosed by these percentages are useful to management in controlling operations and also in planning ahead.

The ratio of prime cost to sales is a key figure for management. Prime cost covers both food (and beverage costs) and labor (including preparation labor and serving), and it is a principal concept in menu pricing. In any comparison between convenience foods and regular foods, no reasonable basis for decision can fail to include the cost of labor. Hence, prime cost is well established as a figure of fundamental importance. And the ratio of prime cost to sales is watched very carefully.

The ratio of sales to man hours is a useful measure of the productivity of labor. Sales per-man-hour can be calculated for each department to provide information for control. Further analysis into hourly sales per-man-hour can be useful in planning to staff for peak loads and in staggering hours of work.

There are several *turnover ratios* that provide insight into operations. The concept of turnover itself is enlightening, implying as it does a cycle of use and renewal. We have seen that part of the cash cycle involves an inventory cycle: inventories are purchased and consumed alternately. A variation of the cash cycle substitutes working capital for cash, so that working capital is conceived as generating sales by being used over and over. Three turnover ratios will be described next.

Working capital turnover is calculated by dividing working capital (current assets minus current liabilities) into sales. It provides an indication of such things as the adequacy of working capital in consideration of the volume of sales and the possibilities for increasing sales without added investment in working capital.

Inventory turnover for food is calculated by dividing food inventory into the food cost of sales. Since the inventory is valued at cost, a proper turnover ratio can be gotten only by dividing into the cost of sales, rather than sales. A refinement of this ratio calls for dividing by average inventory over the period covered. Inventory turnover for beverages is calculated similarly: by dividing beverage inventory into the beverage cost of sales. The number of times a particular inventory "turns over" in a year can point up overstocking and speculation in inventories when prices look "right" at the moment, two practices that should be avoided for reasons described in another chapter.

Promptness of *collections* is measured by dividing average accounts receivable balances into credit sales. Alternatively, the *number of weeks' sales in open receivables* may be calculated by dividing recent average weekly credit sales into total current accounts receivable. Whichever method is adopted, only credit sales should be used in calculating turnover of receivables, because only credit sales create receivables in the first place. Inclusion of substantial cash sales in such a calculation would only distort the result. Furthermore, since collection patterns differ as between house accounts and accounts on credit cards issued by banks, credit companies, and other outside sources, a restaurant that extends credit in more than one way will find that truly significant ratios can be expressed only by analyzing accounts receivable and sales into homogeneous groups.

To illustrate the technique of financial analysis as applied to the restaurant industry, the following section of this chapter represents material excerpted from the Laventhol Krekstein Horwath & Horwath Restaurant Study, co-authored by the writers. The study represents an annual report by our firm on the operating results of the commercial food service industry based on a carefully selected sample of restaurants.

CLASSIFICATION BY LOCATION

Restaurants serving both food and beverages have some variations that can be attributed to location, but results of all "food and beverage" restaurants are similar. However, those that serve only food show several significant differences from the restaurants that serve both food and beverages. For example, in the "food only" category, paper and guest supplies make up over 54 percent of direct operating expenses, while in "food and beverage" restaurants only 11 percent of direct operating expense is in that category. The use of disposable ware in the fast-food operations in the "food only" group is responsible for the great difference. We therefore show separately the operations of those restaurants serving only food from those that also serve some alcoholic beverages. In addition, the "food and beverage" restaurants are further classified by location as follows:

> *Neighborhood*—Situated in areas which are primarily residential but which are near commercial concentrations providing an additional source of business.

> *Center City*—Situated in the central business section of a city.

> *Suburban*—Situated outside of a city.

Net Income

Net income before income taxes showed a very sharp increase in the "food only" category. Although sales volume for that group rose only .7 of one percent, decreases of nearly 4 percent in other controllable expenses and nearly 6 percent in occupation costs resulted in a rise of 127 percent in net income before income taxes. There was a significant drop in the operating results of suburban "food and beverage" restaurants, however, caused mostly by increases in almost all costs which were offset only partly by an increase of 6 percent in sales. The detail for all the groups is shown in Exhibit 1, as follows:

Exhibit 1
Income before Income Taxes—Ratio to Total Sales

	Second Year	First Year	Increase (Decrease)
Food Only	8.4%	3.7%	127%
Food and Beverage			
Neighborhood	5.1	5.0	2
Center City	5.1	5.0	2
Suburban	9.0	10.0	(10)
Total	6.5	6.7	(3)
All Restaurants	6.9%	6.0%	15%

Income before occupation costs of all restaurants in the study was 9 percent higher in total amount than a year ago, and also one percentage point, or 7.4 percent, higher in relation to sales. The detail is shown in Exhibit 2, as follows:

Exhibit 2
Income before Occupation Costs—Ratio to Total Sales

	Second Year	First Year	Increase (Decrease)
Food Only	15.8%	10.9%	45.0%
Food and Beverage			
Neighborhood	13.4	13.4	–
Center City	12.1	12.3	(1.6)
Suburban	17.4	17.6	(1.1)
Total	14.3	14.3	–
All Restaurants	14.6%	13.6%	7.4%

The changes in income before occupation costs of the various categories of "food and beverage" restaurants are summarized as follows:

Neighborhood—no change

The favorable effect of an increase of 2 percent in sales volume was completely offset by the adverse effect of similar increases in prime costs and controllable expenses.

Center City—down 2 percent

Sales dropped 3 percent, and prime costs were down 4 percent, but other controllable costs dropped only 1 percent.

Suburban—down 1 percent

Although sales were up 6 percent, increases in prime costs, and other controllable expenses offset the favorable effect of the rise.

Occupation Costs

In Exhibit 9 which will be presented later, we show a summary of the income and expense ratios before rent, property taxes and insurance, interest and depreciation. The main reason for not including such items in the summary is that we did not receive the details of occupation costs and depreciation from the full sample. The total of rent, property taxes, insurance and interest for all of the restaurants was nearly $4.2 million, a decline of 2 percent, which was a reversal of the trend in recent years. The detail of the ratios to sales, based upon available data, is shown in Exhibit 3, as follows:

Exhibit 3
Occupation Costs—Ratio to Total Sales

| | Food Only | Food and Beverage | | |
		Neighbor-hood	Center City	Subur-ban
Rent	4.0%	5.9%	4.1%	5.0%
Property taxes	.8	.8	.5	.8
Property insurance	.5	.4	.4	.3
Interest	.5	.8	.7	1.2
Depreciation	2.6	1.5	1.8	2.7
Total	7.3%	8.3%	6.8%	8.3%

Property insurance continued to rise significantly in some groups, and for the 80 restaurants studied the rise was nearly 13 percent. Center-city restaurants showed the highest rise, while suburban "food and beverage" operations had a slight decrease. The detail is shown in Exhibit 4, as follows:

Exhibit 4
Property Insurance—Second Year Compared with First Year

	Increase (Decrease)
Food Only	8.1%
Food and Beverage	
Neighborhood	23.1
Center City	25.3
Suburban	(3.7)
All Restaurants	12.7%

Sales

Although total sales volume for all of the restaurants studied was up only one percent, the groups showed varying degrees of change. The greatest improvement reported in dollar volume was one of 6.3 percent in the suburban group, in which there was also a noticeable shift in the relationship of beverage sales to food sales. The sale of beverages provided about 2 percent more of the revenue dollar in the second year than in the first, the second successive year in which such a change took place. An opposite change occurred in the neighborhood group, with the ratio of beverage sales to food sales dropping 10 percent from its earliest level.

The sales per seat for each category of restaurants are analyzed in Exhibit 5, for those restaurants that supplied the data, as follows:

Exhibit 5
Sales per Seat

	Second Year	First Year	Increase (Decrease)
Food Only	$3,805	$3,778	.7%
Food and Beverage			
Neighborhood			
Food	$1,528	$1,399	9.2%
Beverages	496	504	(1.6)
Total	$2,024	$1,903	6.4%
Center City			
Food	$2,377	$2,392	(.6%)
Beverages	750	766	(2.1)
Total	$3,127	$3,158	(1.0%)
Suburban			
Food	$1,286	$1,247	3.1%
Beverages	486	459	5.9
Total	$1,772	$1,706	3.9%
All Food and Beverage			
Food	$1,666	$1,633	2.0%
Beverages	565	564	.2
Total	$2,231	$2,231	1.5%

Cost Per Dollar Sale

With the exception of the beverage cost in suburban restaurants, there were decreases in all of the costs of merchandise sold in all of the groups. The increase in the suburban restaurants' beverage cost, although only 1.3 percentage points, or 4.2 percent, may account for the shift in the sales sources on which we have commented previously.

The drop in the cost per dollar sale in the "food only" category was comparatively sharp and probably the result of a major change in menu prices since there were no significant decreases in wholesale food prices during the year. The detail is shown in Exhibit 6, as follows:

Exhibit 6
Cost Per Dollar Sale

	Second Year	First Year	Increase (Decrease)
Food Only	34.5¢	37.2¢	(7.3%)
Food and Beverage			
Neighborhood			

Exhibit 6 (continued
Cost Per Dollar Sale

	Second Year	First Year	Increase (Decrease)
Food	40.2	41.0	(2.0)
Beverage	31.3	32.2	(2.8)
Center City			
Food	37.2	38.1	(2.4)
Beverage	26.8	27.6	(2.9)
Suburban			
Food	40.3	40.7	(1.0)
Beverage	32.5	31.2	4.2

Payroll

Payroll in the "food only" group dropped 4 percent in dollar amount. Since sales of this group were slightly above those of the earlier year, the ratio to sales dropped to 32.6 percent from 33.0 percent. The payroll ratio rose slightly, however, in each case of the other groups. For the first time in several years, the increase in the total of this expense for all the restaurants was relatively slight—only 2 percent—and the ratio to total sales for all groups also was up only slightly—.2 of one percent.

Prime Cost

Only small changes occured in the prime cost (the combination of cash payroll and cost of merchandise sold) in the "food and beverage" restaurants; however, in the "food only" group, there was a sharp reduction in that very important expense ratio. The prime cost for each group of restaurants is shown in Exhibit 7, as follows:

Exhibit 7
Prime Cost

	Second Year	First Year	Increase (Decrease)
Food Only	67.1%	70.2%	(4.4%)
Food and Beverage			
Neighborhood	66.2	66.3	(.2)
Center City	65.5	65.9	(.6)
Suburban	65.8	65.5	.5
Total	65.8	65.9	(.2)
All Restaurants	66.1%	66.8%	(1.0%)

Other Controllable Expenses

Total controllable expenses for all restaurants in the second year were only one percent higher than the year before, about the same as the increase in sales, so that there was an insignificant rise in the ratio. The direct operating expenses, which make up about

11 percent of controllable expenses, showed very little variation and the ratio to sales decreased from 5.9 percent to 5.8 percent. The detail of those expenses for the second year, based upon the data available, is presented in Exhibit 8, as follows:

Exhibit 8
Direct Operating Expenses—Ratio to Total Sales

	Food Only	Food and Beverage		
		Neighborhood	Center City	Suburban
Laundry and linen and/or linen rental	.6%	1.9%	1.6%	1.7%
China, glassware and silver	.2	.8	1.3	.7
Cleaning and cleaning supplies	.4	1.0	.7	1.0
Paper and guest supplies	2.7	.7	.5	.8
All other	1.0	1.5	2.2	1.4
Total	4.9%	5.9%	6.3%	5.6%

The summary profit and loss ratios for both years reveal the following comparisons as shown in Exhibit 9 (Figure 9-1)

Industry Outlook

Recent years have witnessed an increase in the cost-consciousness of the consumer. Fast-food operations that specialize in low-priced menus and minimum service continue to attract the young people, particularly young families. In some areas, particularly center cities, the trade press reports serious problems in the higher-priced table-service operations. However, imaginative operators, guided by good market information and geared to the fast pace and constant change demanded by our young people, seem to do well. With the only noticeable population change projected being an increase in the 20-year-to-40-year-old group, food service operations must adjust their plans to meet the needs of younger guests.

Exhibit 9

Restaurant Operations: Summary Profit and Loss Ratios

	Second Year	Second Year	Second Year Food and Beverage Restaurants				First Year	First Year	First Year Food and Beverage Restaurants			
	All Restaurants	Food Only	Total	Neighborhood	Center City	Suburban	All Restaurants	Food Only	Total	Neighborhood	Center City	Suburban
Sales												
Food	80.3%	100.0%	74.7%	75.5%	76.0%	72.6%	80.2%	100.0%	74.3%	73.5%	75.8%	73.1%
Beverages	19.7	—	25.3	24.5	24.0	27.4	19.8	—	25.7	26.5	24.2	26.9
Total sales	100.0	100.0	100.0	100.0	100.0	100.0	100.0	100.0	100.0	100.0	100.0	100.0
Cost of sales												
Food*	37.8	34.5	39.6	40.2	37.2	40.3	39.0	37.2	39.6	41.0	39.1	40.7
Beverages	30.0	34.5	30.0	31.3	26.8	32.5	29.9		29.9	32.2	27.8	31.2
Total cost of sales	36.3	34.5	36.7	38.0	34.8	38.1	37.2	37.2	37.2	38.6	35.7	33.2
Gross profit	63.7	65.5	63.3	62.0	65.2	61.9	62.8	62.8	62.8	61.4	64.3	61.8
Other income	1.3	.6	1.4	.7	1.2	2.1	1.1	.3	1.3	.7	1.2	1.9
Total income	65.0	66.1	64.7	62.7	66.4	64.0	63.9	63.1	64.1	62.1	65.5	63.7
Controllable expenses												
Payroll	28.8	32.6	29.0	28.2	30.7	27.7	29.6	33.0	28.6	27.6	30.2	27.3
Employee benefits	3.6	3.9	3.6	3.1	4.3	3.1	3.6	4.4	3.4	3.1	3.8	3.1
Direct operating expenses	5.8	4.9	6.0	5.9	6.3	5.6	5.9	5.3	6.0	6.2	6.3	5.5
Music and entertainment	.9	.2	1.1	1.3	1.1	1.1	.3	N	1.1	1.3	.8	1.2
Advertising and promotion	1.7	1.7	1.7	1.8	2.0	1.2	1.7	1.8	1.6	1.5	2.1	1.1
Utilities	1.6	2.1	1.6	1.7	1.5	1.8	1.7	2.0	1.6	1.6	1.5	1.7
Administration and general	5.2	3.8	5.7	5.8	6.5	4.5	5.5	4.7	5.9	6.0	6.8	4.5
Repairs and maintenance	1.6	1.3	1.7	1.5	1.9	1.6	1.5	1.4	1.6	1.4	1.7	1.6
Total controllable expenses	50.4	50.3	50.4	49.3	54.3	46.6	50.3	52.2	49.8	46.7	53.2	46.1
Income before occupation costs	14.6%	15.8%	14.3%	13.4%	12.1%	17.4%	13.6%	10.9%	14.3%	13.4%	12.3%	17.6%

N=Negligible

*Before credit for employees' meals

Figure 9-1.

CHAPTER 10

Tax Implications of Restaurant Management and Operation

CHAPTER CAPSULE PREVIEW

The measure of success for any business is after-tax income, and in view of the size of tax rates and the great complexity of tax laws, failure to take full advantage of the tax laws can result in substantial and unnecessary sacrifices of after-tax dollars.

In the final analysis, almost every economic decision has tax implications, and making the decision that will have the most favorable after-tax results almost always depends upon knowing the consequences of alternatives *in advance*. Accordingly, tax planning under the guidance of expert tax counsel is a critical factor both in planning a new restaurant business and in its continuing operations thereafter.

A major consideration in establishing a restaurant is selecting the organizational forms which will leave the owner or owners the greatest amount of after-tax profits. Restaurants may be organized as individual proprietorships, partnerships or corporations—or in some variation of these legal entities—and they must choose carefully in order to minimize taxes. Making a wise choice depends upon relating the owner's financial situation and needs to the alternative forms of taxation which apply to the different forms of organizing the business.

CORPORATIONS

By organizing a restaurant as a corporation, the owner can limit his legal liability for corporate debts, and also limit income taxes to corporate rates—stockholders do not report taxable income until they receive dividend distributions. Thus, the corporation in effect sets up a partial tax shield between the business and its owners because the corporation is treated as a separate entity, somewhat independent of its owners.

In addition to sheltering corporate profits which are plowed back into the business, the corporate form offers fringe benefits to the owners which are not available under the other forms of business organization. Owners who are legally also employees of the corporation can benefit substantially from establishing pension plans, deferred profit-sharing plans, and group life insurance and health plans. Such plans may not discriminate in favor of highly compensated employees, but the allowable provisions, nonetheless, offer substantial additional tax advantages.

In turn, of course, corporations have disadvantages which do not apply to the other organizational forms. The income of a business organized in corporate form is taxed twice, first to the corporation and then to the shareholder-owners. While tax law allows a dividends-received credit, the credit is significant only for corporate stockholders and is no more than a token for individuals.

Thus, even when some income is held in the business and not currently taxed, the combination of the two taxes may be higher than if the full income had been taxed at the rate applicable to the owner's total personal income for the year. To a degree, the retention of profits in the business as operating capital can avoid this, but the accumulation of surpluses is limited by law and accumulations deemed unreasonable by the Internal Revenue Service are subject to penalty taxes.

Whether the corporate form may be desirable will depend on such factors as the individual's expected tax bracket for all his income and whether he has income from other sources. For an individual with other sources of income, the corporation can be a disadvantage in another way. When the business incurs tax losses, those losses are not deductible against the stockholder's other income. Furthermore, the amount of business loss which can be carried forward to deduct in subsequent years is limited.

If it is desirable to incorporate for other reasons, partial relief from the disadvantages fo the corporate form can often be obtained by reporting under Subchapter S. Generally a Subchapter S corporation is a small, closely held corporation with ten or fewer individual stockholders, a single class of stock, and other specific characteristics. Since a qualifying corporation may elect to have its income taxed directly to the shareholders, the owners can avoid the otherwise double taxation corporate consequences.

To operate as a Subchapter S Corporation requires particularly meticulous planning to insure compliance with all requirements and to determine which course of action will yield the most favorable tax results. Furthermore, some of the advantages of incorporating have to be sacrificed in order to operate as a Subchapter S Corporation.

For example, deductible contributions to a pension plan on behalf of an owner of more than 5 percent of the stock are limited to 5 percent of salary or $7,500, whichever is lower. In some cases, this provision of the tax law can be an important factor in selecting the organizational form, since pension plans can be a valuable tax shelter vehicle for income which the owners of a business can afford to defer until retirement.

Example:

If your restaurant corporation has elected under Subchapter S to have its income taxed to the shareholders, you may have a unique opportunity for accelerating income if you and your corporation have different tax years. Although the corporation is not taxed, its income is taxable to the shareholders in the year within which the corporate year ends, unless the corporation makes a distribution which is taxable in the year that the distribution is made. To illustrate, your Subchapter S restaurant corporation has a fiscal year ending March 31 and you estimate its net income at $60,000. If the corporation distributes $20,000 before the preceding December 31, you must include $20,000 in your previous year's income, while the remaining $40,000 will be taxable to you in the current year. If you wanted $60,000 taxable in the previous year, you would distribute that amount before the preceding December 31; while if you wanted the $60,000 on your current year's tax return, you would either make the distribution after the preceding December 31, or make no distribution at all.

In general, it should be observed that the corporation is a business form which serves to shelter some current income from taxes, and thus in effect defer it. The sheltered income will sooner or later be taxed when distributed to the owners; thus decisions to adopt the corporate form for a new business require particularly careful consideration of income and loss expectations for as many years ahead as possible. Clearly it can be a highly advantageous form of operating, but it should not be just automatically adopted.

PARTNERSHIP

Unlike the corporation, a partnership is merely a conduit for personal income, not a taxable entity itself. The partnership files an information return with the Internal Revenue Service, and individual partners pick up their shares of total earnings on their own personal tax returns.

While the earnings from the business are currently taxable even if not paid out to the partners, the partnership has other advantages which can make it distinctly preferable to incorporation. For example, partners benefit directly from transactions which are taxed at capital gains rates, whereas in the corporate form of operation, a capital gain transaction does not flow through to the owners' own personal tax returns.

The deductibility of losses is much more favorable for owners of a partnership than for a corporation, which can be particularly important for partners who have income from other sources.

When a partnership owns land and building, the partners receive cash flow and tax losses to offset against taxable income. Depreciation charges produce book losses even though a net cash inflow may be coming in, and thus the losses shelter income against taxation while property values build up for eventual gain.

Compared to ordinary incorporation, the partnership has the same disadvantage as Subchapter S Corporations in allowable tax deductions for contributions to a pension or profit-sharing plan, since each partner is deemed to be self-employed for the purposes of the applicable provisions of the tax law.

Normally, a partner may deduct his share of partnership losses on his personal return for the year within which the partnership year ends. However, the amount deductible is limited to the lesser of his share of the loss or his tax basis in the partnership interest (generally made up of his capital account and his share of certain partnership debt). Partnership losses not allowed currently may be taken in a future year when the partner's tax basis has increased sufficiently. If your restaurant partnership is going to sustain a loss during the current year and you wish to take current advantage of your share of the loss, make sure that your tax basis will be large enough. Conversely, if you wish to defer all or part of the loss until next year, perhaps you may reduce your tax basis by making withdrawals from the partnership in the current year and repaying them in the following year.

It is often said that a Subchapter S Corporation is a corporation taxed "like" a partnership. One very important difference is that deductible Subchapter S losses are limited to the basis in stock plus debt owed the stockholder by the corporation; and inability to use the loss in the year incurred results in never getting use of the loss. Unlike the partnership, the loss can't be used in a subsequent year; it is lost forever if insufficient basis exists at year-end. Therefore, analysis should be made *before* the corporation's year-end to determine if there will be losses in excess of basis; if it appears there may be, perhaps the corporation may be able to defer the losses or perhaps you may make loans to the corporation to increase your basis and thus your allowed loss.

LIMITED PARTNERSHIP

Selecting the most suitable organizational form depends upon relating legal, tax, and other requirements to the circumstances of the various owners; and where their participation in the business will differ substantially, they should consider a limited partnership. For purposes of the individual partners, such a partnership is a hybrid, permitting limited partners to enjoy one of the principal advantages of the corporation: limited liability.

The limited partnership is defined by law as "a partnership formed by two or more persons . . . having as members one or more general partners and one or more limited partners. The limited partners as such shall not be bound by the obligations of the partnership." The limited partner shares pro rata or in any other manner agreed upon by the partners in the earnings, cash flow, and any tax losses which may occur. In practice, the limited partner is usually a passive participant in the business, earning his share of the profits largely because of putting up capital. Accordingly, he is likely to have other assets and other income which he will wish to shelter from any calamitous loss in the new business. Under such circumstances, the limited partnership may be the most appealing organizational form for both the active partner who will be running the business and the limited partner.

Furthermore, the law and regulations applying to limited partnerships permit allocation formulas somewhat proportionate to the partner's cash contributions, with the result that tax deductions resulting principally from depreciation may be allocated predominantly to the limited partners, who are likely to benefit most.

SOLE PROPRIETORSHIP

By all means the simplest form of operation is the sole proprietorship. Income and losses from the business are exclusively the owner's and he has minimal formalities in order to comply with the provisions of the tax law.

The sole proprietor's income is not sheltered from taxes as it can be in a corporation; but, on the other hand, the deductibility of losses is not restricted, and where the owner has other income, he can offset losses against it. In some cases, it may be desirable to operate initially as a sole proprietorship (while there may be losses), and then shift to the corporate form as the business becomes firmly established.

The specific tax attributes of operating as a sole proprietor are the same as those described for the partnership, of course, since a partner is treated as an individual for tax purposes.

MULTIPLE CORPORATIONS

Where restaurants are to be operated at separate locations, the owner should consider the possibility of using multiple corporations. In addition to establishing separate operating companies for each location, the owner may be able to justify separate corporations for individual activities if he can demonstrate that they have a legitimate business purpose.

For example, real estate may be held and operated by a separate realty company, and overall management of all individual restaurants may be separated into a management company which sells its services at a fee to each restaurant. Such separate incorporation may be contested by the government, but it is possible in some cases to establish that they operate at sufficient arm's length to justify their operation as distinct business entities.

In addition to isolating the legal liabilities of particular operating units, the establishment of such separate corporations will have significant tax advantages through 1975, through surtax exemptions presently scheduled to end that year.

The tax advantage is an outgrowth of the tax rate differential for corporate income above and below $25,000:

Less than $25,000	22 percent
$25,000 and more	48 percent

The tax saving for $50,000 of income, for example, if separate operating entities are individually incorporated is $6,500 ($25,000 X 26%). This has been such a substantial incentive to the establishment of multiple corporations that Congress acted ın 1969 to eliminate multiple surtax exemptions over a five-year period, limiting the corporate income taxed at only 22 percent to the following:

1970	$20,833.00
1971	16,667.00
1972	12,500.00
1973	8,333.00
1974	4,167.00

Effective with 1975, a group of related corporations will be allowed only one $25,000 exemption which may be taken by a single member of the group or apportioned among the various members of the group according to Tresury Department Regulations.

The phase out of multiple surtax exemptions may not be total however. It is conceivable that Congress may grant relief for the formation of new corporations to engage in business in separate marketing locations where the parent corporation transferred money or credit to the new corporation to buy inventory, fixtures and similar property from the parent: or where the parent guaranteed leases and furnished organizational experience and business know-how to the new corporation.

Many restaurants expand in this fashion and although a bill to provide relief failed to get out of committee and on the floor of Congress in 1972, the Treasury Department indicated an intent to provide the necessary relief from the 1969 law, which would mean that restaurants and others operating under the same methods would again qualify for multiple surtax exemptions.

As a moderate compensation for the phasing out of multiple surtax exemptions, the Tax Reform Act of 1969 provided that the dividends-received deduction for corporations will gradually increase from 85 percent to 100 percent, thus permitting a larger amount of dividends to pass tax-free between members of a controlled group of corporations.

To qualify for the exemptions, each corporation in the group must, of course, be a legitimately distinct operating entity. The IRS has frequently challenged management companies as not being *bona fide* separate business engaged in substantial and independent activities. Thus, in establishing multiple corporation groups, the owners must work carefully with legal counsel in setting up the individual corporations in a way that will comply with IRS rules and regulations, both initially and in subsequent operations.

These rules and regulations are particularly complex since they deal with various individual transactions among related corporate groups and because the definition of what constitutes a controlled group of corporations varies from one situation to another.

The two basic distinctions are (1) parent-subsidiary relations between corporations and (2) brother-sister corporations commonly owned by non-corporate entities (individuals, trusts, estates, etc.). The first relationship is deemed to exist if the parent corporation owns at least 80 percent of the voting power or value of the outstanding stock. The second relationship is deemed to exist if 80 percent of the voting power or value of the outstanding stock is owned by five or fewer non-corporate entities and if they own more than 50 percent of each corporation in the group.

Thus, where the ownership of a new operation is to be highly concentrated, the owners may expect multiple corporation groups to be subject to whatever limitations currently apply to multiple surtax exemptions. Where ownership is to be distributed among a larger group of individuals (or trusts and estates), the law has leeway for establishing separate corporations which will qualify for multiple surtax exemptions for each corporation.

Distributing ownership among various family members (husband, wife, parents, children, etc.) does not qualify for separate ownership, since the law considers such distribution as "constructive" ownership by a single individual. For example, a total of 20 percent ownership by each of a husband, wife and two children would be treated as a single 80 percent ownership. The same ownership by four brothers, however, would enable the corporations to operate separately and thus qualify each corporation for the full multiple surtax exemption.

Complicating the matter further, rules for precentages of ownership vary by categories of transaction. For example, where the IRS deems that the principal purpose of acquiring control of a corporation is the evasion of tax, the tax benefit is not allowable, but control is defined as at least 50 percent of the voting power or value of the outstanding stock, and separate ownership by family members is not treated as constructive ownership.

In contrast, the 80 percent ownership principle applies to the denial of surtax exemptions and accumulated earnings tax credits where a transfer of property to a new or newly activated corporation is deemed to have tax avoidance as a major purpose.

In the case of various transactions between related corporations in which the IRS has authority to reallocate income (interest charges, various fees, sales, etc.), control is not determined by percentage of ownership at all. Arbitrary shifting of income or deductions between the corporations is *presumed* to constitute control.

Other Advantages

In addition to the tax rate advantages of multiple surtax exemptions, the use of multiple corporations has other advantages which may make them worth considering even if no relief from the phasing out of exemptions is provided.

Each corporation in the group may accumulate earnings up to $100,000 without being penalized with the accumulated earnings tax. Member corporations need not be uniform in corporate structure and the elections they make for various tax purposes. For example, one or more members may be set up as Subchapter S Corporations while the rest operate as regular corporations.

Some Practical Hints to Avoid the Accumulated
Earnings Tax!

In the case of those restaurants large enough to have accumulated undistributed earnings in excess of $100,000, it is very prudent to review annually and to determine whether the restaurant corporation may be subject to the penalty tax on earnings accumulated to avoid shareholder taxation. If there is no proper business reason for an accumulation in excess of $100,000 (may be less for a member of a controlled group) a penalty of 27½ percent on the first $100,000 of current year excess, and 38½ percent above, may be assessed. Alternatives:

Pay dividends during the current year or within 2½ months of year-end. The 2½-month rule allows shareholder income shifting which might be valuable for other reasons.

Make a Subchapter S election for the following year where otherwise possible and advisable, and pay a dividend during the first 2½ months of that following year. This will relieve the current year's problem and yet not increase the income of the stockholder.

Transfer the stock to an affiliated corporation and then pay a dividend which will be subject to the 85 percent (or possible 100 percent) dividends received deduction.

Pay the exact dividend permissible under prevailing legal regulations.

Carefully document the business reasons for accumulating earnings. These should be specific both as to proposed use and amounts needed, and they should be as directly related to the peculiarities of the restaurant business as is possible under the circumstances.

Similarly, member corporations may use different fiscal years, giving them greater flexibility in planning cash flow to pay taxes and other charges against operations. And overall business and tax planning may be facilitated by the use of a number of corporations, since this facilitates sales of a portion of the business, liquidations of particular operations, or spin-offs of one of the components for various purposes.

Another advantage of multiple corporation groups is that pension and other employee benefits do not have to be uniform for all employees, as they would have to be in a single corporation. Thus, if restaurant owners establish a management corporation to provide services to a group of restaurants and realty corporations, the management corporation can establish more generous pensions than for the other corporations in the group, thus serving the owners as an estate planning device for deferring income to their retirement years. Current corporate taxes would be lower, because contributions into the pension fund would not be taxable.

Some of the business purposes for multiple corporations which the courts have allowed include efforts to avoid the effects of pending legislation covering employees under minimum wage laws; efforts to avoid unionization of employees; and efforts to motivate managers through giving them stock in the operations they manage.

Consolidated Returns

If multiple surtax exemptions are phased out, as discussed earlier in this chapter, multiple corporations may still gain some tax advantages by organizing as an "affiliated" group of corporations and thus qualifying to file a consolidated return.

A principal characteristic of the affiliated group is the percentage of ownership. Eighty percent of the voting power and 80 percent of each class of voting stock of each group member must be owned by either the parent corporation or another group member.

While multiple surtax exemptions may sometimes be preferable, consolidating all the income and losses of the group can be advantageous when one or more of the group members has losses. These losses offset the income of other members, and if the group as a whole has a net loss, that loss may be carried forward to offset against income in subsequent years.

Furthermore, unrealized profits from transactions between members of the group are excluded from taxable income, and gain on appreciated property transferred from one member to another is not taxed.

The laws and regulations governing consolidated tax returns by affiliated groups of corporations are highly complex, and accordingly, such returns offer many individuals advantages and many individual disadvantages, restrictions and pitfalls, thus requiring careful planning and continuous expert counsel.

Recapitalizing and Reorganizing Corporations

If the Treasury Department does not provide the prospective rule changes which would preserve some of the advantages of multiple surtax exemptions, existing corporate groups organized to benefit from the exemption rules may find it desirable to reorganize. For example, the concentration of ownership among a group of corporations may have been satisfactory when full multiple surtax exemptions were available but inadequate to qualify the group to file consolidated returns.

Because any change made in corporate structure entails a transfer of assets in one form or another, the change is likely to produce gains or losses, since assets inevitably do not have a constant value. In order to avoid having to pay taxes upon any gains that result from reorganization transactions, taxpayers must comply with the requirements for tax-free reorganizations. Federal income tax law provides for tax-free reorganizations on the principle that in strengthening the corporation such reorganizations benefit the economy at large, coupled with the concept that paper profits should not be taxed.

Any change in a corporation is regarded as a reorganization, and thus meticulous planning is required in order to insure that the change will remain tax-free. Even the initial incorporation of a previously existent partnership or sole propietorship must allow for compliance with reorganization tax rules in order to minimize taxes and, of course, the acquisition of an existing corporation by another corporation has tax features which fall under the rules for tax-free reorganizations.

Tax-free reorganizations are particularly appropriate for increasing ownership concentration to the necessary 80 percent level needed for a corporate group to be considered an "affiliated" group, and thus eligible for the tax advantages of filing consolidated returns. Thus, no gain or loss is recognized by either the transferor or the corporation if property (including money) is transferred to a corporation for stock if the transferor immediately thereafter owns 80 percent of all voting power and 80 percent of the total shares of all other classes of stock.

Without the protection of the tax-free reorganization rules, such shifts of ownership among a group of related corporations could result in significant tax effects, because of prior changes in value in the stock transferred.

The tax rules for reorganization and recapitalization are also important where a new restaurant is to be purchased for adding to an existing group. A basic requirement for effecting such a purchase tax-free is that the transaction must be an exchange of stock for stock so that the stockholders of the acquiring corporation retain a proprietary interest in the acquired corporation, in the form of voting stock.

In acquiring a corporation under a tax-free reorganization, the acquirers must develop a thorough familiarity with accounting methods in use, valuation of assets, any loss carryforwards available and other tax attributes of the acquired corporation. The value of the assets at the time of the acquisition will determine the amount of gain that will be subject to tax when those assets are subsequently disposed of, and thus the tax advantages gained initially could be more than offset by large tax liabilities which might be incurred when assets are later sold.

Tax-free reorganizations can also be important in preparation for going public and insolvency liquidations. When stock is to be offered for public sale in one corporation representing ownership of the whole operation, reorganization is frequently necessary. Compliance with tax-free reorganization rules in insolvency reorganizations under the Chandler Act can minimize the tax consequences.

Recapitalization frequently becomes desirable for various business reasons, and it can be accomplished tax free if the rules are met. Recapitalization was described in one court decision as a "reshuffling of a capital structure within the framework of an existing corporation," and usually entails the replacing of one kind of stock with another. The issuance of a senior security for a junior security, such as bonds for common stock, is least likely to be accorded tax-free status. Exchanges of securities of comparable seniority may sometimes qualify, but the exchanges of junior securities for senior securities seem to be most assured of tax-free status; preferred stocks for bonds or common stock for preferred stock.

OWN OR LEASE DECISIONS

In establishing a new restaurant, the owners need to consider whether it is more favorable to own property outright or under a sale-leaseback arrangement.

Leaseback

Leaseback arrangements have both tax and financing advantages. Where property is sold and then leased back, the owner can deduct rent as an expense against business income. The deduction is higher than if the property is owned, because under a mortgage loan, only the interest—not amortization of the mortgage principal—would be deductible.

The sale-leaseback can also be a financing device where the owner is short on capital, because by selling the property, he realizes capital and yet by leasing it back, he retains use of the property.

In addition to increased working capital and high tax deductions, sale-leaseback arrangements have other advantages. For example; credit restrictions may be less stringent when a business is operating with a lease rather than a mortgage—under which he naturally has a much higher absolute liability.

Sale-leaseback transactions must be carefully structured in order to avoid being disqualified by the Treasury, and they must meet various criteria, such as reasonable sales price, reasonable rental terms, etc.

Sales and leasebacks between related parties are particularly carefully scrutinized by the Treasury. The best approach is for the owner to establish a trust of at least ten-years' duration to hold the property for the family member and to name an independent trustee, so that the taxpayer cannot be deemed to have effective control over the property. In turn, the trustee should have a written lease with the tenant and the lease should provide for clearly reasonable rent and other terms. Under such circumstances, appraisals from duly qualified appraisers can be useful documentation for purposes of justifying favorable tax treatment.

Direct Ownership

In obtaining the tax and financing advantages of leaseback arrangements, the owner sacrifices the right to deduct property taxes, interest, and depreciation. In some communities and under some circumstances, the combination of various local real estate and personal property taxes, interest, and depreciation can yield more favorable overall tax results for direct ownership.

The timing of income and deductions can be an important factor in considering whether to own or leaseback. While the rent deduction is relatively uniform from year to year, both interest on the mortgage and depreciation are heavily concentrated in the early years. Thus, retaining title to property, rather than selling it and leasing it back, provides much more substantial tax shelter in a business's early years.

Circumstances for which owning rather than leasing may be particularly favorable are:

1. Adequate start up and working capital (which means that a sale-leaseback is not needed to finance operations).
2. High income against which the early depreciation and interest deductions and initial losses can be offset.
3. Maximum flexibility in the current or carryover deductibility of losses.

It can be seen that the form of organization and the owners' overall financial condition can play a significant role in own-or-lease decisions. Flexibility in using multiple corporations would be reduced if property is leased. Conversely, if a corporation or corporations are established for the real estate and buildings owned by a restaurant operation, high expense deductions in the initial years for interest and depreciation might result in significant losses. If the group of corporations are operating on the use of multiple surtax exemptions, however, the losses would not be applicable against profits in the other corporations. They might also exceed the limits upon loss carryforward applicable to an individual corporation.

The same amount of tax deductions for losses in a partnership, sole proprietorship, or affiliated corporate group's consolidated return might be more favorable. Where the sole proprietor or members of a partnership have high income from other sources, the deductions might be particularly valuable.

DEPRECIATION

Property used in a trade or business, or which is held for the production of income, is depreciable where its use may be expected to be ultimately exhausted. Thus, land is not depreciable, since it is regarded as of enduring value and not expected to lose its basic utility. To be depreciable, property must have a limited life which can thus be measured and apportioned according to various methods over the period of its use.

Deductions against income for depreciation usually apply to the owner of the property, but where a lease is suitably worded, the lessor acquires the right to claim depreciation. However, he is limited to straight-line depreciation (an equal amount each year for the property's useful life). Hence, only the owner can use accelerated methods of depreciation (which concentrate the bulk of the deductions in the early years of the property's useful life).

The number of years over which property is depreciable is determined either by IRS guidelines or by the facts of the individual case. Taxpayers can use a shorter useful life than those established by the guidelines if they can successfully demonstrate that the shorter life is appropriate for the particular property.

Depreciation of a building does not necessarily have to be based on the useful life of the building as a whole. Taxpayers have the option to use components parts depreciation in which each individual component of the building is assigned its own useful life. These lives may vary from as little as three years for painting, to 12 or 15 years for heating facilities, to 30 or 40 years for the basic shell of the building. The "component parts" method frequently results in more rapid depreciation than if the building is treated as a whole, but it is applied only to totally new property and calls for highly detailed records of the costs of the individual components and a need to justify the cost basis allocated to each component.

For small businesses, an additional depreciation allowance on newly acquired tangible personal property, whether new or used, may be deducted in the first year the property is put in use. The additional allowance is 20 percent of the cost, in addition to the regular depreciation determined on the balance of the cost. This additional "bonus" depreciation is not applicable to buildings or structural components, such as plumbing or heating fixtures, and the deduction is limited to $10,000 cost for qualifying property, thus limiting the deduction to $2,000 (20 percent of $10,000). The property must also be depreciated over a period of six or more years to qualify for the bonus.

For restaurants, this additional first-year depreciation allowance can be a significant benefit, because it applies to various items of property, such as refrigerators, air-conditioners and other equipment items which are not structural components of the building.

Saving Taxes by Properly Using the Investment Tax Credit

The 7 percent investment tax credit for the acquisition of depreciable property is another important tax benefit available for certain depreciable property other than a building and its structural components. The investment tax credit applies in the first year the property is placed in service and in order to qualify for the full 7 percent, the property must have useful life of 7 years or more. For property with useful lives of 3 to 6 years, smaller prorated tax credits are allowed. Lives used for investment credit must be the same as for depreciation purposes.

The 7 percent investment tax credit is available only to the owner of the property, but as a practical matter of economics, he may pass the benefits of the credit through to a lessee.

A Handy Tax Tip!

Even though you could use a five-year life on new restaurant equipment that you purchased, you might find it better tax-wise to use a seven-year life and qualify the equipment for maximum investment credit, as well as for additional first-year depreciation.

Finally, when depreciable property is sold, the sale may generate additional taxes to the extend that the sales price results in "recapture" of depreciation deductions previously taken. For example, if a $10,000 property has been depreciated by $5,000 and is then sold for $7,000, $2,000 would be taxed to the seller as ordinary income. No recapture tax consequences would apply if the sale price were $5,000 or less.

PRE-OPENING COSTS

Before a restaurant is opened, the owners normally incur significant costs. These include investigation expenses before a decision is made, preparatory expenses to set up the business once the decision is made, organizational expenses (attorneys' and accountants' fees) and operating expenses (such as rent, utilities, and salaries) incurred before the restaurant is actually open and generating an income.

The guiding tax principal is that expenses deductible from income are those incurred while "engaged in carrying on a trade or business," and therefore expenses incurred earlier are generally regarded as non-deductible capital expense.

With careful planning, however, at least some of these expenses may be structured so as to qualify for tax deductions. First of all the owners need to start the business as soon as possible, in order to obtain expense deductions for beginning rent, utilities, and salaries as soon as possible. Second, pre-opening expenses should be structured in a way that they will be associated with particular depreciable property so that they are deductible over a period of years as part of that property's acquisition costs. Expenses not directly related to a depreciable asset with a determinable useful life are deemed capital expenditures for an intangible asset and may not be amortized.

The form of organization can be important in this context, because corporations are allowed capital expenditure deductions for organization expenses, but partnerships (or sole proprietorships) are not. Deductions are allowed to corporations for: "Legal services incident to the organization of the corporation, such as drafting the corporate charter, bylaws, minutes of organizational meetings, terms of original certificates and the like, necessary accounting services, expenses of temporary directors and organizational meetings of directors or stockholders, and fees paid to the state of incorporation." Expense deductions may be spread over a period of up to five years, at the discretion of the corporation.

The corporate form has the added advantage that investigatory expenses incurred for a project which is never started are still deductible because the corporation is a going business. If an individual, on the other hand, abandons a contemplated project, his expenses are not deductible. An exception is available for individuals who are engaged in the business of acquiring ventures for resale. Although such an individual may never "engage in the business" which he explored and abandoned, the activity was part of his overall business of seeking business ventures and thus qualifies for deduction.

TAX TREATMENT OF RESTAURANT TIPS AND EMPLOYEE MEALS

A significant problem in the case of the restaurant industry is the tax treatment of employee tip income. While the restaurant employer is not required to withhold the *employer's* share of Social Security taxes on employee tips because they are not considered "wages" for Social Security and withholding tax purposes, the employee must include all tips in his taxable income. In the case of a waiter or waitress who receives more than $20 per month in tip income, however, this tip income must be reported to the restaurant employer who is required to withhold the *employee's* share of Social Security taxes as well as federal income taxes on such tips.

The Internal Revenue Service has provided the forms which follow to assist the restaurant employee in compiling a daily record of tips as well as reporting his monthly total of tips received to the government, respectively.

DAILY RECORD OF TIPS

EMPLOYER'S NAME

MONTH _____ YEAR _____

Date	Tips	Date	Tips
1	$	17	$
2		18	
3		19	
4		20	
5		21	
6		22	
7		23	
8		24	
9		25	
10		26	
11		27	
12		28	
13		29	
14		30	
15		31	
16		Total $	

Form 4070A (1–66)

Figure 10-1. Daily Record of Tips.

Similar tax problems are encountered in connection with the tax treatment of meals furnished by the restaurant to its employees. If meals and/or lodging are furnished to the restaurant employee for the convenience of the employer, they are not regarded as taxable income to the employee, so long as they are furnished on the restaurant employer's business premises (in the case of meals) and the employee is required (in the case of lodging) to accept the lodging on the employer's business premises "as a condition of his employment."

Form **4070** (Jan. 1966) U.S. Treasury Department Internal Revenue Service	**EMPLOYEE'S REPORT ON TIPS**	Social Security Number
Employee's name and address		
Employer's name and address		
Month or shorter period in which tips were received		Amount
from ...., 19......., to ...., 19........		$............................
Signature		Date

Figure 10-2. Employee's Report on Tips.

HOW TO REALIZE REAL ESTATE TAX BENEFITS
IN THE RESTAURANT BUSINESS

We have already examined, in Chapter 6, the deductibility of real estate taxes as an expense for federal income tax purposes and their classification as rent where the land is leased. In addition, one very important point must be made. Where the land is leased and the lessee constructs the restaurant building, a benefit is usually derived for real estate tax purposes in that the valuation assessment of the improved land resulting from the building's construction is delayed until the following assessment date. This results from the fact that the fee interest in the land rests in another person and the taxing authority undergoes a time lag in matching the two separate parties together.

On the other hand, construction of a building on land recently purchased by the taxpayer would normally result in immediate reassessment and inclusion of the building's assessed valuation in the tax base.

HOW TO SAVE TAXES AND IMPROVE EMPLOYEE MORALE
THROUGH A BONUS PROGRAM AND PROFIT-SHARING PLANS

Costs and headaches involved in recruiting and training new employees can be reduced—and work performance improved—with a bonus plan, especially one based on length of service. There's also an added plus—the employer obtains a tax deduction for all such bonus payments.

Employees think more carefully about making a job shift when a bonus program is tied in with length of employment.

Participation in the plan is based on length of service with, of course, the largest payments to the longest-term employees, in accordance with their jobs.

Example:

One midwest restaurant chain sets aside 30 percent of net profits each month. Three years' employment is required for full participation in the plan, with lesser amounts for workers with less tenure. Other restaurants require longer terms of service for full participation.

The payment formula should be kept as simple as possible—based on length of service, salary, and work performance. Complicated formulas can create trouble and destroy the program's effectiveness.

As noted earlier in Chapter 4, from an employee motivation standpoint, it is very important to sell this type of bonus program to the employee. In addition, the restaurant's employees should know in advance what is required in order to obtain maximum benefits under the bonus program, along with those factors which can act to reduce the size of individual bonuses (such as deficient performance, unexplained absences, prolonged tardiness, or other employee deficiencies). It is also a good idea to tie such a bonus program in with the profits of the applicable restaurant operating unit so that the amount paid to the employees is not equal each year. From a psychological standpoint, this device makes the bonus payments appear less like regular pay, but also, from a practical standpoint, allows reduction in the size of such bonuses in a year when profits fall off. Another device which has proved to be very successful is a qualified pension and profit-sharing plan which permits the employer to obtain a current tax deduction for contributions made to the plan without the employee being taxed until subsequent distributions are received by him after retirement. Under the applicable provisions of the Internal Revenue Code, such a plan must benefit employees in general and must cover at least a specific percentage of employees or a classification of employees without discriminating in favor of officers, shareholders, supervisors, or highly-compensated employees. Generally speaking, in the case of profit-sharing plans, the annual deduction is limited based on a percentage of compensation; however, contributions in excess of these limits may be carried over and deducted in succeeding taxable years by the employer.

Suffice to say, profit-sharing plans can go a long way toward boosting restaurant employee morale, incentive, job interest, and ultimate performance.

Some Cases in Point:

The February 1973 issue of "Restaurant World" (Vol. 2, No. 5) cites the following examples of restaurant profit-sharing incentive plans:

"—A Pacific northwest restaurant has used a program of flat payments to food preparation employees for controlling food and labor costs. Payments range from $15 and $20 to dishwashers and kitchen helpers to $50 to chef.

—A California restaurant pays 3 percent of net profits to head chef, 1½ percent to other cooks, 1 percent to cashier, ½ percent to waitresses.

—A midwestern restaurant makes payments ranging from 7 percent to 15 percent of base pay to employees, with attendance, punctuality, and other factors involved in qualifying for money."

CHAPTER 11

How Industry Trends Affect the Restaurateur

CHAPTER CAPSULE PREVIEW

Every trend is an opportunity at the beginning, and a pitfall as its development begins to level off. Those on the bandwagon early benefit substantially. Those who are late to recognize a major trend incur the risk that it has become so much a part of the mainstream that saturation has occured.

Thus, keeping a finger on the pulse of the industry and responding quickly to developing trends may be one of the restaurant operator's most valuable intangible assets.

It has been said that change has become the American way of life. As a result, successful business operations increasingly have come to depend upon structured planning to keep pace with change by anticipating the practical effects of trends. The earlier a business considers developing trends, the less the likelihood that substantial new developments will catch management unprepared.

No industry is immune to change, and restaurants, particularly, need to be sensitive to trends affecting their operations. These may be considered in three principal categories:

1. Sales, costs, and earnings trends which affect the realization of profits from the market.
2. Socio-economic trends which affect the size and character of the market.
3. Trends in operational methods.

Trends may emphasize financial, marketing, or operational considerations, but in the final analysis, all three considerations enter into every trend, because finance, marketing, and operational methods are interdependent.

For example, restaurant franchising, which has been a major trend in recent years, combines all three factors in a unique way. Franchising is a device for convenient financing of a particular new restaurant in a particular location. It is also a valuable form of mass marketing, establishing a national name which has a substantially greater leverage than would the individual outlets with separate names. And it is also a highly efficient streamlining of operational methods through the use of advanced equipment and layout, standardized for further savings through bulk purchases and mass production.

Thus, restaurant operators need to observe the flow of developments in the industry from the multiple perspective of financial trends, marketing, and operations.

FINANCIAL TRENDS

Statistics on how the industry as a whole is performing from year to year can be a valuable benchmark for the individual restaurant to assess its own performance. Performance variations over a period of time may be exclusively a function of the individual restaurant's own operations, but to a degree, they are likely also to be somewhat in phase with trends in the industry as a whole. By comparing detailed operational data with data for similar restaurants, and for the industry as a whole, management can estimate how well they're doing in light of prevailing trends.

The comparisons will show whether the restaurant is outperforming or underperforming comparable restaurants and will identify the operational areas in which the principal differences occur. These differences may result from fundamental operational advantages or disadvantages, or they may signify that management is doing something particularly well or particularly poorly. For example, if a given financial ratio is consistently less favorable than other restaurants, investigation may show an operational problem, and eliminating that problem may increase profitability. Checking performance against industry standards in principal financial areas is a valuable tool for diagnosing various operational problems.

LKH & H Annual Restaurant Study

For the purpose of reviewing and analyzing financial trends, restaurant operators have the Annual Restaurant Study issued by Laventhol Krekstein Horwath & Horwath. The LKHH Study, which is based upon an annual survey of a carefully selected sample of restaurants and presents summary profit and loss ratios for major income and expense items, plus statistics on net income, occupation costs, sales, direct expense, and prime cost, is analyzed in depth in Chapter 9.

The LKHH Annual Restaurant Study, as seen in Chapter 9, classifies restaurants into "neighborhood, center city, and suburban." It also distinguishes restaurants serving both food and beverage from restaurants serving only food. Such classifications not only facilitate comparisons of a restaurant's financial performance with similar restaurants, but also permit the examination of market and operational trends among the different types of restaurant operations.

For example, socio-economic trends have clearly led to a population shift from center city to suburbs, with a comparable change in restaurant markets. Year-to-year changes in the report's financial statistics for each category reflect some of the consequences of the shift and provide a valuable guide to planning restaurant operations for the medium and long term. Viewing statistics from this perspective can be of great assistance in considering whether to expand, retrench, or perhaps, open up in a new location.

MARKET TRENDS

A profile of restaurant operations today compared with 20, 40, or 50 years ago would show striking differences because changing life styles, prosperity, and customs change people's tastes and habits in eating out. Some of these changes are clearly signaled by conspicuous socio-economic and demographic changes. For example, the massive development of interstate highways across the nation created a clear need for restaurants to serve travelers' needs. Similarly, the mass exodus to the suburbs transferred a substantial restaurant demand from the center city to the suburbs and at the same time changed the character of the cuisine and service people expected.

Other changes, however, are more subtle. For example, the public tends to cycles of trading up and trading down in their eating out habits. In some periods, large numbers of people have shifted from low-priced informal service—cafeteria or counter style—to medium-low-priced sit-down service. In other periods, they have shifted from Howard Johnson style restaurants to the low-priced hamburger chains. In recent years, the Longchamps chain in New York quietly closed all but one of its luxury restaurants and opened, with fanfare, a new Steak and Brew chain, trading down to tap an emerging new demand. To some extent, these trends can be mutually reinforcing: trading up for some segments of the market while trading down for family dining. Under such circumstances, restaurants with cuisine, price, and service between these two alternatives may find their patronage falling.

Our discussion of market trends in the restaurant industry would be incomplete without considering the following excerpt from "The Importance of Being Greedy," in the "Modern Living" column of the October 23, 1972 issue of *Time:*

> In Downey, Calif., a man in his early 20's went through the prime-ribs line seven times at Marmac's, a restaurant that provides an unlimited amount of roast beef for only $3.50. If the evening was a total loss for Marmac's, it was for the customer too. He wound up in a hospital, having his stomach pumped out. But less than a week later, he was back in the beef line at the same restaurant.
>
> The Downey episode is just one of many similar instances of gluttony that

occur daily across the U.S. in an ever-increasing number of "all-you-can-eat" restaurants. Apart from regulars, like the dainty, little old lady who routinely gobbles 20 pieces of fried chicken (for only $1.55) on each visit to Shakey's Pizza Parlor in Los Angeles, gluttons have only their appetites in common and are difficult to identify at a glance. Manager Edward White, of Manhattan's Stockholm Restaurant (unlimited smorgasbord for $6.95), still shudders when he remembers the tall, beautifully groomed woman who ravaged his 85-dish buffet. With exquisite technique but total nondiscrimination, she forked slabs of roast beef atop heaps of shrimp, added globs of Swedish meatballs and salted herring, then ladled a quart or so of Russian dressing over the mess. "It looked like an exploding volcano," says White, "and she repeated three or four times." On her next visit, some customers sickened by the sight of the orgy, began to complain, and White politely told the woman she was welcome no longer.

Considerably easier to detect was the mob of high school kids who descended on a Howard Johnson's restaurant in Spring Valley, N.Y. They arrived on chicken night (unlimited amount for $1.69) and devoured 360 pieces of chicken (about 90 lbs.), along with salad and rolls, before vanishing into the night. Another easy-to-spot glutton was the "gigantic man" who waddled into a Sir George's Smorgasbord House branch in the San Fernando Valley. He opened with 2 lbs. of salad, then reduced a chicken to rubble, inhaled two plates of roast beef, and washed it all down with milk. Then he thoughtfully wiped his plate clean with half a loaf of bread, paid his $2.50 check and left. (Inexplicably, he passed up dessert.) Jack LeFever, a vice president of Sir George, while denying that the huge customer was responsible, reports that most of the restaurants in the chain have since stopped advertising its all-you-can-eat come-on. "The policy remains the same," he says, "But we don't plug it any more."

The supreme challenge to gluttons is posed by the $10 Fiesta dinner offered by the Club El Bianco on Chicago's Southwest Side. The three- to four-hour Super Bowl of Gluttony begins with appetizers (bean salad, salami and pepperoni) and a vast antipasto tray, continues with soup, tossed salad, stuffed peppers, ribs, eggplant parmigiana, veal scallopini, chicken cacciatore and piles of pasta. Dessert includes pastries, fruit and cookies, followed by a nut cart. If anyone complains that he is still hungry, Manager Peter Bianco, Jr. has a secret weapon that few could stomach: a huge submarine sandwich topped by a "Champion" trophy. "Nobody's finished the whole thing yet," says Bianco. "If anyone really has, he hasn't lived to talk about it."

Most restaurateurs suffer silently under a gourmand's assault, but they all frown on one particular variant, the "Takeout Artist." At the Stockholm, for example, Manager White caught one soberly dressed couple making off with 4 lbs. of shrimp in a concealed plastic bag after they had finished dining. When White intercepted them, both complained angrily—and the woman dumped the smuggled shrimp on the floor at his feet. A pair of California counter-culturists astounded the manager of Shakey's Pizza Parlor with the huge amounts of food they were putting away—until he found an excuse to open their guitar case and found 200 pieces of chicken stashed inside.

Still, the all-you-can-eat theme keeps spreading, and profits keep rolling in. Explains Larry Ellman, whose 37-unit Steak and Brew chain offers unlimited amounts of salad, drinks, and bread with a modestly priced entree: "The person who eats too much is a fantastic advertisement for us, because he'll tell other people about his great buy." Fifteen Steak and Brew establishments are on the drawing boards, and further expansion seems to be limited only by the output of world agriculture. "We've never run out of food," boasts Robert Gladstone, manager of one of the Steak and Brews. "We let them eat as long as they want to." (Reprinted by permission from TIME, The Weekly News Magazine: Copyright Time, Inc.)

Finally, the following selected excerpts from an article by Eleanore Carruth, "Restaurateurs Need Some New Recipes for Survival," published in the September 1972 issue of *Spectrum '72* (The Journal of the National Association of Hotel-Motel Accountants, Inc.), provide additional meaningful data in properly scrutinizing trends in the restaurant industry.

When the Colony closed its doors last December after half a century of dedication to feeding in style the rich, the wellborn, and the famous (and the drop-ins on society), the news was fit to print not only on the first page of the *New York Times* but also in the *Daily News*, and it became fare for the national television news shows. One did not have to be a habitue of that venerable Manhattan landmark to feel some sense of shock—even of loss—at the notion that the event might indeed signal, as proprietor Gene Cavallero Jr. declared and the headlines proclaimed, "the end of an era."

What was closing up restaurateur Cavallero, however, was not so much the end of society—the inference that the *News* regarded as proper intelligence for *hoi polloi*—but rather the new and general troubles of the dining-out business, be it for society, for businessmen, for tourists, even for some *hoi polloi*. For the Colony was only the latest and most publicized of a lengthy list of recent restaurant casualties in the preeminent American city of the gustatory and culinary arts. Over the past year or so, New York has lost any number of good and well-known restaurants—among them Cafe Chauveron, Cavanagh's, Maud Chez Elle, Toots Shor, and Voisin. A good many others are known to be in trouble, and the guessing is that some of them may fold in the near future. "It's like an epidemic," says Leon Leanides, owner of the highly successful Coach House in Greenwich Village. "When you know business is off all over town, you figure you've been lucky so far, but your time will come."

FALLING BY VARIOUS ROADSIDES

What is happening to the restaurant business in New York has been happening, to one degree or another, in most of the fifteen major cities across the U.S., according to leading restaurateurs and observers of the dining scene who replied to a special *Fortune* survey. The business has been through a shake-out in almost every town, and for most operators, 1971 was the worst period in a long time, until the tag end of the year. Many individual owners reported sales declines of 5 to 15 percent from 1970, which itself was generally a poor year. Profits, of course, were hit much harder, and there were some losses. Not many were able to say that business last year was better than ever, and even most of them felt a pinch on profits.

A number of well-known establishments have meanwhile fallen by various roadsides. In San Francisco, for example, Lupo's went out after thirty-six years in business, Ruggero's was closed for nonpayment of taxes, and La Gare was sold to a chain. In Detroit, the $3-million Mauna Loa was the largest of six top-service restaurants to fold in 1971 (two others in Grosse Pointe changed hands). Childe Harold, among Washington's most expensive dining places, has turned into a steak bar, and some notable (though not famous) names have disappeared even in New Orleans as well as in places like Indianapolis, Atlanta, and San Diego.

Things are not equally tough all over, to be sure; for example, not in Houston. Moreover, there has been a turn for the better lately. The last quarter of 1971, generally speaking, showed a sharp upturn continuing over into January of 1972. There are optimists who feel that once the economy regains prosperity, the industry's troubles will be largely over. They argue from experience that restaurants, being a kind of luxury affair, are early to suffer in recession and slow to recover when the economy picks up again. The behavior of the economy in the past three years or so has been the worst possible one for restaurants: a prolonged, if mild, recession, followed by a slow and sluggish recovery, in which restaurants have had a poor chance to get going—until perhaps now.

But the industry that provides fine dining is also plagued almost everywhere by some long-term problems—the economics of rising costs and prices, complicated by increasing unionization and taxation, and the social problems associated with the decay of the cities, to name a few. Many practitioners of the culinary arts, for all their usual entrepreneurial ebullience, assert persuasively that if they had it to do all over again they would not now start a restaurant. Among the fanciers of fine food there is a noticeable apprehension about the future. Jack Shelton, who regularly reviews the San Francisco restaurant scene for 12,000 subscribers to his newsletter, recently voiced the common concern. "The truly best restaurants will hold their own," he said, "but I don't think we'll ever return to the opulence of the past." Richard A. Blumenthal, executive vice president of Restaurant Associates, which launched such spectacular New York dining establishments as the Four Seasons, the Forum of the Twelve Caesars, and La Fonda del Sol, now says flatly, "Good-to-great restaurants are not the best business to be in . . . ."

Luxury restaurants, moreover, were very good business over these years, especially during the prosperous Sixties. They were the volume producers in a highly fragmented industry. In 1967 there were only about 700 restaurants in the country with annual sales of $1 million or more, according to the U.S. Census of Business, and 2,800 with a volume of between $500,000 and $1 million. Even with inflation pushing some of the latter above the million-dollar mark, there are probably not many more than a thousand establishments of that size in the U.S. today. Not all of them are great or even good by exalted gastronomic standards. What makes success depends so much, after all, on local circumstance and tradition. So some of the big ones are unexpected establishments in some unlikely places: In Detroit, Joe Muer's a seafood place, and the London Chop House, specializing in Continental cuisine. In Milwaukee, two German eateries, Mader's and Karl Ratzsch's, and a hybrid, Frenchy's, serving steak and seafood. In San Diego, Lubach's (fish and steak) and Bali Hai.

Other million-dollar or more eateries include the Tower in San Antonio, Look's Sir Loin in Houston, and the Jockey Club in Washington, D.C. Three in Los Angeles are Le Bistro, Chasen's and La Scala. The venerable Bookbinders's in Philadelphia racked up $3 million in sales last year. In the restaurant towns, of course, there are a large number of high-volume restaurants that do indeed specialize in fine cuisine—La Bourgogne and Ernie's in San Francisco, the grand old names of New Orleans, and, of course, numerous winners in New York, which has the greatest concentration of fine, high-volume establishments in the country. Among those over the mark last year were "21," La Côte Basque, La Grenouille, The Four Seasons, Le Pavillon, the Forum of the Twelve Caesars. Sardis, Luchow's, Quo Vadis, and the now defunct Colony. There are even more in the group just below the million level.

Even in the good years it was a very tough business indeed. Those talented restaurateurs who achieved both high volume and high quality took for granted a work week that would stagger most executives. Henri Soule, for instance, scarcely ever took a day off from Le Pavillon. "You don't have to be gone for a week or even a day," he once explained. "Turn your back on those *types* for only a few minutes and right away they start to slow down." The presence of the host on the premises, moreover, was essential for developing a cadre of customers who become "regulars" because they have a sense of personal identification with the owner.

Total dedication is no assurance of success, however, for as restaurateurs are fond of pointing out, there seems to be a kind of mystique to the business. "You see a swarm of mosquitoes all going to one light on a marquee," muses the Coach House's Leanides. "I often wonder why they don't go to the others. I don't know. And that's the way it is with restaurants."

If a restaurant clicked, it could produce more than a good living for the owner. If he had a million-dollar operation going, he was probably drawing, in salary and profits, 10 to 15 percent of the gross, or between $100,000 and $150,000 in this case. Since the restaurateur is loath to show much of a profit ("Why pay the tax twice?"), he may then distribute hefty bonuses to himself and to key members of the organization. Needless to say, there haven't been many bonuses or even fat salaries around lately, and some owners wonder if those lush days will ever return.

The dominant note of the blues that owners are crying these days is: "Labor is killing the restaurant business." It's a long way from that time in the Thirties when waiters and captains often worked just for tips and sometimes paid to get the job. "For years this industry lived off underpaid labor," says Blumenthal of Restaurant Associates. "Now we are finding out what the economics of the business really are."

For fine restaurants, rising labor costs loom as potential disaster, because a large proportion of their costs are built into the preparation of elegant dishes served in style, and their break-even point is high. But if a restaurateur bases his prices on his costs at an assumed volume, he can make a very high profit if business booms. For every dollar of sales beyond the assumed norm, his profit could increase by 40 or 50 cents.

Conversely, when volume slips, profits go down very much faster than sales. What has been happening in the past few years is that costs have risen, and volume has lagged or declined. And labor costs have been rising faster than almost anything else. It is, after all, at the lower end of the wage scale that the largest advances have been made in recent years, reflecting both the realities of the labor market and the rising tide of unionism in the lower ranks of the labor force . . . .

Fine restaurants represent only a small fraction of the $46-billion industry that feeds Americans away from home, and yet it would be a pity to lose the grace note they add to the quality of life. As something of a national asset, perhaps they deserve, for instance, some special relief from mounting taxes and high rents. But certainly restaurateurs must face harsh new realities. "A restaurateur used to put on a suit to greet the guests, test the consommé, look at the fish eyes, and inspect the meat," says Richard Blumenthal. "Today that's child's play and only part of the business. Now you also have to read the *Wall Street Journal.*"

(Reprinted from material originally appearing in the March 1972 issue of *Fortune* magazine by special permission; ©1972, Time, Inc.).

Population Mobility

A major trend influencing restaurant operations today is increasing population mobility. People not only move more frequently from city to city and state to state, but within a given community they move from one neighborhood to another as family fortunes improve.

Growing mobility and growing income are mutually reinforcing factors which influence operations doubly. Mobility influences the size and character of the market in any given location, both favorably and unfavorably. And greater family incomes generate an increase in disposable income. The increase in discretionary income is more rapid, after basic necessities are taken care of, with a greatly increased economic capability of dining out.

The impulse to dine out is reinforced by a high incidence of working wives. Since they do not wish to cook, they have a greater tendency to dine out than wives who do not work. Even such a basically remote factor as the woman's liberation movement can have an influence, because the working wife will feel less obligation to follow the traditional housewife role.

In turn, the children of working mothers learn to eat out early, and their tendency is reinforced by eating out on their own for school lunches, during recreational activities, etc. Both the example set for them by parents who take them out to dinner more frequently than in prior generations and more money of their own dispose them naturally to eat out. The net effect is to condition a whole generation to eating out as a way of life.

Informality

Socio-economic changes can lead to qualitative as well as quantitative changes. People who patronized one kind of restaurant in the center city prefer different styles in suburban areas, where people prefer restaurants which accommodate their necessarily less formal dress.

Not only have public tastes shifted to greater informality in surburban settings, but this preference has been carried back into the center city. Informality and convenience have been an increasing keynote of successful restaurant operations in recent years. People want familiar foods, including finger foods. They like making their own salads. They accept the convenience of frozen foods and instant coffee. Generally rejected by one generation, these things are routinely emphasized by the next as a basic preference.

Carry-out foods are in greater demand, and people generally want less exotic and less expensive foods. They prefer to dine out more frequently and less elaborately. At the same time, many previously exotic foods, served only in specialty restaurants, have been domesticated, and are routinely served even in quick-service restaurants. Pizza may never replace ham and swiss on rye, yet it has long since ceased to be an unfamiliar foreign food. And today, restaurants as American as apple pie offer Mexican, Italian, and other specialties alongside cheeseburgers and bacon and eggs. The durability of the assimilation process can be seen by a dish like goulash, which many Americans order routinely with no awareness that it was once an exotic dish available only in formal Hungarian restaurants in a few large metropolitan areas.

The public's desire for informality has a substantial influence on a restaurant's whole operations. The decor and service must be compatible with the cuisine, and the facilities can be significantly simpler. Informality permits disposable dishes and flatware, which in turn eliminates warewashing and handling. Serviceable formica replaces formidable oak paneling. Plushness is not only unnecessary but a disadvantage with a clientele that wishes the comforts of home, not the adornment and panoply of a royal court.

The result is smaller space needs, lower equipment costs and smaller staff requirements. (Disposables, of course, increase garbage handling requirements, and as their use increases, restaurants will face some substantial ecological problems for which final solutions are not yet available.)

Overall, the trend to informality leads to distinctly simpler operations—which means less costly operations.

OPERATIONAL TRENDS

As public tastes and markets change, restaurant operational methods also change, partially as a response to external conditions and partially as a purely internal measure of improving profitability.

Restaurant operators are affected by trends in technology, labor, payroll, systems, food supplies, etc.

Technological Trends

Recent years have seen steady improvements in equipment and techniques, and these may be expected to continue. Processing, shipping, and storage equipment are all continually refined, improving restaurant efficiency and changing staffing and scheduling methods.

Technological improvements occur both outside and inside. Suppliers making technological improvements are able to offer restaurants superior service, lower prices, or more conveniently packaged supplies. Technological improvements in equipment used by restaurants enable them to effect economies in their own operations through labor-saving, better layout, smaller space requirements, etc.

Advances in electronic data processing also offer advantages to restaurants. Computers can be used for ordering, planning, and recordkeeping. With the development of minicomputers and the wide expansion of services offered by computer service bureaus, using the computer is practicable now even by relatively small operations. Some restaurants are already using computers effectively, but the trend is nowhere near its maturity, and, therefore, the future should hold significant advantages in this area for most restaurant operators.

Developments in the field of the behavioral sciences offer prospects of benefiting restaurants. Increased understanding of workers' motivations and attitudes leads to new and better ways of combating boredom through greater work involvement, and to ways of reducing frictions that tend to retard efficiency when it develop among employees.

Labor Trends

The availability of part-time workers in our society is on the increase. Married women, working mothers with children in school, and students are all in the market for part-time jobs with flexible hours. At the same time, restaurants have a growing need for flexible staffing. Simpler operations in the face of the new informality and the increasing use of convenience foods are just two examples of trends which affect labor needs, generally reducing kitchen staff requirements and off-hour preparation. Clearly, many restaurants should plan for increased reliance on part-time workers.

This trend will make significant changes in methods of recruiting, training, and supervising employees, and in many cases operational methods and systems will need to be suitably modified in order to accommodate differences between part-time and full-time workers.

Payroll Costs

A distinct trend to rising payroll costs must be a matter of major concern to every restaurant. Keeping costs in line is absolutely essential, because when the economy is sluggish, low volume hurts profits, and when the economy is expanding, rising costs and labor shortages can combine to hurt profits significantly.

Cost pressures show no tendency to abate in the short term. Other industries have had a significant effect on the restaurant industry. Chronic competition for workers becomes particularly severe cyclically: in times of prosperity, the scramble to capitalize on that prosperity drives pay rates up, and with high employment, restaurants are forced to the higher price scales.

These competitive factors are reinforced by the trend to improved technology. Many innovations which save labor also reduce the need for the development of particular skills, thus increasing the restaurant's ratio of unskilled labor to skilled labor. If workers are not bound by the possession of a particular skill, they can take work in another industry just as easily as in the restaurant industry. Thus, two different factors combine to drive costs up in the restaurant industry: labor scarcity in general and the industry's own dependence on unskilled labor for which other industries compete.

Changes in minimum wage requirements have tended to drive payroll costs up, and the trend continues. With the high incidence of unskilled labor in restaurants, minimum wage laws have great impact.

Restaurants are affected both by increases in the minimum wage rate and by growing restrictions on the employment of particular categories of workers, such as women, students, etc. In turn, there has been a distinct trend to eliminate exemptions from minimum wage requirements which the industry has traditionally enjoyed.

Growing unionization also exerts pressure on payroll costs. With organized strength behind demands for higher wages, fringe benefits, and improved working conditions, restaurants may expect substantial increases in payroll costs.

While large restaurants and chains are primary targets for unionization, smaller operations are affected both directly and indirectly:

1. Higher rates for organized restaurant workers in a particular community exert a pressure on pay rates demanded by other workers in that community.

2. As a community's larger units are unionized, organizers turn their attention to the employees of smaller indpendent operations.

Pressure on fringe benefit costs could tend to drive payroll costs up also. The restaurant industry lags significantly behind most other industries, and restaurants may have to begin to catch up. Pensions in particular may become significantly more costly, because of legislation likely to be passed during the 1970's requiring compliance with more stringent standards for funding and other factors which will increase annual costs.

The trend to labor-saving devices may be one of the major compensating factors. Increased mechanization of restaurants tends to reduce the labor intensity, and even if unit costs are inevitably driven up, net costs could well be offset by savings from using fewer employees.

To realize these savings, however, restaurants must effectively modify operational systems with the introduction of each new piece of labor-saving equipment. Higher efficiency is critically dependent upon integrating new equipment into the existing equipment configuration at the lowest cost. This not only means capitalizing fully on the labor—saving properties of new equipment, but also revising operational procedures carefully in order to ensure that the smallest amount of labor cost is incurred in using both new and old equipment.

In the face of all the other trends, cost reduction has itself become an important trend, covering the whole spectrum of restaurant operations. Cost reduction methods should be an integrated management policy which systematically considers each facet of operations for improvements which can pare overall costs. This includes the consideration of the whole field of technological improvements from new equipment to layout to procedural innovations, to use of convenience foods, and to good labor relations.

Thus, restaurants, today, face a period of particularly intensive change. They need to introduce new, improved equipment. Each new facility affects the layout, and thus facilities must often be reorganized to maximize efficiency. In turn, new equipment and layout change operational procedures and work assignments and scheduling. Unless systems are carefully thought out to adjust to the basic changes, the restaurant will not realize the full benefit of any labor-saving innovations introduced.

Good employee relations are a key factor here. Changes can be unsettling, and dissatisfaction and turnover lead to lowered productivity. Thus, restaurant operators must consistently maintain good relations with unions and individual employees, both in general and in specific details of operations. Streamlined operations will tend to increase the incidence of monotonous, repetitive work, and supervisors must seek to compensate by rotating responsibilities, giving workers individual attention, etc. A paradox of the trend to using more unskilled labor is that the skills required of the skilled labor that remains may well have to be significantly higher in order to ensure utmost efficiency. Thus, a part (and hopefully a small part) of the savings realized from using unskilled labor may be absorbed by higher supervisory costs.

Convenience Foods

One of the major developments which will influence restaurant operations in the years ahead is the use of convenience foods. They rely both upon improvements in cooking methods and upon rapid reconstitution for serving. As a result of technological improvements, frozen food can be prepared rapidly for serving by eliminating the thawing stage. The equipment uses infra-red heat or high-pressure steam.

In omitting one stage, the process already saves labor, but the saving is even larger, because preparation outside leaves less work to be done on the premises, and that work requires both less skill and less time. Since convenience foods are pre-cooked, ready for serving, chef skills are not needed.

Pre-fabricated meats need no butchers, and as desserts become increasingly available in convenience food form, bakers and pastry chefs can also be eliminated. Since chefs are the highest labor cost in restaurant operations, savings at both the entree and dessert level can be significant.

The use of convenience foods can either reduce or eliminate the need for chefs, depending upon the kind of cuisine offered, with a significant payroll saving, because both pay rates and work hours are lower. By careful staffing and work scheduling, restaurants can even apply some servers' time in the kitchen to heating frozen foods for serving. Training needs are minimal, and as a result servers can productively apply time which would otherwise be idle.

Convenience foods are likely to become an increasingly important factor in restaurant operations. Techniques used for relatively simple kinds of foods are adaptable to more elaborate cuisines, and they could have substantial effects upon restaurants.

Convenience foods are more economical at the processor's level as well as in the restaurant itself. Processors can use labor more efficiently, thus achieving economies of scale. They are also able to operate at a lower overall cost because they are able to locate their kitchens in marginal low-cost areas.

Despite the higher price tag on prefabricated items, their use can cut a restaurant's prime cost. Butchered cuts of meat may cost more than larger sections, but they obviate the need for a butcher on the premises. Frozen foods may cost more than regular foods, but there is less waste from overbuying or overproducing. Unused portions simply remain in the freezer at the end of the day. Pre-cooked items may cost more than uncooked ingredients, but they can be heated and served by unskilled workers, replacing higher-priced chefs.

By requiring fewer people with lesser skills, convenience foods do more than merely reduce the total cost of kitchen labor. They alleviate problems associated with labor shortages, high turnover, and absenteeism. The result is a welcome relief to restaurateurs.

An Interesting Idea!

A group of midwestern hospitals has banded together, for instance, to establish a central food processing plant. Foods and ingredients are processed at the central point, frozen, and then shipped to each member hospital, which can then assemble patient meals, insert its own seasoning and spices—if the individual patient's diet permits them—and prepare tasty meals at low cost.

Such area plants are also a possible development for restaurants in remote areas or sparsely settled regions which depend now on commercial prefabricated foods but which simply do not have enough demand for certain exotic items to order them economically through a food broker. With their own centralized kitchen serving two or more restaurants, the same process can be followed; fresh foods can be prepared, frozen, and shipped to the client restaurants. The long shelf-life that requires the highly criticized use of artificial preservatives in commercially prefabricated foods is not necessary, the restaurant owners can control the cleanliness of their food from start to finish, and their restaurants can offer gourmet fare prepared by talented cooks at the central processing point.

As restaurants use significant amounts of convenience foods, they can reduce losses and waste. Portions are controlled, and thus there is no waste in preparation, and unused food is kept frozen for use another day. Even the basic handling time is significantly lower than with ordinary foods. Space and equipment requirements are also significantly reduced. With smaller space, the need for air-conditioning is also reduced.

Franchising

Franchised operations have become an important part of the restaurant industry in recent years. Franchises can have a significant effect upon the individual markets in which they operate. National reputation can command a high volume quickly, in competition with other restaurants operating nearby. Franchises often tend to establish, or strongly reinforce, new trends in decor, menu, kind of service, etc. both through the force of multiple operation and as a result of extensive market research skills.

Anyone contemplating opening a new restaurant might well consider the advantages of franchises. A good franchise provides an established name and image which are widely recognized. Ready acceptance is a powerful asset, since it means that the proprietor can expect to begin operating in the black much earlier than with an independent operation.

A franchise offers advantages at every stage. Assistance in financing is available through established connections with sources of funds. Lending sources will generally tend to have greater confidence in a franchise operation than in an independent. Franchises and their employees are also trained in the restaurant business and the franchisor's particular method of operations.

Starting a franchised operation provides the franchisee with a fully developed marketing concept and system for applying and realizing it. Equipment, layout principles, food management principles, and staffing methods are all fully developed by the franchisor, who even provides operating systems and recordkeeping systems.

Furthermore, franchisees continue to benefit throughout their operations from skillfully designed national advertising campaigns for the entire chain.

In return for these various benefits, the franchisee assumes various specific obligations. First of all, of course, he pays part of his profits in the form of fees. He pays an initial fee when he enters into the contract and additional fees, based on revenues, thereafter. He must agree to maintain relatively strict standards of food and service, and he must agree to keep the physical premises in satisfactory condition to meet national standards for the franchise. Most franchise outlets must also conform to specific requirements in construction, display, promotion, etc.

The prudent franchisee investigates carefully before entering into an agreement. He determines the franchisor's general financial soundness. He examines the methods used in the franchisor's financial statements. He investigates the franchisor's credit rating and general standing in the financial community, and perhaps determines how satisfactory that franchisor's relations have been with other franchisees.

He should seek to determine the franchisor's record of dealings with franchisees and the incidence of franchisee failures over a period of years.

The relative care the franchisor uses in selecting and accepting franchisees is also an important factor. The franchisor's own success depends upon having the right people operating franchises, and therefore a failure to examine prospective franchisees critically is questionable.

Another major consideration in investigating the franchise arrangement is the soundness of the franchisor's financing. The franchisee needs assurance of capitalization adequate for fulfilling all his franchise obligations and operations expense until the operation begins to show a profit. Financing terms must also be reasonable in light of prevailing interest rates.

Joint Ventures

An important restaurant trend in the years ahead is likely to be joint-venture operations, a partnership for a specific purpose, most often involving a passive partner with a special interest and an active partner who will operate the restaurant on a day-to-day basis.

The most common potential sponsors of such joint ventures are likely to be companies with an indirect interest in restaurants, such as leisure-time companies and conglomerate companies supplying food.

For leisure-time companies which operate theme parks, campsites, recreation areas, etc., a joint venture is an excellent way of handling the food service part of operations. Operators also benefit through access to captive markets. Restaurants and snack bars at leisure sites may expect expanding markets in the years ahead because of compensating trends such as the rising incidence of tourism, long vacations, long weekends, and possibly the four-day week.

Leisure-site joint ventures parallel franchises in their advantages over purely independent operations. Monopoly conditions offer considerably quicker and surer prospects than a completely independent restaurant. Careful market investigation is necessary, of course, in order to ensure that the leisure site will attract sufficient visitors to support profitable operations. If the investigation shows the leisure-site operation to be basically sound, growth potential could be particularly good, because of the leisure trends cited above.

Joint ventures with conglomerate companies with food processing and distributing divisions may offer significant advantages, both marketing and financial. As further technological innovations are made, operators with first access may have a distinct advantage over competitors.

Some innovations take the form of food products with a strong new market appeal and thus a tendency to increase sales significantly. Other innovations take the form of substantial unit price and handling economies, thus providing higher profit margins at the same sales level.

Such joint ventures with comglomerates offer restaurant operators particular financing advantages also,, since the passive partner has ample funds to capitalize on markets fully, to experiment with new products, and to allow ample time to develop markets without financial pressures.

CHAPTER 12

Site Selection, Feasibility, and Location Planning

CHAPTER CAPSULE PREVIEW

A complete feasibility study includes a number of interrelated phases. Market studies and competition analyses, combined with projections of trends, help to identify suitable locations; but only when a site is finally selected can the market and competition studies themselves become final. The results of market studies and the other phases of the feasibility study provide essential data for the financial analysis; but decisions made in other phases are based to a considerable degree on financial analysis. Accordingly, a study of economic feasibility for a proposed restaurant moves back and forth between the phases, arriving at temporary conclusions that become less and less tentative as the process continues. Thus, the feasibility study is an important part of decision-making in order to attain the starting point for profitable restaurant management.

In the end, the financial analysis phase produces estimated income statements in addition to a pro forma balance sheet that indicates the investment required. And the financial factors are summarized in an analysis of return on investment calculated from either the present value of future earnings or the discounted cash flow. With this basic planning foundation, the restaurant operating cycle can properly and sensibly begin.

HOW TO SELECT THE RIGHT SITE!

A restaurant's site is more or less permanent, and the restaurant itself often gets to be known by its location. Furthermore, the chances of financial success are strongly influenced by the choice of the right location.

And yet, in selecting a site, there is no set formula that will hold for all restaurants. One restaurant may need heavy traffic, while another relies on a neighborhood of a particular type, and a third is able to draw people from a wide area. The only thing they have in common is their dependence on their respective markets; and the selection of a site is, therefore, related to the selection of the market to be served, and sought.

Identifying, evaluating, and selecting markets are functions of the feasibility study. Hence it is useful to put the site selection study in its proper perspective as a part of the more comprehensive study of economic feasibility. Feasibility studies are made before new restaurants are built, or existing restaurants are expanded or relocated.

A feasibility study is a systematic method for evaluating the economic factors at work and the likely results of operations before they are begun. Proposals are subjected to such study in order to protect potential investors and lenders from putting their money in projects whose prospects for success are dim. Another use of feasibility studies is to help select the best alternative from a number of proposals.

In this chapter, we will cover three topics:

1. Analysis of economic feasibility which includes market analysis and financial analysis.
2. Narrowing of alternative locations to the most promising ones for further study.
3. Selection of a specific site.

There is considerable interaction between the factors that make up a complete study. For example, a change in site often means that part of one market will be lost while part of another is gained. Also, elements of the financial analysis will be affected: not only will revenues change, but some costs may be altered. Again, an attempt to reach a luxury market instead of a family market will bring changes in both costs and revenues and hence in the financial analysis. And the selection of a particular kind of operation or a particular site may mean that a larger investment is required, or that more, or less, financing will be available. These factors will be reflected in the return on investment.

These interactions, and many more, make it impossible to proceed in a straight line from market analysis to financial analysis to site selection, completing each phase before beginning the next. On the contrary, it is more likely that tentative judgments and analyses will be made and upgraded as the study moves back and forth between the phases. As final decisions replace tentative ones, the study moves toward a conclusion.

Of the phases of a feasibility study, market analysis is directed toward the measurement of the demand, primarily the unsatisfied demand, for a restaurant of the proposed type among the people who reside, shop, or work in a prescribed area, or pass through it. If more than one type of restaurant is under consideration, then each type requires a market analysis of its own. Potential customers are classified into market segments that reflect relevant characteristics, and the strength of the demand in each segment is measured. Thus, all professionals in a specified area may constitute a market segment, or all teen-agers, or all retired persons, and so on.

In estimating the unsatisfied demand, it is, of course, necessary to take into account the competition, both existing and prospective. Competing restaurants are classified into categories that are described further as offering direct or indirect competition, depending primarily on how closely they attempt to satisfy the same wants and needs as the proposed restaurant. Some categories of restaurant will not be competing at all.

Financial analysis is the phase of the feasibility study that seeks to evaluate the return on investment, after giving full consideration to all initial outlays, start-up costs, and expenses of operation. Both net earnings and cash flow may be compared with the investment required. Revenue forecasts are based on data derived from market analyses, while expenditures reflect alternative locations, styles of operation, kinds of menu, and other factors that influence costs as were discussed in earlier chapters.

The site selection phase of the feasibility study relies on market analysis and financial analysis for evaluation of the markets to be served, the financing that is available, and the accumulation of all revenue and cost data. In addition, there are non-monetary guidelines and criteria to be met.

THE ECONOMIC FEASIBILITY STUDY

Before a prudent investor puts his money into a new restaurant venture or an expansion program, he may seek assurance on several counts: that the risks do not exceed certain limits; that the rewards are likely to meet his minimum specifications; and that the potential rewards are at least commensurate with the risks. Feasibility studies can help him to determine whether to pursue individual projects or abandon them; and comparative analyses of feasibility studies can help him select specific options. In all cases, a feasibility study seeks to present a reliable prediction of results.

To accomplish that objective, we must understand the factors that influence the success of a business. Before we can hope to predict reasonably well the results of a proposed restaurant, we must have a grasp of the environmental factors and the internal factors that contribute to those results. And we must be able to measure these factors. The distinction between environmental factors, sometimes called exogenous, and internal, or endogenous, factors is essentially a matter of controllability. Endogenous factors, by and large, can be planned and controlled, or at least managed, by the restaurateur; whereas exogenous factors, in general, can only be predicted.

With a grasp of the factors involved in success and a way to measure each of them, we are ready to take the next step: Measuring relationships in a manner that permits us to determine the impact that a given variation will have on the final result. With this information, we are equipped to establish break-even points and to predict profitability at various operating levels. From here, we may also go on to more sophisticated types of analysis to ascertain what effect forecasting errors will have.

To sum up, the feasibility study seeks to quantify factors that influence the success of the restaurant, and to establish relationships between variables and results, thereby permitting predictions of results under varying conditions. Thus, the feasibility study provides a basis for judging the soundness of a proposed investment.

This brief discussion leads us to the question: What are some of the elements of success in the restaurant business? To begin with, a successful restaurant needs satisfied customers in sufficient numbers to provide revenues to cover all expenses and leave something over for a reasonable profit. These customers may be shoppers taking time out for a snack, office workers having a quick lunch, theater-goers taking an evening out, or families giving Mother a day off from cooking. Whatever the market segments to be served, the style of service, menus, decor, advertising, and so on will have to be coordinated in making a consistent appeal to those segments. Likewise, the feasibility study will have to reflect all these items and their costs in a unified proposal that retains the same internal consistency.

In determining which market segments to aim at, the restaurateur defines the individual segments, finds out where the customer will come from, what their economic status is, how much they can afford, and what they are willing to spend. Other characteristics are also assessed, such as age distribution, education levels, and housing in the area. And the wants and needs of each market segment are specified.

Facilities and decor are chosen for their appropriateness to the markets to be served and their practicality in providing the right kind of service. There are obvious differences between fast-food counters, cafeterias, and dining rooms; and there are basic differences, too, between cocktail lounges and family restaurants; but even subtle differences can set one restaurant apart from another within its own class. Similarly, there are different kinds of equipment for preparing convenience foods and regular foods, and decisions as to the purchase of equipment must await prior decisions on markets and menus.

The service and menus to be offered, and the prices to be set, will depend on the market segments selected and the practices of the competition. The feasibility study must comtemplate the standards of quality that will be maintained and the cost of quality and service. The restaurant must be competitive in what it offers and it charges.

Quality and service are provided by an organization with appropriate skills and motivation, as well as supervision and management. Convenience foods require lesser skills, as compared with regular foods. The turnover will vary with the kind of service offered, and so will the requirements for waiters and other personnel. Organizational specifications incorporated in the feasibility study must be consistent with the nature of the operation.

The location must be convenient to the markets that are selected, but the meaning of convenience may vary. For fast-food customers unwilling to cross a busy street, convenience means being on the right side of the street, perhaps not more than a few doors away from a busy store or group of stores. But for an elegant dining room, convenience may mean having adequate parking facilities on a suitable highway within several miles of a populated area. Convenience is often a relative matter: of two similar restaurants catering to the same market, the one with only a slightly less convenient location may suffer for it severely while its competitor reaps large rewards from what appears to be only a minor advantage.

Adequate capitalization is also required for successful operation. Besides buying, constructing, or renting suitable premises, equipment, and furnishings, provision must be made for hiring and training a staff, for advertising in advance of the opening, and for providing flatware, linens, and a basic inventory of food, beverages, and supplies of all kinds. In addition, there must be sufficient working capital to meet bills and payrolls through the initial period, when losses may be incurred, and during regular operation thereafter.

Starting with this brief survey of the factors that foster or impede successful operation of a restaurant, we can proceed to a more detailed discussion of the elements of an economic feasibility study.

Market Demand Analysis

The basic purpose of a market demand analysis is to estimate the number of customers with sufficient accuracy to provide reliable forecasts of the revenues to be derived from carefully defined operations. Definitions will include descriptions of the markets that will be appealed to; the demand analysis evaluates the strength of these markets.

A single restaurant may want to serve several markets. It may see a potential for serving breakfast to people on their way to work, lunch to workers in nearby buildings, and dinner to theater-goers or local residents. It may also go after families on weekends. What is the potential of a given market segment, and how do we go about estimating it?

Another way of putting the question is: Of the population of office workers, or residents, or theater-goers, how many can be expected to want to eat out or to take advantage of the availability of a place where they can eat out? This is the total potential market for all restaurants in the area of certain types.

A starting point can be found in population statistics for the region being studied, combined with general data from the National Restaurant Association and other sources. Rough assessments of market segments in given areas can be made with such figures.

Since a restaurant is meant to operate for a long period, and markets can be expected to undergo continual change, a market analysis must examine trends and portents of things to come. A static picture of the situation as it is now should be regarded only as a starting point for an investigation of the dynamics of the locality, including the economic and sociological forces at work to produce change in the future. Forecasts should then contemplate the impact on the restaurant of the impending changes.

In any study of socioeconomic conditions and trends to evaluate present prospects or predict future outlook, it is necessary to segment the total market by socioeconomic characteristics. For example, a proposed specialty restaurant may see as its principal source of customers a high-income professional group. This group then becomes a specific segment for careful analysis by itself. If the restaurant can appeal to more than one market segment, then each segment is analyzed on its own, and an overall potential is estimated by grouping appropriate segments. There may be a different grouping for each meal period, in order to provide as reliable a forecast as possible by meal period for the financial analysis phase of the complete feasibility study.

In evaluating the market for a particular type of restaurant at a specific location, there is always a question as to how wide an area should be included. Looking at the matter from another viewpoint: How far will people travel or walk to get to the restaurant? The answer in each situation will depend on several factors.

Meal periods have a good deal to do with the distances people will go, mainly because of time limitations. The two most hurried meals of the day are breakfast and lunch. Eliminating those who breakfast at home and those who skip breakfast or start their coffee breaks early at their desks, there remain those who will stop off for breakfast at a restaurant. These people are not easily persuaded to stray from their accustomed paths, usually the shortest and most direct route from home to work. Therefore, the restaurant that seeks to capitalize on the breakfast trade must locate where the morning traffic is.

At lunchtime again, people are prevented from going far afield. Whether walking or driving, they allow only a short interval for getting to a restaurant. So the restaurant that wants to attract people for lunch must locate near where a substantial number of people work.

Dinner is usually more relaxed. There is more time, and people are willing to travel further. Just how far they will go depends on how strong the attraction is. Accordingly, the farther removed a restaurant is from its market, the greater its reliance on an exceptional quality or some unique feature.

The type of restaurant being considered is closely related to meal periods in which it will operate, and considerations of distance are similar to those already discussed. If a restaurant is counting on distinctiveness to draw people long distances, then it will have to be truly unique. In general, people eating out of necessity will tend to prefer nearby restaurants, whereas those who want more than just "food" should be willing to travel.

How far is far? Distance is a relative matter, depending on the availability of transportation and its quality. If people are to come by car, then the quality of roads and the normal conditions of traffic flow will affect accessibility. Plans for road construction and repair can be an important factor in site selection and in the evaluation of the market.

It is generally assumed that, of two comparable restaurants, the one closer to the market will draw more people than the other. When the restaurants lie in the same direction from the market, the nearer one is in a strong competitive position, with an ability to intercept a larger share of the volume. Consequently, in locating a restaurant, it is often essential to evaluate neighboring sites and select the most convenient, in order to prevent a competitor from opening there later.

Finally, when people walk to a restaurant, even short distances can be significant. If there is a marked difference in traffic on two sides of the same street, then the side with the heavier traffic is preferred, because people dislike crossing a busy thoroughfare. And if there is a break in a row of stores, people are often reluctant to continue on past the break.

For those restaurants that depend on passersby dropping in, traffic counts may tell the story adequately, but for a restaurant expecting to serve an area, a market study should include data describing the characteristics of that area. Such sources of secondary data as the Census Bureau and its publications are valuable aids in constructing a market profile for a given area. When such a profile has been constructed, ratios and other measures of relationships may be derived from general market studies and applied to the profiles to afford better insights into the nature of the opportunities that the markets offer.

This manipulation of figures has a purpose: to estimate the market potentials that exist, so that we may judge whether the market is adequate to support the proposed restaurant. As a simplified example of the calculation of a market estimate, take a restaurant that expects to serve families whose income is over $15,000. The statistics of the proposed location indicate that the area population is 100,000, and that there are 5,500 households with incomes over $15,000. Market studies that are available indicate that such families spend $480 annually, on the average, eating out. The potential sales to this particular market segment are $480 x 5,500, or $2,640,000.

General market statistics can be treacherous, however, and great caution must be exercised in using them. For, statistics that describe a large population over a wide area cannot be expected to apply precisely to any particular locality within that area. Extrapolating outside the area is even more hazardous. The more dissimilar, or heterogeneous, a population is, the less representative an average of the whole will be for any particular part.

One way to overcome the problems inherent in general statistics is to search for specific secondary statistics derived from studies of limited populations similar to those under investigation. County-wide data may be useful in evaluating a section of the county. And if two neighboring counties have similar characteristics, a study of the spending habits of middle-income people in one county may be helpful to an understanding of the spending habits of middle-income people in the other county. This principle may be carried further afield, but when questions arise as to the applicability of data from one source to calculations involving another location, original (primary) research into the two areas may be necessary to establish that they are (or are not) alike in important respects.

Primary research within a defined area, properly carried out, is capable of providing the most valid statistics for that area. But primary research is costly. Accordingly, a decision to extend or limit primary research is based on an assessment of its costs and the benefits to be derived from the greater accuracy that such a study will lend to the ultimate estimates of market potential. Sometimes, a limited primary study is sufficient to verify the conclusions of a less expensive study based on secondary information.

If a primary market study is to be undertaken, its cost can be held down by careful preparation. Sampling techniques permit us to draw reliable inferences concerning a whole population from a limited number of responses drawn from a carefully selected sample. The selection process must assure that the sample is truly representative of the whole.The questionnaires that are used in gathering data must also be constructed carefully to elicit accurate responses and to secure the kinds of information that will be useful to the study and the decision-making process that follows. Questions should direct responses that will permit precise descriptions of market segments and their characteristics—more properly of those characteristics that are relevant to the study. And they should ask such questions as how often people dine out, where they dine, and how well satisfied they are at present.

The entire market study should be designed in such a way as to bring out a complete definition of the market: how it is segmented, what its composition is, what groups it comprises, and how large each group is. The individual segments require further definition in the form of market profiles describing the wants and needs of the people included in the segments. These wants and needs should be quantified to indicate relative strength. Finally, market opportunities should be assessed from summary data for the various combinations that would be attracted to specific types of restaurant. These are the elements of a market demand analysis.

Location and Site Analysis

Having found that an adequate market does exist for a proposed restaurant, we turn next to the question of where to put it. First we will define a limited area, or location, that suits our purpose best. Then we will investigate specific properties, or sites, within the favored location.

Since the location must be convenient to the market, we will begin with the market analysis and derive basic facts from it. We have already identified the market segments to which we will direct our appeal; now we will want to know where those market segments are. How are they scattered around the market area, where are they concentrated, what routes do they travel? In defining the preferred location, we will take all these things into account, because we want to put our restaurant where it has the best chance of drawing the greatest number of people in our chosen market. In the simplest terms, that means meeting them more than half way. The restaurant stands still, and customers have to come to it, but we can make it easy for them to reach us. We can locate in as close proximity to the market as possible, where access to the restaurant is unimpeded.

With this objective in mind, the mechanics of defining suitable and preferred locations can be reduced to plotting population densities on a map and then drawing the boundaries of locations that meet the criterion of convenience. A map that shows both roads and topography can save time in selecting a site.

The selection of a site involves convenience and much more. Insofar as convenience is concerned, the proper selection of a location ensures that sites within it are near enough to the market. Nevertheless, accessibility to individual sites may vary. One may be on a side road, another on a highway, and a third at the intersection of major traffic arteries. One may be at a bus stop, while another is several blocks away. One may be at a shopping center with a parking lot, while another has poor facilities for parking, or none at all.

If the preferred locations run through several communities, then the characteristics of the communities should be considered and compared. Especially if land is to be purchased and a building constructed, the restaurateur as an investor in real estate (which he is about to become) will want to evaluate the prospects for his investment. Will it appreciate by taking part in the growth of a thriving community, or is it likely to lose much of its value as the neighborhood deteriorates? In considering this question, it is useful to examine trends in population and construction, practices with respect to zoning and the granting of variances, the quality of schools and community services, and the impact of regional demographic developments and road building plans for a broad area.

The characteristics of the individual lots are also important considerations. Will it be expensive to clear the land; do outcroppings of bedrock present construction problems; will it be necessary to grade the parking lot; does an irregular shape restrict the usefulness of a substantial part of the lot; will poor drainage hamper operations or cause flooding? Some lots are undesirable because they slope away from the street, or because there are nuisances nearby.

Finally, each lot is subject to its own economics. Financing may be easier to arrange for some lots; sometimes a seller is willing to extend more favorable terms than can be arranged elsewhere. Property taxes, water, and rubbish removal charges may vary. If higher costs are offset by advantages, the restaurateur may be willing to incur them; but in making such a decision, he must be fully informed as to the cost of land, including its preparation for use by clearing and grading; the cost of construction, including the elimination of problems and preparation to bring in utilities; and the carrying costs of debt service, taxes, insurance, and other charges.

We noted earlier that the parts of a complete feasibility study are so interrelated as to preclude movement from one phase to another in a precise sequence without backtracking. We observe this condition once more in connection with site analysis and competition analysis. The competition can only be fully described when the site has been selected, but surely no one would want to select a site without analyzing its competitive position, at least tentatively. An effort must be made to permit such tentative analysis, because it would be too costly to prepare a detailed analysis of competition for every site that may be under consideration at any time during a feasibility study. With this interrelationship in mind, we turn next to the analysis of competition.

Competition Analysis

A market analysis must go beyond analysis of potential customers to analysis of the attempts being made (and going to be made) by others to satisfy the demand that exists. Accordingly, part of the feasibility study must be dedicated to finding out all we can about the competition and the related demographics.

Among the things essential to know about the competitors is what they are selling. Their menus, prices, and specialties; presence of a bar and entertainment; meal periods served. In short, the food, beverages, and services offered to customers, and the appeal that is used to attract business.

Since management is the key factor in the success of a business, it is useful to evaluate the management of each competitor. How well do they run their restaurants? Of importance also are questions related to their expansion plans and their ability to carry them out. Will financing be available, and the talent to run a larger enterprise? Are uninspired managements allowing their facilities to become obsolete in the face of opportunities to revitalize and grow?

On the other hand, there may be reasons why restaurants are deteriorating or closing. Perhaps there are no restaurants in an area; some may even have tried and failed. It is well to investigate the causes of such phenomena. To put the issue more broadly, an effort should be made to discover the problems that others have encountered in each area, whether they have overcome those problems or not.

However, the basic objectives of a competition analysis remains to find out how well the competitors are fulfilling the needs of the customers. Is the demand adequately supplied? This question obviously relates to the specific market segments that are chosen by the proposed restaurant. Is there an unsatisfied demand among those market segments for the new restaurant to fill?

Related to this question is the loyalty of customers to the existing restaurants, for the strength of that loyalty will be a determining factor in setting limits on the ability of the new restaurant to penetrate the market and capture a share of existing business. It is easier to take away customers who are dissatisfied than those who are well pleased.

In the end, competition analysis seeks to ascertain the share of market held by each competing restaurant, and to estimate how the market will be divided up in the future. The proposed restaurant's share of the future market provides a forecast of revenues to be used as a basis for the financial analysis part of the feasibility study.

Financial Analysis

In essence, the financial analysis summarizes the findings of other phases of the feasibility study, or at least the relevant business facts for the surviving options as to markets, locations, menus, and so on.

Included in the financial analysis is a capital investment budget, with its detailed statement of the investment required for land, building, furnishings, equipment, and working capital. Provisions must also be made for pre-opening expenses and operating losses that are likely to be incurred before the restaurant is established as a profitable activity. Sources must be lined up to supply all of the needed capital in advance. Money borrowed later, under pressure, can be very expensive.

Also included in the financial analysis is an operating budget with estimates of revenues and expenses in detail. Net return is predicted on the bottom line. Such expenses as depreciation and property taxes must be consistent with the capital investment budget for assets to be acquired; and such expenses as advertising, payrolls, and supplies must be consistent with volume levels as reflected in estimated revenues.

Several threads are woven in the estimate of revenues. Evaluations of market segments, projections of trends, calculations of market share, and forecasts of local and general business conditions become part of the determination of demand. Meal periods, menus, prices, and turnover help to establish dollar volumes. And the capacities of kitchen and serving areas set limits on volume.

Decisions on other matters also affect the financial analysis. For instance, the decisions as to whether to apply for a liquor license will determine whether there will be beverage sales. If local laws forbid the sale of drinks in some locations but not in others, the financial analysis will quantify the effect: it will show the difference in sales and earnings potential between locations.

Estimates of operating costs must incorporate a great many factors. The size of the operation and the number of food areas and work situations will influence the space requirements for service, production, storage, and preparation. The type of seating and quality of service will affect labor costs. Seat turnover by meal period will influence not only revenues and costs, but also the relationship between them. This relationship will also be affected by the size of the average check. The ratio of food cost to sales will be influenced by the type of menu, and also by pricing policies. These factors will help to determine gross margins. The decor and the kind of fixed assets purchased will push overhead costs up or down. All of these items will become parts of the estimated income statements that financial analysis produces.

Factors originating outside the business also influence the estimated income statement. Labor market conditions, by which we mean both the availability of all types and levels of labor and the going pay rates in the area, are reflected in labor costs. Supervisory and administrative costs are subject to analogous considerations.

The potential labor market consists of more than just numbers of people and levels of ability. It is essential, at the outset, that the restaurant operator summarize and carefully calculate tentative employee needs. He must also appraise the available and potential labor market in the area in and around the selected site. Is there a good market and, if so, how easily accessible is your selected restaurant site to public transportation lines? If there is no convenient means of transportation via public conveyance, your labor market immediately becomes more limited. Once construction has begun and is being monitored, the time arrives actively to seek the personnel to staff the restaurant.

Before beginning the interviews, the restaurateur must be sure to know exactly what he is looking for. Training of employees is an expensive process. A conference with his team of advisors would be worthwhile, as they are aware of the personnel that will be needed to enable the restaurater's operation to run smoothly. Once a decision on the necessary staff has been reached, a complete list of job descriptions of all positions should be prepared. If you already are operating one or more restaurants (hopefully with success), even though you know the requirements of each position in your present restaurant, have you ever compiled a complete list of duties for each of these jobs? What happens if an employee leaves and has to be replaced? It is difficult to train someone if the job is not defined. Make an analysis of all the positions which will be needed to staff your restaurant, then enumerate, in detail, what the duties of each position are.

It is to your advantage to prepare these job descriptions before you begin placement interviews. Once you know what types of jobs you have available, it is also wise to set up the criteria by which you can judge applicants. There should be at least minimum requirements for each position, and you should not employ anyone who doesn't meet the standards that you have established.

Remoteness from suppliers of certain food items or supplies may cause significantly higher costs to be reflected in estimates. Local tax rates are certainly reflected, as well as insurance rates which may be affected by the quality of fire and police protection.

Then there are policy matters that are also included, in some way, in the estimated income statements. These policy matters range from the amounts to be spent on advertising and promotion to the fringe benefits to be provided to employees and executives and to the precise manner and cost of financing the restaurant.

Having established what investment is required and what net earnings may be expected from the proposed restaurant, the financial analysis proceeds to evaluate the return on investment. The purpose of this evaluation is to ascertain whether the proposal meets the restaurateur's minimum criterion for investment of his funds. This purpose may be extended to compare two or more alternatives and determine which offers the best prospect of an adequate return.

In brief, an analysis of return on investment establishes the annual earnings expected over a number of years, reduces these future earnings to present value as a common base, and then compares the total present value of future earnings to the total investment required. A businessman evaluating an investment by this method would want to see a present value of expected future earnings that exceeds his investment by a minimum percentage of his own choosing.

The concept of present value being central to calculations of return on investment, a few words on present value are in order at this point. The concept is based on the fact that a thousand dollars in hand now is worth more than a thousand dollars that will come to us next year, because we have the use of the first thousand dollars for a full year before we can begin to use the second thousand. The measure of the differential between the two sums is the interest that a thousand dollars earns in the intervening year. Hence, by discounting the second thousand dollars to account for a year's interest cost, we bring it down to present value. Similarly, a thousand dollars due in two years can be discounted for two-years' interest cost to bring it down to present value. Incidentally, the calculations are made easy by references to tables of present value at varying discount rates for varying numbers of periods. These tables are employed to reduce future net earnings to present value in calculating return on investment as part of a feasibility study.

We have been discussing, up to this point, calculations of return on investment based on net earnings as determined by the methods of accrual accounting. There is another way to look at the return an investment throws off. Many businessmen, especially in the real estate business (ownership of restaurant property does have its real estate business aspects), prefer to examine the cash flow that their cash investment will generate. The major difference between the accrual and cash bases in evaluating return on investment is in the handling of depreciation charges.

Future cash flow can be discounted to present values just as well as future net earnings; and the total discounted cash flow can then be compared with the required investment of cash to determine whether the investor's criterion will be met. In essence, this is the concept that underlies discounted cash flow techniques.

The highly sophisticated investor may want to incorporate in the financial analysis a sensitivity analysis that indicates what effect variances from the basic assumptions would have on the outcome. What would net earnings be if seat turnover is 5 percent less than anticipated, or if the average check is lower by 10 percent? What would happen if population growth differs from the projection by stated amounts, or if family incomes fall short of expectations? Some variables have little impact, while others can be very serious. Sensitivity analysis attempts to provide an understanding of such relationships. By combining this type of analysis with assessments of the probabilities that specified variances will occur, a prospective investor can acquire fuller comprehension of the risks he is assuming and the rewards he may realistically expect.

Index

INDEX